Clinical Phonology

Second Edition

PAMELA GRUNWELL
Professor of Clinical Linguistics and Head of the School of Speech Pathology at Leicester Polytechnic

CHAPMAN & HALL
London · New York · Tokyo · Melbourne · Madras

Published by Chapman & Hall, 2–6 Boundary Row, London SE1 8HN

Chapman & Hall, 2-6 Boundary Row, London SE1 8HN, UK

Chapman & Hall, 29 West 35th Street, New York NY10001, USA

Chapman & Hall Japan, Thomson Publishing Japan, Hirakawacho Nemoto Building, 7F, 1-7-11 Hirakawa-cho, Chiyoda-ku, Tokyo 102, Japan

Chapman & Hall Australia, Thomas Nelson Australia, 102 Dodds Street, South Melbourne, Victoria 3205, Australia

Chapman & Hall India, R. Seshadri, 32 Second Main Road, CIT East, Madras 600 035, India

First edition 1982
Second edition 1987
Reprinted 1992

Printed in Great Britain by Ipswich Book Co, Ipswich

ISBN 0 412 44500 X (PB)

A catalogue record of this book is available from the British Library.

Contents

Preface

During the past two decades speech pathologists have become increasingly interested in linguistics and linguists have begun to find disordered language an interesting topic of academic enquiry. A variety of publications, mainly journal articles and papers in volumes of collected articles, have appeared illustrating the applications of phonological frameworks of description to clinical data. This book has developed from annual attempts to introduce this new and rapidly expanding area of study to prospective and qualified speech therapists. *Clinical Linguistics* has now become the generally accepted designation for the whole area of study of this new, hybrid subject, thus my choice of title to indicate that this book is concerned with the clinical applications of linguistics at the phonological level.

I have restricted the coverage to phonology for two reasons. First, in regard to clinical practice, the introduction of phonological principles has promoted a radical rethinking of the nature of certain disorders and appropriate assessment and intervention procedures. It is now appreciated that it is inappropriate to designate all mispronunciations as indicative of speech/articulation disabilities. This has led to more insightful differential diagnoses and consequent treatment programmes. Secondly, in applying phonological principles to clinical data, linguists and speech pathologists have drawn upon a variety of theoretical frameworks for their analytical procedures, thus creating a ready-made area of study. There seemed, therefore, a need for an introduction to the different theories of phonology and a survey of their applications to clinical practice.

In lecture courses and seminars over the years I have found that each phonological framework, together with its applications, needs to be considered within its own terms. I have retained this organisation here. Each chapter is fairly autonomous and can, for the most part, be read in its own right, except that Chapter Two provides the principles basic to all phonological analyses and should be read before later chapters and after Chapter One. Only those phonological theories which have been applied to clinical data are discussed in the subsequent chapters. Chapter Three considers the traditional applications of phoneme theory in clinical practice. Chapter Four extends phonemic concepts to analysing clinical data in terms of an independent phonological system. Chapter Five considers Distinctive Feature Theory and Chapter Six Generative Phonology, both as applied to clinical data. Chapter Seven discusses normal and disordered child speech in terms of the concepts of Natural Phonology. Chapter Eight summarises the basic principles of clinically applicable phonology.

At the end of each chapter, except One and Eight, there are sets of exercises in the analysis of clinical data. These are designed to facilitate understanding of the principles and procedures described in the chapter and to promote confidence in the use of phonological analysis so that the reader may more readily apply the procedures in the assessment of disordered speech. Most of the data used in the examples and exercises have been collected by the author from children with phonological disability. This is the clinical population that has been most frequently and fruitfully investigated using phonological procedures. I must also acknowledge that it is this group of language-handicapped children that I personally find most interesting, from both theoretical and practical points of view. Where appropriate, reference is also made to other types of speech and language disability where I, or other investigators, have found phonological procedures applicable.

The book has been written on the assumption that most readers will have a knowledge of articulatory phonetics and be familiar with phonetic transcription. It does not, however, require the reader to possess more than an introductory level of study of general theoretical linguistics. The book was written primarily for prospective speech pathologists and therapists and practising clinicians. It is hoped, however, that students of linguistics, both undergraduate and postgraduate, will be encouraged to explore a different dimension of their subject as presented in this book. There is also much that will be of interest to the student of child language and psycholinguistics in the sections which consider the implications of applying phonology to clinical data.

American readers should note that all the examples and data samples are taken from British English speakers with non-rhotic accents. There is therefore no word final or preconsonantal /r/ in words like *ear*, *sugar*, *soldier*, *feather*, *arm*, *card*, *birthday*. Also symbolisation of the vowel system, especially the diphthongs, follows the tradition of British phonetic studies.

I have to acknowledge the contributions of many present and former colleagues and students to the development of this book. Their interest and the challenge of explaining clinical phonology to them has continued to stimulate my own enthusiasm for the subject. In addition, I have especially appreciated my discussions with practising clinicians. I wish to express my particular thanks to Sue Huskins for asking me to explain phonological theory, and thus becoming the sounding-board for the original draft of the book, and for providing such provocative feedback. I am also grateful to John Connolly, Howard Jackson, Fiona Macdonald, Elizabeth Owens and Marion Shirt for reading and commenting on parts of the manuscript. Naturally, the final version is entirely my own responsibility. I must also record my debt to all the children and patients, whose speech I have had the privilege to study. I hope this exercise in Clinical Phonology will prove to have been of benefit to them and others who suffer from similar handicaps.

Pam Grunwell
Leicester

Preface to the Second Edition

In this second edition I have retained the organisation of the first edition. New sections have been added to each chapter from Three through to Seven reviewing clinical assessment procedures, based on the analytical frameworks described in each of these chapters. In addition the discussion in Chapter Seven of phonological processes in disordered speech has been considerably extended to include new information from recent studies. The final chapter has been comprehensively revised to reflect the shift in orientation towards the cognitive aspects of phonetics and phonology. There have also been numerous small changes throughout the book.

Many colleagues and students have provided me with comments and suggestions which have contributed to the evolution of this second edition. I wish to express my particular thanks to Martin Ball, Eeva Leinonen-Davies, Pippa Line and Andy Spencer. I am especially grateful to Jane Russell for her generous support and enthusiasm and her perceptive comments on the clinical relevance of phonological concepts. As with the first edition, this exercise in Clinical Phonology is dedicated to people whose speech disorder handicaps their ability to communicate; I hope that this book will contribute to the alleviation of their disabilities.

Pam Grunwell
Leicester

1

The Contribution of Phonology

The traditional foundation for the study of speech disorders has been the study of phonetics, which is the science of speech. As an applied science in the study of disordered speech, phonetics has enabled speech and language pathologists to describe speech sound disorders and to explain these disorders as resulting from articulatory speech production errors. However, speech is usually the manifestation of language. *Phonology* is that branch of the linguistic sciences which is concerned with the study of *spoken language.*

The nature of some speech and language disabilities has frequently been misinterpreted because of a failure to appreciate the crucial distinction between the phonetic description of speech and the phonological description of spoken language. This distinction has implications for both the theoretical characterisation of certain disabilities and the clinical management of patients with such speech problems.

Consider the following three extended definitions of the 'domain of phonetics' provided by eminent linguists and phoneticians.

> If the linguist [or linguistic phonetician/phonologist] is asked whether two 'sounds' are the same or different, or how many 'sounds' there are in a given language, he must know whether the question is one of substance or form; whether these 'sounds' are to be regarded as physical entities which can be described without knowing to what language they belong or whether they are to be described in terms of such differences and similarities of sound as are functional in the language (by 'functional' is to be understood 'relevant for the purpose of

communication'). In the first case he will give a PHONETIC description of what he hears or analyses instrumentally; in the second he will give a PHONOLOGICAL description. (Lyons 1969: 99)

The study of the total range of speech sounds that can be made by human beings is the concern of GENERAL PHONETICS.

All human beings have substantially the same speech apparatus, so that the total repertory of human sounds is effectively the same for the whole species, but the selection made from this total repertory varies quite considerably from community to community. The study of speech as a universal human phenomenon is PHONETICS. The study of the systematic organisation of selected speech sounds in the spoken forms of individual languages has variously been called FUNCTIONAL PHONETICS, PHONEMICS or more commonly nowadays, PHONOLOGY. The business of PHONOLOGY is to abstract, describe and classify as neatly as we can the recurrent sound units used to build up the spoken forms of a given language and to state the rules for their use. (Henderson 1971: 38–9)

Phonetics is the study of the sensible manifestation of language. It is, therefore, concerned with the acoustical properties of speech, with the motor behaviour of the vocal organs that produce the acoustical signal, and with the way the signal is processed in the human auditory system. In studying these topics sight must never be lost of the fact that we are dealing with *manifestations of language* [P.G.'s italics], and not just the arbitrary acoustical signals produced by the human vocal tract and perceptible to our auditory system. Linguistic considerations and, in particular, facts concerning the limitations that different languages impose on the phonetic shape of words and utterances must therefore be taken into account on a par with articulatory and acoustic data. (Halle & Stevens 1979: 335)

These definitions pin-point the distinction between a phonetic and a phonological description of speech. In a *phonetic analysis* one is describing what types of sound the human individual is, or is capable of, producing. The term 'sound', by the way, should be taken as referring to both segment-size units, which are commonly called 'speech-sounds', and to differences in humanly produced sound that stretch over longer pieces of utterances, for example pitch, loudness, rate, voice quality, etc., although this book will concentrate entirely on the segmental aspects of speech. In addition, it should be noted that a phonetic description may be couched in articulatory, auditory or acoustic terms, or a combination of these, though articulatory descriptions will be used almost exclusively here. In contrast to the general descriptive approach of a phonetic analysis, the aim of a *phonological analysis* is to provide a description and classification of the sound differences in speech on the basis of their communicative function and organisation in the spoken medium of language.[1]

A simple, though not unrealistic, example of different types of speech deviations can illustrate the clinical applications and implications of this fundamental distinction. Many languages, including English, have an [s] in their pronunciation system. The articulation of this sound can be summarised in a label such as 'voiceless fortis apico-alveolar (or lamino-alveolar) grooved median fricative'. In a full phonetic description there would need to be much more detail; for example, acoustic and auditory characteristics would also be outlined. These details are not material to the present issue. In fact, for a phonological description of the functions of this sound in the sound patterns (the phonological system) of English, even the label given above contains unnecessary details. A description which would uniquely specify the phoneme /s/[2] as different from all the contrastive consonantal types of segment in English would need to include the following articulatory features:

/s/ is: voiceless/fortis as opposed to /z/ which is voiced/lenis;
alveolar as opposed to /θ/ which is dental and /ʃ/ which is palato-alveolar;
fricative as opposed to /t/ which is plosive.

It is well known that the articulation of [s] presents difficulties for certain individuals. These speakers may use phonetically very different articulations from those used by normal speakers of their language and the result is a different phonetic segment. A possible deviant pronunciation is the use of [ɬ], that is a 'voiceless fortis apico-alveolar lateral fricative'. Comparison with the phonetic label for [s] indicates that there is a major phonetic difference in the articulation of these sounds, in that [s] is a *median* (grooved) fricative and [ɬ] is a *lateral* fricative. Comparison with the phonological description for an English /s/, however, reveals no significant differences; both sounds are fortis, alveolar and fricative. The implication of this is that if an individual with a speech deviation consistently uses [ɬ] where a normal speaker of English would use [s] he is still able to signal all the consonantal contrasts in the phonological system of English, and therefore he can realise the language adequately and efficiently in the spoken medium. His speech may sound rather bizarre and the [ɬ] will probably be obtrusive, which are in themselves sound reasons for offering remedial assistance to such speakers; but it is unlikely that such a speaker would fail to make himself understood on any occasion. This type of speech disorder involves a *phonetic deviation* in the pronunciation patterns of the language.

During the development of speech, young children at the earliest stages of learning to talk often do not use the [s] type of sound very much at all. For most words which in the normal adult pronunciation would contain an [s], a child may use, for example, [t] instead of the fricative.[3] The adult pronunciation system includes the phoneme /t/ as a contrastive consonantal sound type, which can be uniquely specified as different from all the other consonants in the system in that it is:

voiceless/fortis	cf.	/d/;
alveolar	cf.	/p/, /k/;
plosive	cf.	/s/.

It will be evident, therefore, that the use of [t] where an adult would use [s] will affect the child's ability to signal consonantal contrasts and thus he will fail to realise the English language adequately in its spoken medium. For example, both *tea* and *sea* will be pronounced [ti], *nice* and *night* as [naɪt], etc. The difference in the pronunciation patterns here results in a *phonological deficit* in the child's speech at this stage in its development.

To continue this illustration one step further, it is sometimes the case that speakers who have difficulties with the articulation of [s] also encounter difficulties with [ʃ]; and where either of these sounds occurs in the normal pronunciation the speaker who uses the deviant [ɬ] articulation may well use it for both. In this instance, not only does the use of [ɬ] involve a phonetic deviation, it also results in a phonological deficit, as the speaker will be unable to signal the difference between *sew* and *show*, both [ɬoʊ]; *ass* and *ash*, [aɬ]; etc.[4] There are, obviously, different treatment implications to be drawn depending on whether the differences between the patterns used by the deviant speaker and the normal patterns involve phonetic deviations and/or phonological deficits. A person with a straightforward phonetic deviation will have to be made aware of his mispronunciation and assisted in the mastery of a new articulatory gesture. A person with a phonological deficit will have to appreciate that his speech is communicatively inadequate, and then he will need to acquire the new phonological contrast in his pronunciation system together with the normal articulatory gestures that signal the contrast.

This illustration not only serves to indicate the fundamental necessity of the distinction between phonetics and phonology, it also encapsulates the multifaceted contribution of phonetic and phonological studies to the clinical practice of speech and language pathology. For even in this simple example we can see that the distinction between phonetics and phonology enables us to assess the difference between normal and disordered speech, and indeed between different types of disordered speech. From this assessment we are able to diagnose different types of speech disorders and their communicative implications. Finally, on the basis of this information we can plan and implement the most appropriate treatment according to the different characteristics of the disordered pronunciation patterns. Let us therefore examine the contribution of phonology in these more general terms.

ASSESSMENT

In order to analyse and assess the characteristics of a speech and/or language disability the clinician must have detailed knowledge of the normal pronunciation patterns of the individual's speech community. This is provided for British English in such phonetic texts as Gimson 1980; Hughes & Trudgill 1979; Wells 1982. There will therefore be no further discussion of normal pronunciation patterns here, except as is necessary for the explanation of examples. As a considerable number of the patients seen by speech pathologists are children, the clinician also requires knowledge of the normal patterns in the development of spoken language, in order to compare the speech of the child patients with that of children developing speech normally. In Chapters Four and Seven information is provided about normal phonological development, since the procedures discussed there are particularly appropriate to the assessment of child speech.

It would also be useful for the purposes of both assessment and diagnosis if there were detailed descriptions of the phonetic and/or phonological characteristics, of different types of disabilities. This type of information is available in many general speech pathology textbooks, although it is often phonetically rather superficial and lacks a linguistic framework of description. More detailed, linguistically-oriented descriptions include, for example, Crystal 1980: Chapter 4; Edmonds & Shriberg 1983; Grunwell 1981b; Ingram 1976: Chapter 5; Lesser 1978: Chapter 8; Stoel-Gammon & Dunn 1985. On the basis of such descriptions clinicians can examine an individual's speech for the occurrence of similar characteristics and thus identify the type of disability (see Chapter Eight for specific examples of diagnostic characteristics).

Clinical phonology contributes more than just information required for the clinical procedures of assessment. It also provides the principles which underlie the construction of the assessment procedures and the frameworks of analysis and appraisal. In order to make a comprehensive and relevant assessment it is essential to acquire adequate and appropriate data from the patient. This involves both the speech sample to be elicited and the way it is recorded (i.e. transcribed) by the clinician. For example, the data base must seek to be representative of both the potential targets for the individual (i.e. the phonological system of his language) and his present performance. The recording or transcription, furthermore, must make available all the information about his speech that may be required in the assessment. These aspects of assessment will be discussed in Chapters Two and Three.

Once the data have been elicited and recorded they must then be assessed. Here one finds the most obvious contribution of clinical phonology: the applications of the *principles of phonological analysis.* By applying a phonological framework of analysis to the assessment of disordered speech the clinician is able to discover the regularities in the data and to appreciate the potential communicative inadequacies consequent upon the speech deviations. There are several different theoretical frameworks of phonological analysis that have been applied as the basis for clinical assessment procedures. These are the main concern of this book. It is obviously important that the clinician is aware of the basic principles which underlie these procedures, as well as how to carry out the analyses themselves. It is also important that the clinician should be aware of any explanatory, that is psycholinguistic, hypotheses associated with any procedure and therefore be able to evaluate whether any particular procedure is appropriate and applicable in the assessment of different types of speech disabilities. Therefore these implications are also discussed in respect to the procedures presented in this book.

DIAGNOSIS

A major diagnostic contribution of clinicial phonology has already been encountered, viz. the differentiation between a phonetic deviation and a phonological deficit. Indeed it is no exaggeration to state that the distinction between phonetics and phonology is crucial in the classification of types of speech and language pathologies. Furthermore, for some types of speech disabilities a differential diagnosis can be made on the basis of phonetic and/or phonological descriptions of the disordered speech.[5] In Chapter Eight the distinction between phonetic and phonological speech disorders is defined and explored further in relation to specific types of pathologies.

Another dimension of diagnosis is also dependent on phonological information. This is the differential diagnosis between delayed or deviant speech development in children. Chapter Four and especially Chapter Seven contain some discussion of this aspect of clinical phonology, since this diagnosis must be based on descriptions of normal development.

Finally, in regard to diagnosis, if speech assessments and analyses are designed and administered according to phonological principles, the descriptions of the disordered speech data will take account of the communicative implications of the disorder and the diagnostic characteristics of pathologies will be much more informative. It is therefore hoped that wider and more frequent application of the procedures outlined in this book, as and when appropriate of course, will lead to more informed diagnoses.

TREATMENT

Appropriate treatment procedures must be based on a detailed description of the 'correct' target behaviour. Therefore the description of normal pronunciation patterns required for assessment purposes is also needed in the delineation of treatment aims. Equally, a comparison between the normal and disordered pronunciation patterns will enable the clinician to specify the changes that intervention must facilitate.

As the brief example above demonstrates, the clinical applications of phonology can be extended to influence the principles of treatment. This example illustrates that the distinction between the phonetic and phonological aspects of speech patterns has major implications for therapeutic methodology. Each of the various different frameworks of phonological analysis and assessment discussed in the subsequent chapters of this book suggest different methods of approach in remediation. But all share in common the fundamental principles that treatment aims and procedures should be specifically designed and delineated and that they should be directed at changing the disordered *patterns* in a person's speech (see further Chapter Eight).

In the applications of phonology to the basic clinical tasks of assessment, diagnosis and treatment, one can see therefore the relationship and implications between the three activities. Reliable and relevant assessments are dependent upon adequate and appropriate descriptions and comparative analyses of the disordered speech behaviour. These in their turn lead to explicit statements of identifying characteristics and informative diagnoses of different types of disorders. On the basis of such descriptive assessments and diagnostic classifications, explicitly principled treatment strategies appropriate to each type of disability, or quite often each individual patient, can be defined.

This type of approach to the theory and practice of speech and language pathology is not, of course, unique to clinical phonology. It is in fact a specific application of the 'behavioural model' of investigation (see especially Crystal 1980; Chapter 1). In this model the clinician focuses on describing what the person *does* when he is talking, and from this description the clinician derives treatment aims, programmes of intervention procedures, and predictions, or prognoses, about the outcomes of treatment. Fundamental to this approach is the *detailed description* of the person's behaviour and *identification of patterns*, or regularities, in the disordered speech.

This book concentrates on the description and analysis of disordered speech *production*. The focus is, however, even more specific than this statement implies. Phonology, as indicated at the beginning of this chapter, is concerned with speech in its linguistic function. Therefore clinical phonology is primarily concerned with the linguistic implications of disordered speech; so there will be no detailed discussion here of the speech mechanisms themselves and the articulatory or neurophysiological breakdowns that may, or may not, underlie different types of speech disorders.[6] The concentration is entirely on the identification of the abnormal speech patterns to which we can attribute communicative breakdowns at the *phonological level of the linguistic organisation* of spoken language. it must, of course, be appreciated that this approach cannot stand on its own. The clinician must also make a comprehensive assessment of a person's speech production abilities, including not just an examination of the speech production mechanism and its phonetic functioning, but also an assessment of the aural reception mechanism and its auditory functioning. This latter should include an auditory phonemic discrimination test, i.e. an investigation of the person's ability to perceive the phonological contrasts used in the normal pronunciation of his language. These procedures are, however, well-established clinical practice, and they are not the province of this book. Phonological analysis and assessment are relatively speaking more recent additions to the battery of clinical procedures. Being less familiar and requiring different types of theoretical knowledge and technical expertise, they are sometimes misunderstood and misapplied (see especially Carney 1979). This book aims therefore to provide a theoretical and practical introduction to the principles and procedures of clinical phonology.

Each chapter considers a different approach to phonological analysis and description that has been shown to have clinical applications. The procedures for carrying out an analysis within each framework are detailed and exemplified. The clinical implications of each framework are examined and evaluated. Specific formal clinical assessment procedures employing each of the frameworks are outlined and reviewed at the end of each chapter. In the final chapter we return to more general considerations and explore further the implications of clinical phonology for progress in the science of clinical speech pathology. It is intended that with this theoretical background and the practice in analysis provided by the exercises, the clinician will be able more easily to perform phonological assessments and to plan and implement phonological therapy. It is also hoped that this knowledge and experience will enable clinicians to evaluate and select clinical phonological assessment procedures appropriate to their needs, and from using these procedures to gain a greater understanding of the nature of a person's communicative disabilities.

NOTES

1. For discussion of this use of the term 'medium' see especially Abercrombie (1967: Chapter 1).

2. For an explanation of the term 'phoneme', and of the use of different types of brackets, see Chapter Two below.

3. For further discussion and analysis of this and other patterns in child speech, see Chapter Seven below.

4. Like this first illustration of the clinical applications of phonological principles, all examples in this book involve disordered pronunciations of consonants. These are most frequently encountered in clinical practice and have formed, almost exclusively, the subject of all previous studies of clinical phonology. For an explanation of the representation of vowels used here see Appendix.

5. It should be noted that throughout this book the 'phonetic and phonological characteristics' of a speech and/or language disability are the characteristics of disordered speech *production*. While it is acknowledged that in many, if not most, pathologies other aspects of the patient's communicative abilities are also important, these are not relevant to the concerns of this book which is concentrated upon the analysis of a patient's spoken language.

6. There is, however, a discussion of the interaction of phonetic and phonological aspects of certain types of disabilities in Chapter Eight.

2

Basic Concepts and their Clinical Applications

All frameworks of phonological analysis describe patterns in pronunciation with reference to two basic concepts: system and structure. Indeed, these concepts of system and structure are fundamental to all types of linguistic analysis. They are defined in the first section of this chapter and discussed with reference to their clinical relevance.

The second section of the chapter discusses the principles and procedures of phonemic analysis. While this approach to analysis is related to a specific theoretical framework, it is directly derived from another basic concept: that of contrastive function which is fundamental to phonology. In essence, the concept of contrastive function encapsulates the primary role of phonology in the linguistic system of a language, and of languages in general; sound differences, while having no inherent meaning in themselves, signal meaning differences. Thus an examination of this concept and how it is applied through phonemic analysis to phonetic data, both normal and clinical, provides an appropriate starting point for our exploration of clinical phonology. In addition, historically and theoretically phonemic analysis provides the basis and the point of departure for the theoretical frameworks and their clinical applications discussed in Chapters Five, Six and Seven. Also it is, at least on the face of it, the theoretical basis of the traditional assessment procedures discussed in Chapter Three. An understanding of this conceptual framework is therefore required in order to evaluate the theoretical validity of these procedures. The concept of contrastive function *per se* is, however, most rigorously applied in the analytical procedures outlined in Chapter Four.

The final section of the present chapter discusses phonetic

representation. The recording of spoken data using the techniques of phonetic transcription is essential for all clinical applications of phonological analysis. The type of transcription made directly from a person's speech is inextricably linked to the phoneme principle. For this reason, and for their primary place in the process of phonological investigations, procedures of phonetic transcription are therefore most appropriately discussed in this chapter.

SYSTEM AND STRUCTURE

A phonological analysis of a speech sample will describe the organisation of the speech units with reference to their function of 'transmitting the messages' of the language. It goes without saying that in order to do so there must be a range of different sounds that can be used to signal different meanings. Hence the basic phonological concept of SYSTEM.

A system is a set or inventory of different sound units which are in a relationship of replacement or substitutability. When one unit is replaced by another unit a difference in linguistic meaning is signalled. Each of the units is therefore said to have a contrastive function; it contrasts or is in opposition to all the other units; its linguistic value is that it is different from all the other units in the system. The relationship of replacement or contrastivity is called a PARADIGMATIC relationship. A paradigm, or list, of units can be drawn up that may replace one another and in so doing change the meaning that is signalled.

e.g.	*eye*	/aɪ/	
	ear	/ɪə/	
	air	/ɛə/	
	oar	/ɔ/	
	'ow'	/ɑʊ/	? cry of pain
	'oh'	/əʊ/	? cry of surprise
	'oy'	/ɒɪ/	? call of attention
	'oo'	/u/	? cry of excitement[1]

It will be obvious from the above examples that spoken language would be extremely limited if it had to rely solely on a single system of different holistic units to signal its meanings.

There is, however, a second dimension of phonological

organisation. This is based on the concept of STRUCTURE. In analysing the structure of spoken language the phonological description is concerned with the relationships of co-occurrence and combination of units, and with the distribution and arrangement of units within larger-sized units. The description of structural patterns states the SYNTAGMATIC relationships between phonological units. For example, in English:

(1) /s/ can combine with /p/ and /r/, in that order, and occur before /aɪ/ to form *spry* /spraɪ/;
(2) /s/ can combine with /p/, in that order, and occur directly before /aɪ/ to form *spy* /spaɪ/;
(3) /p/ can combine with /r/, in that order, and occur directly before /aɪ/ to form *pry* /praɪ/;
(4) no other ordered combination of these three consonants before /aɪ/ (or indeed any vowel) occurs in adult English; that is */psraɪ/, */prsaɪ/, */psaɪ/, */rsaɪ/, */rpaɪ/, */sraɪ/ are not only words that just happen not to exist in English (but could be created if a new word was required at any time), but are in fact not possible as words of the language because they contravene the structural patterns of English phonology.[2]

The statements of the structural patterns in the phonology will thus detail the possible combinations of units, and by implication the restrictions on these possibilities; these are the PHONOTACTIC possibilities and restrictions. Generally speaking, the phonotactic analysis describes the patterns in the combinations of segments with respect to their co-occurrence in syllables. The structure of the SYLLABLE is:

C	V	C
consonant	vowel	consonant
nonsyllabic	syllabic	nonsyllabic
onset	nucleus	termination
initial		final

V, the vowel element, is the syllabic nucleus; it is the essential element of the syllable. C, the consonant element, is the nonsyllabic marginal element, occurring initial or final in the syllable, as the onset or termination respectively. A syllable may have no onset, for example *arm* /ɑm/, *it* /ɪt/; or no termination, for example *car* /kɑ/, *toe* /təʊ/; or neither, for example *eye* /aɪ/, *oar* /ɔ/; or both, of course, for example *might* /mɑɪt/, *calm* /kɑm/. A syllable with no termination is called an OPEN syllable; a syllable with a termination is a CLOSED syllable.

Phonotactics is usually concerned with more complex patterns than this; as illustrated above, it describes the possible combinations of consonants at the two positions in syllable structure. In the adult English pronunciation system up to three consonants can occur in sequences at the initial onset position and, in more careful styles of pronunciations, up to four in the final termination position, for example *texts* (tɛksts/. Hence the following formula details the structure of the English monosyllabic word:

$$C_{0-3}\ V\ C_{0-4}$$

When two or more consonants co-occur at the same position in syllable structure they constitute a CLUSTER.[3] As is evident from the example above there are restrictions on the occurrence and sequence of consonants in clusters. As onset (or syllable initial) clusters have already been introduced, the above example will be extended to illustrate some of the restrictions on the combinations of consonants in this position in adult English (an exhaustive description of the phonotactic possibilities can be found in Gimson 1980: 237–54). With two-place initial clusters: C_1C_2

(1) where C_1 is /s/, C_2 must be one of /p t k m n w l j (f)/ (there are only a few words beginning with /sf/, e.g. *sphere, sphinx*);
(2) where C_2 is one of /w r l j/, C_1 may be one of a large number of consonants, predominantly obstruents, including /p t k b d g f θ/ etc.

With three-place initial clusters: $C_1C_2C_3$

(1) C_1 is /s/;
(2) C_2 is one of /p t k/;
(3) C_3 is one of /w r l j/.

Thus, three-place clusters are a combination of the two types of possible patterns in two-place clusters. There are, however, further restrictions on the combinations of consonants in initial clusters in adult speech. For example:

(1) /pb/ cannot precede /w/; thus */pwæm/, */spwɪŋ/ and */bwɪk/ are impermissible adult forms;
(2) /td/ cannot precede /l/; thus */tli/, */stlɔ/ and */dlʌm/ are impermissible adult forms.

As the above examples are intended to suggest, such restrictions may not apply to the pronunciation patterns used by children (see Chapter Seven). As well as defining impermissible forms, the phonotactic analysis also classifies as '*possible forms*' sequences that are not existent vocabulary items of English at present. For example, the following are 'possible' words in English: /snɜtʃ, flɪg, skrɛm/.

The discussion of initial cluster patterns above has outlined in some detail the adult possibilities. This information is important for the understanding of the development of these patterns in children (see Chapter Seven). Since this is an aspect of the phonological development of English which has been fruitfully investigated in some depth, it clearly must be included in any consideration of the clinical applications of phonology. The patterns in adult initial clusters also provide an appropriate illustration of further aspects of a structural description to be introduced later in this chapter. The phonotactic possibilities in termination (or final) clusters are less simply stated; there is a much greater range of possible combinations, e.g. /-sp, -ps, -sps, -ls, -lz, -lp, -lps, -lpt, -lpts, -mz, -lmz, -mp, -mpt, -mpts/ etc. This book is not intended as a textbook on the phonology of English; examples are drawn from English to illustrate the phonological concepts discussed because of their familiarity. As the details of final clusters are not required for such purposes, no discussion of them will be included here (for the details see Gimson 1980: 246ff; Grunwell 1985c: 21, 74–76).

The discussion so far has been confined to single syllables and all examples have been monosyllabic words. Much of our speech, however, consists of words of more than one syllable. Here the problem immediately arises of deciding where one syllable ends and the next begins. The general rule is to apply the structural possibilities in monosyllables to the structure of each syllable in a multisyllabic word. The vowel nucleus of each syllable is readily identified; the permitted combinations of initial and final consonants are those possible in monosyllables. Thus, in a word like *extreme* the syllable division may fall in one of three places, as indicated by the placement of the stress mark and the comma:

	(1)	/ɪk,'strim/
	(2)	/iks,'trim/
	(3)	/ɪkst,'rim/
but	(4)	*/ɪ,'kstrim/
and	(5)	*/ɪkstr,'im/.

For the author, (1) is the most likely pronunciation; (2) may be used, especially for emphasis; (3) is unlikely. Consonants that form a sequence across a syllable boundary are called ABUTTING consonants (following Abercrombie 1967: 76). In (1) /k/ and /s/ are abutting, in (2) /s/ and /t/ are abutting, etc.

While the rule referring to monosyllabic patterns solves one problem of syllable division, another dilemma still remains. If there is only one consonant between two vowel nuclei, to which syllable should it be allotted? There are, on occasions, good reasons for leaving such 'ambisyllabic' consonants in this ambivalent status of being 'shared' by both syllables (see Ingram 1981; also Crystal 1982). There may, however, be a need to allot such consonants to one or other of the syllables; if so this must be done on a principled basis. An operational principle is provided by a statistical study of the distributional characteristics of English segments (O'Connor & Trim 1953). This upheld 'the often heard dictum: "If possible a syllable should begin with a consonant"' (ibid.: 120). Thus, whenever there is a single consonant between two vowels it should (almost) always be analysed as the onset consonant of the second syllable: for example *rabbit* /'ræ,bɪt/, *sugar* /'ʃʊ,gə/, *feather* /'fɛ,ðə/ (the comma indicates the syllable division).

As well as statements describing the possible combinations of segments in syllables, the consideration of structural patterns must also analyse the distributional possibilities and restrictions of individual segments. Again to take some simple examples from adult English, there are well-known restrictions on the following segments:

(1) /h/ only occurs in syllable onsets;
(2) /ŋ/ only occurs in syllable terminations;
(3) /w j/ only occur immediately prevocalic (i.e. before a vowel).

When combinations of consonants in clusters are considered, however, the restrictions are more complex, as described above. With such patterns it may be appropriate to set up subsystems of mutually replaceable segments for each position in the structure. Thus, the subsystems in three-place initial clusters are:

C_1	C_2	C_3
/s/	/p/	/w/
	/t/	/r/
	/k/	/l/
		/j/

This type of description, where a different system of units is set up for each position in the structure, is called a POLY-SYSTEMIC analysis. It is often found to be particularly appropriate in the clinical analysis of disordered speech (see Chapter Four).

This section has been concerned with emphasising that the patterns of pronunciation involve not only systems of different sounds but also regularities in the ordered combinations of these sounds into sequences which form the words of the language. Consideration of some data samples of disordered speech demonstrates the clinical applications of the concept of structure. With reference to the possibility of combining consonants to form clusters, there may be evidence of restrictions in a child's patterns that do not operate in the adult system.

DAVID 5;9 (1979)
Single onset consonants include:

[ɹ,w]	*river* [ˈɹɪvə,ˈwɪvə]	*water* [ˈwɔtə]
[j]	*lock* [jɒk]	
[p]	*paper* [ˈpeɪpə]	
[b]	*bottle* [ˈbɒkəɫ]	
[t]	*tea* [ti]	*Common* [ˈtɒmən]
[d]	*donkey* [ˈdɒŋki]	*game* [deɪm]
[k]	*candle* [ˈkandʊ]	
[s]	*soldier* [ˈsoʊdə]	
[f]	*feather* [ˈfɛvə]	*thumb* [fəm]

Onset consonant clusters are restricted to:

[p b t d f]+[ɹ]		
[pɹ]	*pram* [pɹam]	*play* [pɹeɪ]
[bɹ]	*bread* [bɹɛd]	*black* [bɹak]
	train [tɹeɪn]	*slide* [tɹaɪd]
[tɹ]	*crab* [tɹab]	*claw* [tɹɔ]
	queen [tɹin]	*squirrel* [ˈtɹɪɹʊ]
[dɹ]	*draw* [dɹɔ]	*straw* [dɹɔ]
	grape [dɹeɪp]	*glove* [dɹəv]
[fɹ]	*thread* [fɹɛd]	*flag* [fɹag]
	swing [fɹɪŋg]	
(Note:	*smoke* [moʊk]	*snow* [noʊ]
	spoon [bun]	*stove* [toʊf])

In this sample it will be seen that a much wider range of consonants occurs in single onset position, initial in a word, than in word initial onsets with clusters of consonants. In David's speech at this time, onset clusters are restricted to two places, and the systems at each place in structure would appear to be:

C_1	C_2
[p	[ɹ]
b	
t	
d	
f]	

Another type of distributional restriction often found to be characteristic of very young children's speech, but generally associated with disordered development in children over the age of 2;6–3;0, is exemplified in the following sample.

ALISON 5;3 (1977)

meat, me [mi]	*nice* [naɪ]	*name* [neɪ]
purse [pɜʔ]	*take* [teɪ]	*clothes* [koʊ]
bread [bɛ]	*dog* [dɒ]	*gun* [gʊ]
	this [dɪ]	
fork [fɔ]	*thumb* [s̪ʊ]	
	seat [si]	*horse* [hɔ]

	shoot [suʔ]
one [wɒ]	*like* [laɪ]
red [wɛ]	

There are virtually no final (or terminating) consonants at all in this child's speech; there is, however, a relatively wide range of consonants used in word-initial onset position. Alison's data sample thus indicates a structural pattern which is restricted to open syllables; her patterns of consonant distribution are therefore very different from those of adult English.

A third type of distributional restriction is exemplified in the data sample of Rachel.

RACHEL 5;7 (1979)

pussy cat [ˈpəhitat]	*tiger* [ˈtaɪ-ə]
bathing [ˈpeɪ-ɪŋ]	*coffee* [ˈtɒhi]
birthday [ˈpɜheɪ]	*gollywog* [ˈtɒhiˈwɒ]
feather [ˈfɛhə]	*seven* [ˈsɛhə]
	soldier [ˈsoʊ-ə]
	sugar [ˈsʊhə]
	ladder [ˈsahə]
	lollipop [ˈsɒhiˈpɒp]
washing [ˈwɒhɪŋ]	*yellow* [ˈjɛhoʊ]
robin [ˈwɒhɪ]	
orange [ˈɒhɪŋ]	
holding [ˈoʊ-ɪŋ]	

Here, while there is a relatively wide range of consonants in onsets initial in words and some consonants also occur in terminations final in words, within words the range of consonants is restricted to [h] or zero. This is another distribution pattern which is often encountered in the speech of children with disordered phonological development and which is very different from the target patterns of adult English.

As is evident from these examples, in analysing and assessing the speech patterns of any individual it is important to investigate the distribution and combinations of segments that occur as well as the range of different sounds that are used.

PHONEMIC ANALYSIS

So far the concept of SYSTEM has been given only a very brief and somewhat oversimplified examination. Nevertheless, it is evident that underlying the operation of a system of phonological units, as outlined above, is the fundamental concept of contrastive function: sound differences signal meaning differences. However it is not the case that every phonetically different segment necessarily functions as a different phonological unit. In carrying out a phonological analysis it therefore has to be established whether each perceptible phonetic difference signals a difference in linguistic meaning, and if not which phonetic differences serve a contrastive function. This is the basis of the *phoneme principle.* The phonemes of a language are the minimally distinct (i.e. different) segments that signal the meaning differences in the language. Their basic phonological characteristic is their *contrastive function*: their basic phonetic characteristic is that they are *different* from one another; thus they are distinctive sound units. Based on this set of criteria for the identification of phonemes is one of the important 'discovery procedures' in phonemic analysis: that of the 'substitution test', which uses words that are *minimal pairs.* Minimal pairs are words that differ in one segment only and have different meanings. The latter property indicates that the phonetic difference between the two segments is distinctive (see further in Chapter Five). Thus it is demonstrated that the segments fulfil the contrastive function and are realisations of different phonemes. For example, the following are minimal pairs in normal adult English:

tin	/tɪn/	*bitter*	/'bɪtə/	*bit*	/bɪt/
din	/dɪn/	*bidder*	/'bɪdə/	*bid*	/bɪd/

By drawing up lists of minimal pairs the system of contrastive segments can be established for each position in structure. For example, the minimal pair *tin/din* can be extended to include *pin/bin/kin/fin/thin/sin* . . . ., etc.; these are part of a minimal set. Segments that occur at the same position in structure and signal a meaning difference are in *parallel distribution.* They constitute the system of contrastive segments at the particular position in structure, and as such they are in a paradigmatic relationship of mutual replacement, as is shown by the substitution test procedure.

In clinical analysis the occurrence of minimally-different words provides evidence to establish whether two or more phonetically different segments are contrastive in the pronunciation patterns investigated. For example, from the following data it can be established that [p] and [t] are contrastive in word-initial syllable onsets in the speech of this child.[4]

PAUL 6;11 (1975)

bath, bat [paʔ]	*cat* [taʔ]
bees, peas [pi]	*tea, key, cheese, tree, green* } [ti]
bite, buy [paɪ]	*kite, sky* [taɪ]
box [pɒʔ]	*dog, got* [tɒʔ]
blue [pu]	*two* [tu]

This procedure for analysing the system of contrasts relies on the recognition of the phonological identity of segments in different utterances and in different phonetic contexts. It is often possible, however, to detect quite considerable phonetic differences in the pronunciation of the same phonological unit. For example in adult English the plosive in the termination position of a word like *bit* might be:

(1) released with audible plosion [bɪtʰ];
(2) unreleased [bɪt˺];
(3) accompanied by a glottal stop [bɪʔ͜t], etc.

These variant pronunciations tend to occur quite randomly; that is they are not usually predictable in terms of any phonological or other linguistic factors. These different segments are therefore in *free variation.* They do not signal a difference in meaning.

In analysing a speech sample in a clinical assessment it is likewise important to recognise that certain phonetic differences may not be used consistently to signal meaning differences. For example, Paul's data also include:

PAUL 6;11 (1975)
brother [ˈpəðə, ˈbəðə]
cart [tɑ, kɑ]
dog, got [dɒʔ, tɒʔ].

From these variant pronunciations of the same word it can be concluded that [pb] are in free variation, as are also [tdk]. (It has already been demonstrated in the immediately preceding sample of Paul's speech that the set [pb] is in contrast with the set [tdk].) Clearly, in the devising of treatment aims the recognition of this situation is of considerable significance. In order to assist Paul to achieve a more normal pronunciation pattern, it would be necessary to develop a consistent contrast between these free variants. This is an example of a very common situation in speech disorders, especially in children; the clinical task here is not one of facilitating the actual pronunciation of sounds, but rather of developing a system of stable contrastive segments.

The following data illustrate another pattern of free variation often found in clinical data.

MARTIN 6;3 (1975)

lip [wɪʔ, ʋɪʔ]	*wing* [wɪŋ, ʋɪŋ]
lock, *rock*, *watch*, *yacht* } [ʋɒʔ]	*lots*, *yacht* [wɒʔ]
rug [wəʔ, ʋəʔ]	
red, *yes* [ʋɛ]	*race* [weɪ]
line [ʋaɪn]	*white* [waɪʔ]

Here the variation is between two phonetically similar segments, one of which occurs in normal adult speech, the other does not. Therefore, in terms of an expansion of the child's patterns towards the normal adult target pronunciation, this type of free variation does not constitute the basis for the establishment of a potential contrast. This type of variation would thus need to be inhibited. In addition, of course, Martin, like Paul, needs to develop a wider range of *consistently* different contrastive segments to signal the meaning differences between the words he is using.

In examining the variation in children's speech in this framework of analysis it is important to recognise that one is describing only one of several possible dimensions of variability in children's pronunciation patterns. The above examples have illustrated free variation which is, as it were, internal to the child's own patterns. In phonological analysis for clinical purposes we must also consider variability in the relationship between the pronunciation patterns of the disordered speaker and those of the normal target pronunciations. For example, Paul's free variation in his use of [t; k] results in his attempts at words with target /k/ being unpredictable: some may be pronounced with /k/ realised as [t], others as [k] and yet others with one or other of these consonants on different occasions (i.e. in free variation). There is therefore a variable correspondence between the adult and child pronunciations: where the adult has one possibility, the child has more than one (and often several). This issue of variability, and especially the variability and predictability of relationships between target and child pronunciations, recurs throughout subsequent chapters. In the present chapter, however, the focus is upon an examination of how phonemic principles can be applied in the description of the internal organisation within a child's pronunciation patterns. It is to this theme that we now return.

In the discussion of *structure*, above, restrictions on the distribution of segments were illustrated. It was suggested that a polysystemic approach setting up different systems of contrastive segments for each position in structure was a particularly appropriate procedure for handling this type of patterning. In contrast to the polysystemic approach, the principles of phonemic analysis require the classification of different segments which occur at different positions in structure as phonologically identical *under certain specified conditions.* Thus the phonetically different segments in the onsets

(1) *tin* [tʰɪn]
(2) *stick* [stɪk]
(3) *trip* [t̠ɹ̥ɪp]

and the terminations in:

(4) *bit* [bɪt˺]
(5) *width* [wɪt̪θ]
(6) *wished* [wɪʃt̠]

are classified as being members of the same phonological unit, that is as *allophones of the same phoneme.* These allophonic variants only occur at certain places in structures; their phonological contexts of occurrence can thus be delimited and described, for example:

(1) [t^h] occurs as single onset consonant in a stressed syllable;

(2) [t] i.e. unaspirated, occurs after /s/ in stressed syllable onsets;

(3) }
(6) } [t̠] occurs before and after post alveolar consonants e.g. /r ʃ tʃ/;

(4) [t˺] i.e. unreleased, frequently occurs in word-final position;

(5) [t̪] occurs before dental consonants /θ ð/.

These variants are *context-conditioned* and their occurrence is predictable (in contrast to allophonic variants that are in free variation). Such rule-governed variants are said to be in *complementary distribution.* They cannot, normally, replace one another as they only occur in mutually exclusive contexts. Here once again phonetically different segments are not signalling a difference in meaning; the phonetic difference is not linguistically significant.

This type of patterning may be a relevant aspect of disordered speech, as the following two examples illustrate.

ROBERT 4;6 (1977)

spade [beɪt]   *skate, gate* [deɪt]
pig, big [bɪt]   *stick* [dɪt]
fork [bɔt]   *talk* [dɔt]
Bob [bɒp]   *dog, cot* [dɒt]
soup [dup]   *cup* [dəp]
stove [doʊp]   *shed* [dɛt]

Here, regardless of the characteristics of the target adult pronunciations, all word-initial onset consonants are lenis/voiced and all word-final terminating consonants are fortis/voiceless. Thus [b] and [p] are in complementary distribution and could be classified as members of the same phonological unit; similarly [d] and [t] are members of the same unit.

In the following sample the pattern is more complex.

DARREN 6;3 (1975)

seat, feet [θit]   *four, saw, sort* [fɔ, ɸɔ]
three, sea [θi]   *fat, flat* [fat]
ship [θɪp]   *frog* [fɒk]
fit, sit [θɪt]   *shop* [fɒp]

shake [θeɪk]	*show, sew* [foʊ]
same [θeɪ]	*thumb* [fə]
shed, sledge, fell, thread } [θɛ]	*thirteen* ['ɸɜʔi]
	fourteen ['ɸɔʔi]
fair [θɛə]	*sausage* ['fɒʔɪ]

Here three phonetically-different voiceless fricatives [θfɸ] occur in word-initial onset position. It is evident, however, from the variant pronunciations of *four, saw, sort,* that [fɸ] are in free variation. The occurrence of [θ] versus [f ~ ɸ], on the other hand, is totally predictable:

(1) dental fricative [θ] only occurs before [i, ɪ, eɪ, ɛ, ɛə], i.e. front close vowels;
(2) labial fricatives [fɸ] only occur before open and back vowels.

The two phonetic types of fricatives are thus in complementary distribution and should be regarded as members of the same phonological unit.

From this example it can be seen therefore that free variation and complementary distribution involve two very different types of variability in a speaker's pronunciation patterns. Free variation entails unpredictable variable pronunciations. Complementary distribution entails variable pronunciations which are dependent upon certain specifiable contextual conditions and which are therefore predictable. Nevertheless, the clinical implications of occurrences of complementary distribution such as those illustrated above are essentially similar to those indicated in the discussion of free variation. The treatment aims must be to change the patterns so as to establish as contrastive the segments which are being used by the child but which at present do not have the phonological function of signalling meaning differences. However, given that in the instance of complementary distribution, a child's pronunciations are predictable, the treatment programme can be planned more systematically with the aim of bringing about the hoped-for change in a regular way.

In this outline of phonemic analysis, a fundamental principle has been implicitly invoked in all the examples discussed so far: this is that all the allophones of one phoneme are phonetically similar. Phonetic similarity is difficult to delimit as many of the above examples suggest. In adult English phonology /t/ and /d/ clearly share many phonetic characteristics, but are sufficiently different to function contrastively. In Robert's pronunciation patterns [t d] do not function contrastively and would be analysed as members of the same phonological unit. Similarly, /f/ and /θ/ are contrastive in adult English, but not in Darren's speech patterns. There would appear to be no strict principles or limits to apply in identifying phonetically similar segments. Furthermore, when analysing the pronunciation patterns of normal languages, phonologists take into account not just the phonetic characteristics of variants, but also other aspects of phonological patterns in establishing the allophones of phonemes, (see especially Sommerstein 1977: 20–2).

With regard to the range of phonetic differences, allophones of the same phoneme may differ in voicing, in place or manner of articulation, or in other phonetic characteristics; but they do not usually differ in all of these simultaneously, in a single variant. For example, in certain accents of normal adult English:

(1) /r/ has both voiced, e.g. *grab* [gɹæb], and devoiced, e.g. *crab* [kɹ̥æb], variants;
(2) /p/ has both bilabial, e.g. *helpless* [ˈhɛɫpləs], and labiodental, e.g. *helpful* [ˈhɛɫp̪̆fʊɫ], variants;
(3) /j/ has both approximant, e.g. *you* [ju], *view* [vju], and devoiced fricative, e.g. *pew* [pʝ̊u], *cue* [kʝ̟̊u], variants;
(4) /l/ has both velarised and non-velarised variants, e.g. *local* [ləʊkəɫ].

Defining phonetic similarity has therefore presented theoretical phonologists using phonemic analysis with a problem. The problem of delimiting phonetic similarity is not, however, a particularly important issue in the applications of phonemic analysis to the practical clinical tasks of assessment and treatment planning. The main aim in applying the phonemic principle to disordered speech data is to discover whether and which different phonetic segments are being used consistently to signal contrasts in meaning. The types of non-contrastive variants that are most commonly encountered in the clinical context are well-represented in the data samples quoted above. Variation is most often observed to occur between segments that in the normal adult system signal a contrast, cf. Paul, Robert, Darren. There is a second type of variation that is also frequently encountered and this is exemplified in the samples of Martin and Darren. Here, two phonetically very similar segments are in free variation; typically, one of the variants is used in the normal adult pronunciation, the other is not. As the practical purpose of the analysis is to provide a description of the pronunciation patterns which will form the basis of a plan to change those patterns identified as deviant, it is unnecessary to spend time deciding whether two segments share sufficient phonetic characteristics in common to be classified as members of the same phonological unit. The clinically-essential point is to recognise when two or more phonetically-different segments are *not* functioning as contrastive segments because they cannot or do not consistently signal meaning differences. In these circumstances they cannot be analysed as different phonological units.

There is one final issue to be considered with regard to the clinical applications of the concepts and principles of phonemic analysis. The procedures of analysis based upon these principles have been presented thus far as a descriptive framework within which to make statements about an individual's pronunciation patterns. These statements are said to describe the regularities — or the phonological organisation — in the individual's spoken language based upon a recorded sample of speech. The concepts, such as the 'phoneme', upon which these statements are founded, are abstract analytical devices. In the approach outlined above, if the phoneme can be said to 'exist' it is as a unit of classification which enables the analyst to discern the patterns in the data. There is no explicit or implicit assumption that the resultant analysis is in any way 'real'. That is, it has *not* been claimed nor assumed that it might be a formal representation of the way the speaker organises his pronunciation patterns in the neuro-psycholinguistic planning of his utterances. The analysis is 'data-oriented' rather than 'speaker-oriented'; it describes the data but does not explain the behaviour of the speaker.

This is an issue which will be explored in more detail in Chapter Seven. However, as an illustration of the complexity of the points at issue, we will briefly consider some of those which are pertinent in the context of the phonemic framework of phonological description. As has been pointed out in the preceding paragraph, the analytical statements tend to be entirely based on samples of an individual's speech output alone, when phonological analysis is employed in the clinical context. Furthermore, these samples are often rather restricted in size and in type of utterances elicited. There is generally no attempt to obtain from the speaker judgements or intuitions about the phonological status of the sounds he is using; e.g. whether the words as he pronounces them are perceived by him as sounding 'same' or 'different'. Of course, as these speakers are very often young children it must be acknowledged that obtaining reliable data of this nature would be extremely difficult, if not impossible. Furthermore, on the rare occasions when children have been asked about their speech, if sensible responses have been obtained, these appear to contradict the spoken data, as perceived of course by the normal-speaking adult listener. Children often appear to perceive as different utterances which adult listeners judge as being the same. For example, many children refuse to accept an adult's 'imitation' of their own mispronunciation as a pronunciation of the assumed target word. However, their attempts to correct the adult's 'error' generally do not sound to an adult any different from the child's original mispronunciation: for example, a child pronounces /f/ as [w]; an adult (in a rather painful position) says 'you're standing on my [wʊt]'; the child responds (without removing his foot) by correcting the adult: 'not [wʊt ... wʊt]'. This type of response from children has become known as the 'fis phenomenon' since the first report in the literature described an incident in which a child rejected in a similar way an adult 'imitation' of his pronunciation of *fish* as [fis] (Berko & Brown 1960).

This presents a perplexing state of affairs. One possible interpretation is that children not only perceive differences in the speech of others but also make corresponding differences in their own speech in a way which at the time are not readily detectable by a normal adult's auditory mechanism. Acoustic evidence, based on spectrographic analysis, has been advanced in support of this viewpoint (e.g. Macken & Barton 1979; Smit & Bernthal 1983; see also for a discussion of this issue Menyuk, Menn & Silber 1986). Where such acoustic evidence does not support this interpretation, then a different explanation has to be formulated. It must be assumed that the adult's perception of the child's speech production is accurate: phonetic differences are not being made by the child to signal words that he appears to 'know' are different in meaning. As he does not accept the adult's mispronunciation, it would appear that he also in some sense 'knows' the correct pronunciation, at least in regard to its perceptual characteristics when presented through the interpersonal auditory channel. There is apparently a specific perceptual failure to detect the mismatch (or in this instance, the match) between the output of his own speech production patterns and the adult's. His intra-personal self-monitoring is apparently inefficient and/or inadequate. Furthermore, to account fully for these phenomena it can be argued that the child has separate and different perceptual and production systems in his phonology, (see especially Straight 1980).

For any individual child either explanation could apply, or indeed both for different instances of what appears to be the same behaviour. While such explanations are still, in our present state of knowledge, largely in the realms of speculation, they are important as they represent attempts to develop an understanding of the nature of the phonological behaviours we are describing. Until we return to this issue in Chapter Seven, however, the phonological analyses in the following chapters will be presented as simply descriptions of the pronunciation patterns of the speakers, formulated by the clinical linguist/clinician.

PHONETIC REPRESENTATION

Any type of phonetic representation, or written transcription, of speech is made up of two pieces of written information. The first, and most obvious, is the TEXT, which is usually referred to as the 'transcription'. This is a written representation recording the pronunciation(s) used for the spoken utterances transcribed. The second part of a transcription is the CONVENTIONS. These are statements describing the phonetic values (usually articulatory, but some are auditory, or even essentially acoustic, e.g. for vowels) of the symbols which are used in the text. For example [x] represents the occurrence of a voiceless fortis velar fricative; the use of [$_{\omega}$] beneath [$\underset{\omega}{t}$] indicates that the fortis alveolar plosive was pronouncd with labialisation (lip-rounding). These conventions obviously need to be known or available to the reader/user of the transcription for him to analyse the pronunciations represented in the text and even perhaps to read the text aloud in imitation of the original speaker. It is clear, therefore, that interpretation of a text is dependent upon the conventions. In using phonetic transcription, however, there is an interdependence between text and conventions, with the phonetic information about the speech recorded being distributed differently between the text and the conventions according to the type of transcription employed.

The type of transcription that is generally regarded as the simplest, from the point of view of text, has the most complex and lengthy conventions. This is PHONEMIC TRANSCRIPTION (frequently referred to as a 'broad' transcription). This transcription has an inventory of symbols only as large as is required to represent unambiguously the system of contrastive segments (i.e. phonemes) of the accent of the speaker whose speech is being recorded. There is thus a different symbol for each phoneme. In order to interpret the precise phonetic value of any symbol in the text, a very detailed set of conventions is required. These must describe all the variant pronunciations of each phoneme symbolised by the one symbol, with indications as to the distribution and contexts in which the allophones occur. For example, in the following utterance it is quite possible that each /p/ symbol represents a perceptibly different sound:

Pooh spotted Piglet from the treetop
/ˈpu spɒtɪb ˈpɪgləp frəm ðə ˈtritɒp/
(1) (2) (3) (4) (5)

(1) /p/: an aspirated fortis labialised bilabial plosive, aspirated initial in a stressed syllable, labialised before /u/ [p̫ʰ];

(2) /p/: an unaspirated fortis bilabial plosive, unaspirated initial in a stressed syllable preceded by /s/ [p˭];

(3) /p/: an aspirated fortis bilabial with no approach phase for the complete closure (this having been accomplished for the preceding /b/), aspirated initial in a stressed syllable [pʰ];

(4) /p/: an unaspirated fortis labiodental plosive, anticipating the place of articulation of the following fricative /f/ [p̪];

(5) /p/: an unreleased fortis bilabial plosive, unreleased in utterance final position [p˺].

(Note: Phonemic transcription is always enclosed in SLANT brackets, viz. / /; allophonic transcription (see below) is always enclosed in SQUARE brackets, viz. [ ].)

In any utterance of this sentence by a normal speaker, /p/ (1), (2) and (3) are almost certain to be realised as described above; /p/ (4) and (5), however, are possible variants that some speakers may only occasionally or even never use. It is evident, therefore, that a phonemic transcription is not a particularly detailed record of how a speaker realises a specific utterance on one specific occasion.

More information can be gained about the pronunciations used on a particular occasion from an ALLOPHONIC TRANSCRIPTION, (often ambiguously referred to as a 'narrow' transcription; see below). In this type of representation some of the information that is contained in the conventions of a phonemic transcription is transferred to the text; thus the phonetic details of the pronunciations of the different allophones of a phoneme are recorded in the text. An allophonic transcription of the pronunciation of the utterance described above might be:

['p̪̆ʷʰu: sp˭ɒtɪb̥ 'pʰɪgləp̪̆ fɹ̥ɪə̃m ðə 't̠ɹ̥itɒp˺].

The conventions for this text would require more symbol and diacritic definitions than for a phonemic transcription, for example:

[ʷ] labialisation
[ʰ] aspiration
[p̪̆] fortis labiodental plosive
[˺] unreleased plosive.

However, there would not need to be a long list of allophonic variants for each phoneme with specifications of their distribution and contexts of occurrence.

Both phonemic and allophonic transcriptions are based on a detailed phonological analysis of the pronunciation patterns of the accent (or idiolect) being transcribed. This implies that the range of possible segment types is known and the rules for their distribution and combination are also known. To all intents and purposes one uses these types of transcription only when one is transcribing the speech of a normal mature speaker speaking normally in an accent which has been analysed by a linguistic phonetician. Both phonemic and allophonic transcriptions are SYSTEMATIC TRANSCRIPTIONS, where ... 'the transcriber knows in advance what all the possibilities are ...' (Abercrombie 1967: 128). Systematic transcriptions are particularly useful for pedagogic purposes: for example, for indicating the pronunciation of words in dictionaries; for teaching about the pronunciation of a language to speech therapists, mother-tongue and foreign language teachers; for highlighting, using if necessary allophonic transcriptions, the language- or accent-specific variants or phonetic realisations in teaching the pronunciation of foreign languages, or of different accents for dramatic purposes.

The opposite, as it were, of a systematic transcription is an IMPRESSIONISTIC TRANSCRIPTION (this is also sometimes called a 'narrow' transcription; cf. above). Here 'an almost infinite number of possibilities stretches before a transcriber ...' (Abercrombie 1967: 128). The objective in this type of transcription is to record in as much detail as possible all the phonetic phenomena observed. The transcriber must be prepared to draw on his knowledge of the total range of human articulatory possibilities, to use all the resources of his notation system and even to devise new notational devices to represent sound types not encountered before.[5] In making an impressionistic transcription the observer does not know, or acts as if he does not know, the pronunciation patterns he is recording. A transcriber may choose to disregard previous descriptions of an accent when recording the speech of a different person who apparently uses the accent (this is an especially advisable approach if the previous descriptions were made some time ago, or were based on the speech of a different generation or social group). More obviously the transcriber who is attempting to record for the first time a language which has not so far been analysed by phoneticians will of necessity make an impressionistic transcription. In this instance, the transcription will form the 'raw data' of a phonological analysis of the language and the subsequent conventions for systematic transcriptions. An impressionistic transcription is always enclosed in SQUARE brackets.

To sum up, therefore, there are the following:

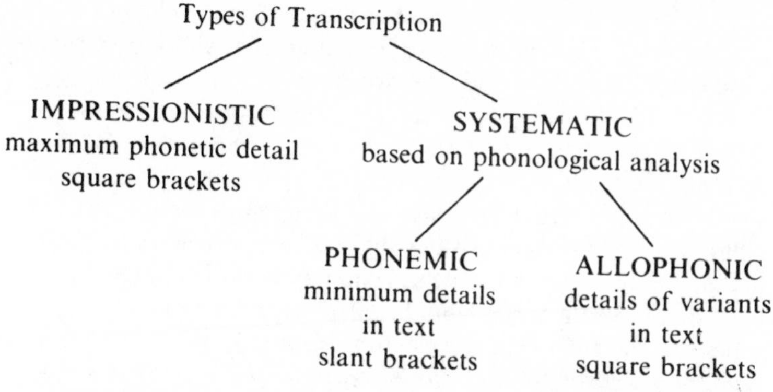

Types of Transcription

IMPRESSIONISTIC
maximum phonetic detail
square brackets

SYSTEMATIC
based on phonological analysis

PHONEMIC
minimum details
in text
slant brackets

ALLOPHONIC
details of variants
in text
square brackets

Transcription, as indicated at the beginning of this chapter, is one of the essential clinical phonetic and phonological skills of the speech pathologist and therapist. This is because every transcription is not simply a representation or a recording of the utterances transcribed, it is the beginning of the discovery procedures which culminates in a phonetic and phonological analysis of the speaker's pronunciation patterns. Indeed, the transcription itself is an ANALYSIS of the speech observed. The symbols represent the transcriber's classifications of the sounds heard into the categories of description provided in the set of notational conventions employed in making the transcription. Therefore only those sound differences can be recorded in the transcription which are allowed for in the conventions. If a transcriber was working on the basis of the categories available in a phonemic transcription of normal English, it would not be possible to record the occurrence of such phonetic sound types as [ɬ; ç; ɰ̢; ɟ]; these would have to be represented as realisations of some English phonemic type, though there would probably be some controversy between transcribers as to which phoneme to allot each of these segments to, if one were to attempt such an exercise. More significantly, such a transcription would obscure, indeed fail to record, very important clinical information about a speaker's characteristic pronunciations, which if these sounds occurred as realisations of the English targets : /s/; /ʃ/; /r/ /ʤ/ respectively, would be obtrusive and probably unacceptable to the native English-speaking population at large.

Let us examine a different example to explore these two points further; that is, the importance of an appropriate type of transcription and the significance of the transcription as the starting point of one's analysis. Supposing a young child were to say the word *pin* with a clearly aspirated plosive at the beginning, that is [p^{h}ɪn], and the word *spin* with a perceptibly unaspirated plosive initially and no preceding fricative, that is [p$^=$ɪn], if one was only using a phonemic framework of transcription based on the adult English system both utterances would be represented by /pɪn/ and thus fail to record that the child was making a consistent difference between words containing the two types of targets. To illustrate further, a child may consistently use a fortis labiodental plosive for the initial consonant in the following words: *four, foot, fan,* that is [p͆ɔ, p͆ʊt, p͆an], and a fortis bilabial plosive in *paw, put, pan,* that is [pɔ, pʊt, pan]; however, once again a phonemic transcription based on normal English pronunciation would not distinguish between these minimal pairs in the child's speech, recording them as /pɔ, pʊt, pan/ for both 'f' and 'p' words. Therefore one would fail to represent the child's phonological abilities in one's transcription and in the subsequent analysis. Clearly, a phonemic transcription is not the type of notational tool the clinician requires in such circumstances.

Nor does an allophonic transcription of the type described above meet clinical requirements (but cf. Gimson 1980: 58, where 'allophonic' appears to embrace 'impressionistic' as used above). Allophonic transcriptions are made of speech that 'obeys the rules'. Individuals with speech that is regarded as immature, disordered or deviant are clearly not 'obeying the rules' of the pronunciation patterns used by their speech community. The clinician needs to discover in what ways the particular individual is different from his speech community in the pronunciation patterns that he uses. Of course, in order to detect the differences the clinician must know what are the 'correct' or accepted pronunciations; he will therefore have to be familiar with the phonemic and allophonic representations of the speech of normal speakers. To find out how a speaker differs from the norm it is obviously inappropriate to analyse that speaker in terms of that normal system; to analyse the differences in the speech of a disordered speaker, a detailed phonetic recording is needed of the individual's pronunciations, which can then be analysed and compared with the norms of his community.

The implications of the foregoing illustrations are clearly that the clinician should be attempting to make an impressionistic transcription. Phoneticians are always quick to point out that an impressionistic transcription is an extremely difficult and highly skilled exercise requiring ... 'long training, continual practice and familiarity with the whole of human phonetic capabilities' (Abercrombie 1967: 128). There is no doubt that to transcribe all the aspects of an utterance impressionistically is a complex procedure requiring considerable phonetic expertise. For clinical purposes, however, it is often quite adequate and appropriate to treat selected aspects of the speech with an 'impressionistic ear' and to record the other aspects using some level of systematic notation.

A very common experience with children with developmental speech disorders in particular, is to find that the patterns of vowel usage mostly, if not entirely, conform to those of their peer group and the speech community at large. The children's speech problems are largely confined in effect to the patterns of consonantal usage (Grunwell 1981b: 22). A systematic transcription can therefore be used for representing most of the vowels in such cases. The transcriber's attention should be concentrated on recording in as much detail as possible the phonetic characteristics of the consonants used by the child. For example, to return to the examples cited above, if the transcription recorded that *pin* was realised as [p^{h}ɪn] and *spin* as [p$^{=}$ɪn], and the text of the speech sample was subsequently found to contain *top* [t^{h}ɒp], *stop* [t$^{=}$ɒp], *cool* [k^{h}uɫ] and *school* [k$^{=}$uɫ], analysis would indicate a consistent pattern in the child's pronunciations. Furthermore, it would reveal that the child was indeed signalling the meaning differences between the pairs of words, a fact concealed in the representation of his pronunciations in terms of the adult phonemic system. In addition, knowledge of the allophonic variants in the adult system provides for further understanding of the child's pronunciations, as these match the allophonic, context-conditioned (non-distinctive) voice onset time differences (i.e. aspirated *v.* unaspirated variants of voiceless fortis plosives) characteristic of the normal adult pronunciations. There are clearly implications for a different approach to intervention in this situation, from that in which it would have been assumed, on the basis of an inadequate transcription, that the child said /p/ for both 'p' and 'sp'. Indeed, the use of slant phonemic brackets here is theoretically as well as practically inappropriate, as this implies that the child's pronunciation contains the adult phoneme /p/ with the same contrastive value as in the adult pronunciations; that is that the child has completely acquired the mature adult phonology. This is clearly not so in this example which, by the way, is not unrealistic; some children in the early stages of speech development do distinguish the two adult forms in the way illustrated above.

There is, of course, the possibility that the clinician, like the phonetician investigating an unknown language, may reach a state in the analysis of the patient's speech where it would be possible to make a systematic transcription of this disordered idiolect of English. This would require an extensive sample of the individual's speech, collected in a relatively short period of time, transcribed impressionistically and glossed for meaning. This sample would then have to be analysed exhaustively according to the principles of phonemic analysis discussed in the preceding sections of this chapter and using some of the procedures described in Chapter Four. The polysystemic approach adopted there, however, where a different system of consonant contrasts is analysed for each place in structure, would not be used, as the traditional systematic transcription requires the statement of a single system of phonemes (i.e. the 'monosystemic' approach). This being so, a systematic transcription requires the analyst to make a judicious choice of a single symbol to represent each phoneme, each of which may have a wide range of variants differing in a variety of different phonetic features in different contexts.

To illustrate with a simple example, if a child consistently uses only voiced plosives in syllable onset position, word-initial and within words, and only voiceless plosives in syllable terminations in word-final position, it is evident that the child is using the voiced and voiceless variants in complementary distribution (see the example of Robert's speech above and Chapter Seven). One would therefore have to represent these two variants in a systematic transcription with one symbol and have to decide, for example, whether to use the symbol |b| or |p| to represent both these phonetically-different segments in the systematic transcription of the child's speech. A systematic transcription of a child's speech patterns is usually enclosed in vertical brackets, viz. | | (Smith 1973).

In the clinical context, it is not particularly appropriate to conceal the fact that the child uses both voiced and voiceless plosives. Although the therapist needs to appreciate that the child does not use the 'voicing' difference contrastively, he must also be aware of the fact that the child does use both voiced and voiceless types of plosive and that his usage is patterned, though non-contrastive. It may be that an appropriate treatment strategy could modify this pattern and thus extend the number of contrasts used by the child relatively rapidly and easily. Therefore, for most routine clinical applications the devising of a systematic set of conventions for the interpretation of a list of symbols representing the minimum inventory of contrastive phones (the patient's 'phonemes') is inadvisable; indeed it is, from the practical point of view, unnecessary and often clinically inappropriate. This in no way should be taken to imply that an analysis of the child's own pronunciation patterns is unnecessary. As will be emphasised in Chapter Four, particularly in cases of developmental phonological disorders in children, this is the most advisable and appropriate procedure to adopt.

It should be noted that the foregoing types of transcription are the three possible ways of recording in phonetic representation the segmental aspects of *actual spoken utterances.* There is another very different type of representation known as a *systematic phonological* or *underlying abstract* representation. This will be defined in the context of the theoretical approach to which it relates, generative phonological analysis (see Chapter Six).

EXERCISES

1. Which of the following are possible English words? Those forms that are impermissible you should mark with *; give the reasons why you think that they could not be 'words' of English.

1. [sglip]	9. [kwɛb]
2. [ksɔd]	10. ['sɹʊkən]
3. [θweɪd]	11. ['twɒmblɪ]
4. ['fɹænlɪt]	12. [splɑʊʧ]
5. ['sdupə]	13. [nkəʊm]
6. [mlɑʃ]	14. [bwɪns]
7. [stɹeɪʤ]	15. [ʃɹɒl]
8. [ɪn'fjutɪk]	16. [tlɜvd]

17. ['swuʒən]
18. [ʧkæmp]
19. [skɹɒɪld]
20. ['fnlɪkə]

2. What restrictions do you observe on the distribution of consonants in the following data sample? Draw up a list of consonants, i.e. the system, that may occur at each position in the structure represented.

JAMES 4;6 (1978)

1. *brush* [blʌ]
2. *sugar* ['ʃʊʔə]
3. *cushion* ['kʊʔə]
4. *table* ['teɪʔə]
5. *glasses* ['glɑʔɪ]
6. *dog* [dɒʔ]
7. *tricycle* ['ʧaɪʔəʔə]
8. *plate* [pleɪʔ]
9. *pigeon* ['pɪʔə]
10. *clap* [klæʔ]
11. *jeep* [ʤiʔ]
12. *chicken* ['ʧɪʔə]
13. *patch* [pæ]
14. *bridge* [blɪ]
15. *sock* [ʃɒʔ]
16. *chopper* ['ʧɒʔə]
17. *gas* [gæ]
18. *dragon* ['ʤæʔə]
19. *butcher* ['bʊʔə]
20. *pretty* ['plɪʔɪ]

3.1 Which of the following pairs of words are *NOT minimal pairs*? Explain your decisions.

1. /meɪk/ — /meɪd/
2. /pɒt/ — /tɒp/
3. /pɪl/ — /bɪl/
4. /sʌn/ — /fʌn/
5. /ʧɑts/ — /stɑʧ/
6. /kæt/ — /kɑt/
7. /bəʊ/ — bəʊt/
8. /'vɪʒən/ — /'vɪlən/
9. /tɔt/ — /kɔk/
10. /praʊd/ — /kraʊd/

3.2 Find minimal pairs for the following pairs of English consonant phonemes in the syllable positions indicated.

(a) *Syllable Onset, Word Initial*

1. /b/ — /v/
2. /t/ — /ʧ/
3. /s/ — /ʃ/
4. /d/ — /g/
5. /w/ — /r/

(b) *Syllable Onset, Within Word*

1. /b/ — /m/
2. /d/ — /ð/

3. /s/ — /z/
4. /t/ — /k/
5. /r/ — /l/

(c) *Syllable Termination, Word Final*

1. /p/ — /b/
2. /n/ — /ŋ/
3. /d/ — /ʤ/
4. /ʃ/ — /t/
5. /l/ — /g/

4. From the data given below which consonants can be established as having contrastive function? Cite the data which support your analysis. Onsets and terminations should be analysed separately. For which consonants do you require further data?

CLIVE 5;8 (1979)

1. *teeth* [his]
2. *shop* [hɒp]
3. *red* [wɛd]
4. *pin* [pɪn]
5. *badge* [badz]
6. *fruit* [hut]
7. *peg* [pɛd]
8. *glove* [hʌf]
9. *cheese* [hiz͓]
10. *dish* [dɪs͓]
11. *net* [nɛt]
12. *bridge* [hɪd͓z͓]
13. *tin* [tɪn]
14. *bat* [bat]
15. *sun* [hʌn]
16. *get* [dɛt]
17. *hit*, *sit* [hɪt]
18. *swing* [wɪn]
19. *mat* [mat]
20. *ship* [hɪp]
21. *brush* [hʌs͓]
22. *desk* [dɛs]
23. *fish* [fɪs]
24. *head*, *thread*, *bread* [hɛd]
25. *some* [hʌm]
26. *top* [tɒp]
27. *bed* [bɛd]
28. *juice* [hus͓]
29. *sleep* [hip]
30. *dead* [dɛd]

5. From the data given below, which consonants would you classify as *free variants* of one phonological contrastive unit? Which consonants consistently operate contrastively to signal meaning differences?

PAUL 6;11 (1975)

1. *saw* [s͓ɔ]
2. *see* [s͓i, θi]
   sleeve [s͓i]

8. *sheep* [s͓ip]
9. *flame* [feɪ]
10. *shirt* [s͓ɜ]

3. *show* [θoʊ]
4. *fall*, *four* [fɔ]
5. *same* [s̪eɪ, seɪ]
6. *snow* [s̪oʊ]
7. *fish* [fɪʔ]
11. *feel*, *three* [fi]
12. *some* [sʊ]
13. *first*, *thumb* [fɜ]
14. *fun* [fʊ]
15. *six*, *ship* [s̪ɪʔ]

Do the following additional data support your analysis?

16. *finger* ['fɪʔθə, 'fɪʔs̪ə]
17. *window* ['wɪʔθə, 'wɪʔsə]
18. *something* ['θʊʔθɪ]
19. *water* ['wɔʔs̪ə, 'wɔʔsə]
20. *thimble* ['fɪʔθʊ]

6. From the data given below, which consonant phones would you classify as *free variants* of one phonological contrastive unit? Which consonants consistently operate contrastively to signal meaning differences?

PAUL 6;11 (1975)

1. *knee* [ji]
   leaf [ji, li]
2. *right*, *white* [waɪ]
3. *lets*, *net* [nɛ]
4. *moon* [mu]
5. *like* [jaɪʔ, laɪʔ]
6. *wellies* ['wɛji]
7. *nose* [noʊ, joʊ]
8. *rock*, *watch* [wɒʔ]
9. *me* [mi]
10. *looks* [jʊʔ]
11. *nail* [neɪʊ, jeɪʊ]
12. *men* [mɛ]
13. *lock* [nɒʔ]
14. *lolly* ['nɒni]
15. *went*, *red* [wɛ]
16. *mine* [maɪ]
17. *telly* ['tɛli, 'tɛji]
18. *new* [ju]
19. *nine* [naɪ]
20. *lost*, *not* [jɒʔ]

7. From the data given below, which consonant phones would you analyse as being in *complementary distribution*? State which phonetically different segments you would group together as variants of phonological contrastive units (phonemes) in the child's system? Give the reasons for your classifications. Which consonants can you establish as contrastive and why?

BARRY 5;0 (1974)

1. *ship* [dɪp]
2. *brush* [bʌt]

3. *digging* [ˈdɪgɪn]
4. *top, shop* [dɒp]
5. *glass* [gat]
6. *truck* [ʤʌk]
7. *toffee* [ˈdɒdi]
8. *cake* [geɪk]
9. *kitchen* [ˈgɪʤɪn]
10. *plate* [beɪt]
11. *satchel* [ˈdaʤəɫ]
12. *cap* [gap]
13. *fishing* [ˈdɪdɪn]
14. *dish* [dɪt]
15. *cough, cross* [gɒt]
16. *picking* [ˈbɪgɪn]
17. *chop, drop* [ʤɒp]
18. *skipping* [ˈgɪbɪn]
19. *frog* [dɒk]
20. *soldier* [ˈdoʊʤə]
21. *dressing* [ˈʤɛdɪn]
22. *face* [deɪt]
23. *chicken* [ˈʤɪgɪn]
24. *flat* [dat]

8. From the data given below, which consonant phones in onsets would you analyse as being in *complementary distribution* and therefore as variants of one contrastive unit? State the contextual conditions in which the variants occur. Which phones would you analyse as *free variants*?

DARREN 6;3 (1975)

1. *lip* [ðɪp]
2. *wear* [ðɛə]
3. *rat* [ʋat, wat]
4. *walk* [wɔk]
5. *red* [ðɛ]
6. *look* [βʊk]
7. *white* [waɪt, βaɪt]
8. *wind* [ðɪ]
9. *race* [ðeɪɬ]
10. *lorry* [ˈwɒhi]
11. *leg* [ðɛk]
12. *robin* [ˈwɒʔɪn]
13. *wool* [ˈwʊʊ]
14. *lazy* [ˈðeɪhi]
15. *read* [ˈði]
16. *watch* [wɒɬ, βɒɬ]
17. *letter* [ˈðɛhə]
18. *wheel* [ˈðiʊ]
19. *roof* [wu, βu]
20. *rock, lock* [ʋɒk, βɒk]

9. Analyse the onset consonants in the data below, using the concepts of phonemic analysis. Your analysis should answer the following questions:

(a) which phones are contrastive?
(b) which phones are free variants of a single contrastive unit?
(c) which phones are in complementary distribution and what are the conditioning contexts?
(d) what criteria determine the grouping of phonetically different phones as phonologically the same unit?

TANYA 8;0 (1977)

1. *climb* [tɬaɪm]
2. *park* [pɑʔ]
3. *top*, *chop* [tɒʔ]
4. *black* [plaʔ]
5. *dress* [tɬεʔ]
6. *boy* [pɒɪ, bɒɪ]
7. *juice* [tu]
8. *prince* [plɪn]
9. *track* [tɬaʔ]
10. *pen* [pεn, bεn]
11. *blue* [plu, blu]
12. *stick*, *skip* [tɪʔ]
13. *twelve* [tɬεʊ]
14. *boots* [pu]
15. *turn* [tɜn, dɜn]
16. *claws* [tɬɔ]
17. *brown* [plɑʊn]
18. *cry*, *dry* [tɬaɪ]
19. *peas*, *bees* [pi]
20. *dark* [tɑʔ]
    cart [tɑʔ, dɑʔ]
21. *box* [bɒʔ]
22. *chair* [tεə, dεə]
23. *tree* [tɬi]
24. *put* [pʊ]
25. *get* [dεʔ]
26. *plane* [pleɪn]
27. *tea* [ti]
28. *big* [bɪʔ, pɪʔ], *pig* [bɪʔ]
29. *please* [pli]
30. *crane*, *train* [tɬeɪn]
31. *peg* [pεʔ]
32. *glue* [tɬu]
33. *pram* [plam]
34. *toy* [tɒɪ]
35. *green*, *queen* [tɬin]
36. *pan* [pan, ban]
37. *ten* [tεn]
38. *grapes* [tɬeɪʔ]
39. *bread* [plεʔ]
40. *cut* [tʊ]
    jug [tʊ, dʊ]

10. The following data are extracted from an IMPRESSIONISTIC TRANSCRIPTION of a sample of speech of a child aged 3;6. List the CONVENTIONS for this TEXT, detailing the symbols and diacritics separately. What important information do you think would have been overlooked if the transcription had been made using the conventions of an adult phonemic systemic representation?

    1. *spinning top* ['ɸp˭ɪnɪn ˌtʰɒʔ]
    2. *racing car* ['ʋeɪs̬ɪn ˌʈʰɑ]
    3. *petrol garage* ['pʰεʈʂʊ ˌɖaʊɪɖ̥ʐ̥]
    4. *two wheeler bike* ['tʰuwiɰə ˌbaɪʔ]
    5. *engine driver* ['εn̠dʐən dʋaɪb̬ə]
    6. *snowball fight* ['n̥ᶠoʊbɔʊ p̃aɪʔ]
    7. *fruit shop* ['p̃ʋuʔ ʂɒʔ]
    8. *apple, pear, orange and cherries* ['apʊ 'pʰεə 'ɒʊɪndʐ ən 'ʈʂεʋɪs̬]
    9. *lots of birthday presents* ['ɰɒʔs̬ə 'bɜfɖ̥eɪ 'pʋ̥εz̠ən̪ʈs̬]

10. *three box of smarties* [ˈp̃ʊi bɒʔs̺ə ˈm̥ᶠɑtis̺]
11. *the little girl playing* [d̪ə ˈɰɪʔʊ ˈd̪ɜʊ ˈp̥ɰeɪjɪn]
12. *my swing in the garden* [maɪ ˈʍĩn ĩnə ˈd̪ɑdən]
13. *my daddy smoke a pipe* [maɪ ˈdadi ˈm̥ᶠoʊʔ ə ˈpʰaɪʔ]
14. *me going to play school* [ˈmi ˈdoʊĩn tə̥ ˈp̥ɰeɪ çcuʊ]
15. *the teacher read us/a stories* [d̪̥ə ˈtʰit̪sə ˈʋidə ˈθt⁼ɔʊɪs̺]

NOTES

1. The functions of these sounds as emotional cries, of course, are not strictly linguistic, but paralinguistic, as they do not have arbitrary and conventional meanings like the four words. American readers are reminded that the pronunciation system transcribed is a British English accent in which there is no word final or preconsonantal /r/.

2. *before a linguistic unit (i.e. in this context, a phonological structure) indicates an impossible form in the language being discussed.

3. This is the correct phonological term. Not infrequently the term 'blend' is used in the speech pathology literature. This is to be avoided when referring to the spoken medium, since it misleadingly gives the impression that the sounds are somehow 'mixed' together. It appears to have derived from usage in literature on the teaching of reading, where it is used ambiguously to refer to sequences of *letters*, representing phonological clusters in speech, and letter sequences representing single phonological units; e.g. 'sh' /ʃ/, 'ch' /tʃ/, 'dge' /dʒ/ are termed 'blends' as well as 'pl', 'tr', 'kw', etc. It is therefore ambiguous as well as inaccurate to use this term.

4. It is important to appreciate that in this and all subsequent examples in this chapter, including the exercises at the end, the principles of phonemic analysis are being applied in order to establish the contrastive segments in the child's pronunciation patterns, irrespective of their relationships to the adult target pronunciations. As indicated in the discussion of free variation, investigating these relationships involves very different considerations which are explored in later chapters.

5. The need to extend existing notational systems is very frequently found when the immature speech of children or disordered speech is being transcribed (see Ingram 1976: 92; PRDS 1983).

3

Clinical Assessment of Speech: Analysing Errors in Pronunciation

It frequently does not require specialist knowledge to recognise that a person has a communication disorder. One of the simplest types of language disability to identify is one which affects the pronunciation of spoken language. Here a person's speech is so different by comparison with the normal-speaking population as to render it obtrusive and more often than not difficult to understand. Phonetic training is not required to recognise that in such a case a person's speech is disordered. Most normal-speaking adults, moreover, can distinguish the speech *differences* that arise from sociolinguistic variations in regional, cultural and social background, that is accent differences, from the more or less idiosyncratic *deviations* (or 'defects') that occur in the speech of a person with a communication disorder. It has to be acknowledged, however, that while lay people can make this distinction, they often are under the mistaken impression that speech pathologists can and do deal with both types of problems. It is interesting to find that children too are frequently aware that some of the members of their peer group are developing different or unusual speech. In literate societies, the non-specialist is often able to describe the specific 'defects' of speech in terms of the 'sounds' or 'letters' that are mispronounced.

It is the theoretical and practical study of phonetics which provides the specialist, the speech pathologist, with the knowledge and skills necessary to analyse the nature of a person's pronunciation problems. Phonetics has long been a basic component in the education and training of speech pathologists. Yet, until comparatively recently the established routine assessment procedures and diagnostic categories for describing disordered pronunciation were apparently simple extensions of the layman's view of 'defective speech'. Speech disorders were, and in many quarters still are, defined as involving 'errors' in the production of speech sounds. This approach even now remains the basic framework of description and classification, as the following quotations indicate:

> Articulation is defective when phonemes are perceived as omitted, substituted or distorted. (Perkins 1977: 255)

> an articulation error, or disorder, is a non-standard production of one or more speech sounds. There are three basic types of articulatory defects: omissions, substitutions ... and distortions. (Emerick & Hatten 1979: 158)

> [the classifications] ... reflect the traditional distinctions in the study of articulatory disability. The first refers to *correct* phones, that is the target phone has been correctly articulated ... [the second] ... refers to *omitted* phones, in relation to the target syllable. The third ... refers to the *substituted* phones which T considers to be abnormal, in relation to the target phone. (Crystal 1982: 67)

> There are three general ways in which a speech sound is produced in error: (a) distortion, (b) substitution and (c) omission. (Newman, Creaghead & Secord 1985: 74)

These definitions differ little from those proffered thirty years ago (e.g. Van Riper & Irwin 1958: 77–8). Of course all the recent texts quoted above discuss the adequacy of such classifications and introduce linguistically influenced approaches in subsequent sections. Nevertheless, the traditional framework continues to be proposed as the fundamental model in clinical speech pathology practice by many authorities. The assessment of speech is initially and therefore primarily presented as 'error analysis'.

In this chapter therefore we shall examine the traditional error analysis procedures and evaluate their effectiveness as an approach to the clinical assessment of speech disorders. This discussion provides the background against which to view the introduction and impact of assessment procedures based on phonological analysis, which are considered in subsequent chapters. Before we consider error analysis, however, it is first of all necessary to examine the speech data that are routinely elicited for a speech assessment and the methods whereby they are most commonly obtained. The first section of this chapter therefore presents through critical discussion the principles and procedures for constructing and obtaining suitable samples of speech for clinical assessment. The second section discusses general issues raised by the traditional error analysis approach. The third, and final section briefly reviews a selection of three specific clinical assessment procedures which employ the error analysis approach.

CONSTRUCTING AND OBTAINING THE DATA SAMPLE

In order to identify a speech 'error' it is necessary to have a clear definition of:

(1) the range of possible speech patterns that can occur and that could therefore provide instances of types of errors;
(2) the types and range of speech behaviours that are considered 'correct' or acceptable.

The most common source of this information is a linguistic description of the phonemic system used by the adult speakers of the language, English for the purposes of this book. As it has been found that consonants are most often 'mispronounced', error analysis assessment procedures concentrate almost exclusively on the consonant phonemes of English. For the majority of English accents, these are 24 in number:

m n ŋ
p b t d ʧ ʤ k g
f v θ ð s z ʃ ʒ
w l r j h

Some procedures assess an inventory of 25 consonants, including [ʍ], for example in 'what, which, where', as phonemically distinct (e.g. Templin & Darley 1960; Goldman & Fristoe 1972, see below). This pronunciation of the small number of 'wh' words has a low and decreasing frequency of occurrence, and is now used consistently in very few accents. Furthermore, it can be more economically and plausibly treated, as a cluster /hw/ (see Gimson 1980; 216).

As is evident from the quotations cited above, assessment based on analysis of errors involves an evaluation of a speaker's production of each one of these phonemes ('sounds') separately, by comparison with the normal pronunciation. This type of assessment is an attempt to investigate the paradigmatic dimension of the speaker's sound production patterns. But in most procedures consonants are not, of course, elicited in 'isolation'; nor could they be. Even if a speaker were asked to produce or imitate them 'on their own' or in 'nonsense words', they would almost always be said with a supporting vowel, usually voiceless or voiced 'schwa': [ə̥] or [ə] for most English speakers; (hence the term 'consonant', which means 'sounding with something'). Usually the pronunciations of consonants are assessed by their occurrence in words. This entails consideration of the syntagmatic dimension of sound production and opens up the possibility of assessing the speaker's pronunciations of consonants in different positions in phonological structures. Indeed, the distributional possibilities of consonants should routinely be taken into account in assessing speech. This includes both the restrictions on the distribution of consonants: for example /ŋ/ never occurs in initial position in a word; and the frequent occurrence of certain consonants in clusters: for example /s/ in both initial and final positions in a word is frequently followed and preceded, respectively, by other consonants. A comprehensive description of the normal pronunciation patterns (e.g. Gimson 1980) will provide a full account of its syntagmatic as well as its paradigmatic aspects; a comprehensive assessment procedure should attempt to make an equally full evaluation of a speaker's performance in both dimensions.

The most common procedure used to obtain a speech sample for assessment by error analysis is to have a person say a set of words which have been pre-selected because they contain the target behaviours that are to be evaluated. The technique used to ensure that a person says the selected words is to ask him to name a set of pictures or objects; this picture-naming game is usually called an 'articulation test'. This assessment procedure as a technique for obtaining a speech sample is considered below, towards the end of this section. We are first concerned here with the phonological criteria which must be taken into account when obtaining a speech sample for error analysis.

These are relevant not just to the construction of published materials, but also in the devising of a clinician's own personal set of elicitation materials, which many practitioners use in addition to standardised assessments.[1]

A speech sample should contain all 24 target consonant phonemes if the speaker's pronunciation patterns are to be properly assessed. It should also reflect the structural possibilities of the normal pronunciation system, and therefore the 24 consonant phonemes should be sampled at all possible positions in structure and in all possible clusters. As far as the phonotactic possibilities of English are concerned, this is a clinically unrealistic requirement (cf. McDonald 1964a,b). Hundreds of words would have to be elicited to ensure a comprehensive sample; most people, and especially children, would tire of such a 'game' long before the full 'test' could be administered. The solution to this problem is almost always an unsatisfactory compromise. Traditionally, consonants are elicited in 'initial', 'medial' and 'final' positions in words and in a few 'initial' and 'final' clusters. With regard to clusters, in many published materials there is often little evidence of a systematic attempt to sample comprehensively or representatively the different types (e.g. as outlined in Chapter Two for initial clusters). Consequently, a sample elicited using such tests is almost always inadequate with regard to the range of possible targets, especially in the structural dimension (for further discussion of published tests of articulation on this point see Grunwell 1980b).

Another equally fundamental flaw lies in the structural classification of the distribution of segments. The traditional unit of description is the 'word'; yet the 'word' is not a *prime* unit of phonological analysis. As with other levels of linguistic analysis, phonological patterns are described in terms of units which have a hierarchical relationship to each other. It will be evident, from the preceding chapter, that a segment-sized unit is a basic concept in phonological description, and that the unit upon which the description of structural patterns is based is the syllable. The structures of syllables are described in terms of combinations of segment-sized units. On the basis of their functions in syllable structure segments are classified into two basic types: vowels and consonants. Another term for the segment-sized unit is a PHONE; this term is equivalent to 'phonetic segment'.[2]

Phones combine in temporal sequences to constitute

syllables. With regard to the higher-level units which are constituted of syllables, these should strictly speaking be units of rhythm and intonation. This would maintain the description within a purely phonological frame of reference; the syllable is the unit that carries the stress and tone contrasts which form the suprasegmental, prosodic patterns at the level of the utterance in the phonological organisation of spoken language. In linguistic analysis, the 'word' is a lexico-grammatical unit. From a practical point of view, however, the 'word' is clearly the smallest naturally occurring, linguistically defined unit that is easy to elicit spontaneously. Furthermore, the word is more often than not taken as the unit of meaning whereby phonemic contrasts are established in phonological analysis. Thus, there are obvious theoretical as well as practical precedents for its use in phonemically based assessment procedures; though it must be acknowledged that in these assessments the 'word' appears to be defined by its conventional orthographic characteristic as that unit which is bounded by spaces on either side in the written medium.

It is not relevant to debate here the problems of defining the concept of 'word'. The traditional, orthographic unit, in fact, is adequate to illustrate the points that need to be made with regard to its use as a unit of phonological analysis. As indicated above, in investigating the distribution of consonants, three places in word structure are routinely recognised: INITIAL, MEDIAL, FINAL. In a consistent phonological framework, however, the word should be specified as the structural unit above the syllable; that is words are constituted of sequences of syllables. Syllables, it will be recalled, have maximally three positions in structure: CVC. Words may be constituted of one or more syllables. A word that is constituted of more than one syllable therefore has potentially four positions in structure for the distribution of consonants. For example, a disyllabic word may have the structure; CVC,CVC, for example *basket*; or CVC,CCVC, for example *penguin*; or CCVCC,CVC, for example *priesthood*; etc. The four positions in word structure are thus:

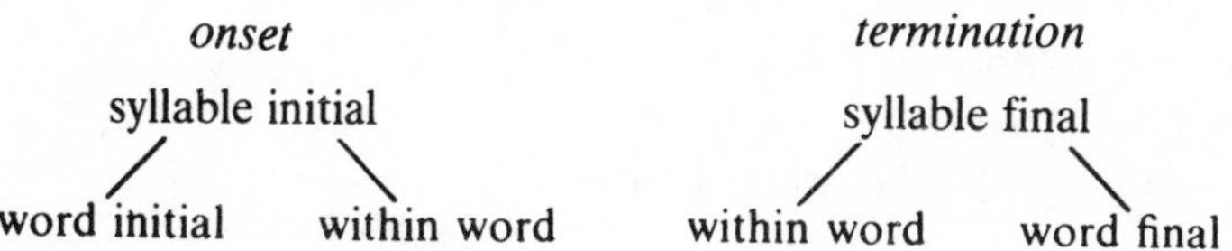

For example:

(a) *basket* /'bɑs,kɪt/
CVC,CVC
(1) (2)(3) (4)

(1)	/b/	syllable initial word initial	'Initial'
(2)	/s/	syllable final within word	'Medial'
(3)	/k/	syllable initial within word	
(4)	/t/	syllable final word final	'Final'

(b) *penguin* /'pɛŋ,gwɪn/
CVC,CCVC
(1) (2) (3) (4)

(1)	/p/	syllable initial word initial	'Initial'
(2)	/ŋ/	syllable final within word	'Medial'
(3)	/gw/	two-place cluster, syllable initial within word	
(4)	/n/	syllable final word final	'Final'

(c) *priesthood* /'prist,hʊd/
CCVCC,CVC
(1) (2) (3) (4)

(1)	/pr/	two-place cluster syllable initial word initial	'Initial'
(2)	/st/	two-place cluster, syllable final within word	'Medial'
(3)	/h/	syllable initial within word	
(4)	/d/	syllable final word final	'Final'

Thus, the traditional term 'medial' is ambiguous as to whether the segment is in onset or terminating position with regard to syllable structure. This is a distinction that can be important in describing the patterns in clinical data, as is illustrated by the following sample.

BECKY 5;8 (1978)

basket ['baʔtɪt]	*castle* ['datəɫ]
christmas ['wɪʔmə]	*crossing* ['wɒtɪn]
costume ['dɒʔtum]	*dancing* ['dantɪn]
icecream ['aɪʔwim]	*pencil* ['bɛntəɫ]
sisters ['tɪʔtə]	*pussy* ['bəti]

Here it is quite clear that the realisations of 'medial' /s/ are consistently different, depending upon its position in syllable structure, either in onset or termination. It is important that a framework of analysis and assessment recognises the possibility of such patterns in the data of speech disorders. In practice, many speech assessment materials and procedures do not distinguish between these two types of 'medial' consonants

The selection of words to be used for a speech assessment should also take account of certain other phonetic phenomena, as well as such non-phonetic factors as familiarity and, in articulation tests, picturability. The pronunciations of sounds in single words and more especially in connected speech are frequently influenced by adjacent or nearby sounds. These voluntary variations in pronunciation are different from the automatic variant realisations of phonemes in different contexts. It must be assumed, though it is rarely stated, that the assessment of a 'correct' pronunciation takes into account the normal range of allophonic variants (but see further below). The other type of voluntary variant realisations, however, are avoidable, and are indeed avoided in certain styles of speaking. They are usually attributable to the influence of other sounds in the context and are most commonly the result of *assimilation.* Where the influencing sound is adjacent to the sound affected, this is termed *juxtapositional assimilation.* If possible one should avoid including words in which the sound to be tested is liable to assimilation in a speech assessment procedure. For example, if the word 'red' is used to sample word final /d/, the object pictured must be chosen carefully as many word initial consonants will influence the pronunciation of final /d/, for example 'red pencil' [ˈɹɛb ˈpɛnsɫ], 'red crayon' [ˈɹɛg ˈkɹeɪən]. Thus a speaker might fail to produce the intended target 'correctly', but nevertheless use a perfectly normal and acceptable pronunciation involving assimilation, affecting the place of articulation of /d/.

As assessment procedures are intended for use with speakers who have been identified as exhibiting pronunciation difficulties, it may be considered desirable to reduce the level of difficulty of some of the items tested by sampling the targets in 'simple' contexts. Normal speakers occasionally experience pronunciation difficulties with complex sequences of consonants, especially when speaking very rapidly, under stress, or when fatigued or intoxicated. In such circumstances '*assimilation at a distance*' may ocur, for example 'soldier' pronounced as ['ʃəʊdʒə], 'packet' as ['pætɪt], as well as the more obvious changes in the order of sounds, usually called '*slips of the tongue*', for example 'a cup of tea' [ə 'tʌp əf 'ki]. As individuals with speech disorders might be expected to experience considerable and recurrent difficulties with complex sound sequences, there are clearly sound reasons for not using, for example, 'soldier' to sample word-initial /s/, or at least not using *only* this word to elicit this sound. A speaker must, however, be able to produce consonants 'correctly' and in the right order in all contexts, if his pronunciation is to be acceptable. Therefore while assessment procedures should attempt to sample sounds in contexts most likely to result in successful production, where assimilative and contextual influences are eliminated, a speaker's performance of more complex articulatory sequences should also be investigated.

Another aspect of normal informal speech is a tendency to elide consonants in certain contexts; for example, in complex sequences of consonants it is quite common for one or more segments to be omitted. Thus, the first syllables in 'postman', 'handbag' and 'sandwich' are usually pronounced with a single final consonant: /'pəʊsmən/, /'hæmbæg/, /'sæmwɪdʒ/. The definition of a 'correct' pronunciation should be realistic and words selected to sample the pronunciation of consonant clusters and sequences should not be susceptible to elision of the intended targets.

Assimilation and elision involve variations in acceptable pronunciations due to stylistic differences. Accent differences also result in a variety of 'correct' pronunciations and these should be taken into consideration both in assessing an individual's performance and in devising an assessment procedure. Locally acceptable pronunciations must be marked 'right', even though for other regional and social communities they would be deemed 'wrong', 'childish' or 'defective'; for example, in the English West Midlands a pronunciation [wiŋg] for 'wing' is acceptable, as is ['fɛvə] for 'feather' in the East End of London. The omission of initial /h/ ('/h/ dropping'), for example 'horse' [ɔs], and the use of an intervocalic glottal stop as an allophone of /t/, for example 'bottle' ['bɒʔəɫ], are common in a large number of urban English accents in the UK and eastern USA.

The need to accept local pronunciations may invalidate some

standardised articulation tests, if certain items cannot be scored. For a standardised assessment procedure to have general clinical application it should not have a restrictive accent bias. Many accents, for example, have an [n] pronunciation of the final consonant in the present progressive verb morpheme '–ing', but use /ŋ/ in other words such as 'long', 'sing', 'ring', etc. It is therefore inadvisable to sample for /ŋ/ only using an '–ing' verb form. Also, tests which include words sampling post-vocalic /r/ are inapplicable in many British English communities, if the aim of the assessment is to compute a standardised score. This renders the large number of widely available published procedures, which are American in origin, inappropriate for use in British clinical practice (and vice versa).[3]

The discussion so far has been concerned with the phonetic aspects of selecting items and words to be tested in a speech assessment. The methodology, as well as the construction, of such a procedure can also be considered from a phonetic point of view. Some years ago, Higgs (1970) took a rather sanguine view of the most common clinical procedure for speech assessment, the 'articulation test'. In her estimation, it is potentially an effective technique for obtaining a representative sample of a person's, especially a child's, speech in a short space of time.[4] In one sense, the representativeness of the sample depends on the test construction (and it appears to be this sense that Higgs intends). In this sense, the test must sample comprehensively and appropriately an individual's production of the pronunciation patterns of his speech community. We have reviewed this aspect of 'articulation tests' in the preceding discussion.

There is, however, another sense of the term 'representative' in relation to a person's speech production; and this raises an extremely important question about the articulation test procedure as a clinical tool. The point at issue is: are a person's responses in such a situation — a picture-naming game — representative of his habitual pronunciation patterns? Not infrequently, the instructions for administering an articulation test suggest that the answer to this question should be 'unlikely' or even an unequivocal 'no'. Many tests allow the examiner to provide the name required (i.e. 'a model for imitation') when the examinee does not know the word (e.g. Templin & Darley 1960: 5; Anthony *et al.* 1971: 7,48). Some other measures of articulation are, at least in part, based on reading aloud (Templin 1957: 12). The devisors of both the Templin–Darley

Tests and the Edinburgh Articulation Test cite validation studies which demonstrated that modelled ('imitated', or 'repeated'), responses were not significantly different from 'spontaneous naming'. Nevertheless, in the author's experience it is inadvisable to accept without question the equivalence of the two types of speech production for all speakers, and most especially children with speech difficulties. Responses that occur after an examiner's model should always be indicated in the transcription of the speech sample, for example, with (M) (i.e. 'modelled') in the margin (cf. Anthony *et al.* 1971: 48). When analysing the data, these can then be examined individually and as a group for any obvious or consistent differences from the 'spontaneous' responses.

One might well ask whether these so-called 'spontaneous' responses are really representative of naturally occurring speech. Normally only very young children (0;9–1;6 according to Crystal, Fletcher & Garman 1976: 85) produce one word at a time. In the speech-disordered population, severely mentally retarded and/or linguistically retarded children are restricted to single-word utterances, as are some severely impaired acquired dysphasics. For most speakers, both normal and disordered, an utterance is more than one word in length and is not a 'naming' act. This artificiality of the procedure is a shortcoming which is frequently found to be a major disadvantage in clinical practice. It is quite common to find that a person may perform satisfactorily on an articulation test, where utterances are restricted to single words, but will continue to use disordered and inadequate patterns in his everyday speech. It is therefore essential for a clinician to obtain a varied data sample if a realistic speech assessment is to be made.

Even if there is no appreciable difference between the pronunciation patterns used in articulation test responses and conversational speech, there is another good reason for obtaining data of the latter type. The responses to the assessment procedure are known to the examiner; it is therefore difficult to gauge from the pronunciation of these how understandable a person's speech would be in a more natural context. A clinician's impression of the severity of a person's communication problems may not be particularly accurate if based solely on articulation test responses. 'Intelligibility' is a notoriously difficult variable to measure as it is never independent of other variables, such as knowledge of context, hearer's knowledge of the speaker and of his preceding utterances, hearer's experience of disordered speech, etc. In routine clinical practice one can therefore only attempt an 'expert's impression' as to the adequacy of a person's pronunciation patterns for normal communication purposes. However, for this to be a realistic and valid opinion it must be based on more than the analysis of responses to an articulation test.

Despite the drawbacks that foreknowledge of the test responses may have, this information is crucial for analysing the articulation test. Obviously one has to know the word that is being pronounced if one is to assess whether the pronunciation is 'correct' or not. It is also necessary to know the target pronunciation in order to identify where the 'errors' are in the incorrect pronunciation of the word. The analysis of these errors forms the focus of the second part of this chapter. There is, however, one final point about the assessment procedure itself which relates to both of the dimensions discussed above, its construction and methodology, and to the classification of 'errors'.

Most currently available articulation tests attempt some degree of representativeness in their construction. However, they generally provide only one opportunity to sample each item tested in each position in word structure. This does not allow for the possibility that the 'same' item may be pronounced differently in a different word or even in the same word on a different occasion. In fact, most speakers with disordered pronunciation patterns tend to be variable in their speech production. Some exhibit extreme variability, which may be a characteristic of their disability. It is therefore essential that the sample which forms the basis of a speech assessment should be large and sufficiently varied in its content to allow each item tested to occur more than once at each position in structure. In this way it is possible for the clinician to detect any variability in the speaker's pronunciation of the same target types.

The conclusion one must draw from the whole of the preceding discussion is that in many instances articulation test procedures probably do not meet their own requirement to elicit a representative data sample. In order to satisfy these criteria for representativeness, it is suggested that 100 different words is the minimum size of an adequate sample; 200–250 words is preferable in order to ensure that there is a possibility of discovering any variability in a person's pronunciation patterns (Grunwell (1985c). To sum up the points made above positively, an adequate data sample should fulfil the following criteria:

(1) be representative of the normal pronunciation patterns in both (a) system and (b) structure:
i.e. (a) the full phonemic inventory of contrastive consonant sounds,
(b) their possible combinations in clusters and sequences;

(2) take cognisance of the normal range of (a) stylistic and (b) sociolinguistic variation:
i.e. (a) contextual factors in connected speech,
(b) accent differences;

(3) be obtained from a variety of 'talking situations' to allow assessment of:
(a) any differences in the pronunciation of individual words in isolation and the pronunciation patterns in spontaneous conversation,
(b) the amount (if any) of variability in pronunciation patterns,
(c) the adequacy of the pronunciation patterns for normal communication ('intelligibility of speech'),
(d) the effect (if any) of providing a 'model for imitation'.

DESCRIBING THE 'ERROR'

The first stage in assessing the responses to an articulation test is to decide whether the pronunciation of the target item is 'correct' or not. Apart from an ability to attend selectively to one segment in a word, this appears to require no specialist skills; indeed, at least one test is designed to be used in this way (Goldman & Fristoe 1972: 8; see further below). The assessment of whether the pronunciation is 'right' or 'wrong' must, of course, be informed by knowledge of the testee's sociolinguistic background. Indeed, Anthony *et al.* (1971: 2) criticise other published tests for not providing a definition of 'correct' pronunciations. Their comments are undoubtedly valid in regard to the specific points they take issue with: first, the scoring of an alveolar flap pronunciation of an intervocalic /t/ as 'wrong' in an American context, where it is a common normal adult realisation (Templin 1957: 49); secondly, the inclusion of a test item liable to juxtapositional assimilation (Renfrew 1966). Both of these are in contravention of the criteria for defining the target discussed above. It would be extremely difficult, however, to provide a comprehensive description of acceptable pronunciations that would be applicable throughout the English-speaking world. The only practical solution is to emphasise once again that clinicians must take into account the local accent in assessing responses to articulation tests.

The traditional framework of error analysis requires a classification of the errors as 'substitutions', 'distortions' or 'omissions', as well as the occasional 'additions'. In the first two textbooks referred to above, the following definitions are given for these types of errors:

> With omissions, phonemes included in normal pronunciations are absent ...
> With substitutions, incorrect phonemes are substituted for those which would normally be heard ...
> With distortions, the correct phoneme is approximated but not closely enough to be normally acceptable ...
> Additions ... improper addition of phonemes to words. (Perkins 1977: 255)

> omissions of sounds ('kool' for 'school'), substitution of one standard sound for another ('thoup' for 'soup'), and distortions (substitution of a nonstandard for a standard sound). Some writers list additions (the intrusion of an unwanted sound) as another type of articulatory disorder. (Emerick & Hatten 1979: 158)

Michel (1978: 425–6) provides similar definitions for the omission, substitution and addition categories, but extends the description of a distortion:

> Distortion: the phoneme is replaced by a production that is slightly to severely off the target, or by a sound not found in that language.

This suggests that there is subclassification of distortions into 'mild' and 'severe' types (Snow 1963: 278; Goldman & Fristoe

1972: 12, see further below). Unfortunately, little or no guidance is given as to how the two subtypes are to be differentiated. Goldman & Fristoe, for example, describe a severe distortion as an 'indistinct sound'. More recently it has been suggested that it is inappropriate to identify distortions as a separate category of error:

> the use of the term 'distortion' is a curious one since it is really better described as a substitution in which the replacement segment is an incorrect variation within the perceptual boundary of the target sound. (Bernthal & Bankson 1984: 17; see also Bernthal & Bankson 1981: 177; Newman, Creaghead & Secord 1985: 75).

As is pointed out subsequently in these three textbooks this definition does not really solve the problem of defining 'distorted substitutions'. For example, should one classify the pronunciation of target /s/ as [ɬ] as a distorted variation of a substituted phoneme /l/, or as a distortion of the target phoneme /s/?

The definitions of the categories of 'omissions' and 'additions' are similarly subject to some debate. 'Additions' apparently are confined to the insertion of 'standard sounds' or 'phonemes'. 'Distortions' or 'non-standard sounds' do not occur, or cannot be analysed and classified as additions according to many definitions of this category. This framework is therefore unable to handle instances where a transitional sound occurs in the movement from one articulatory position to another, for example the fricative that may occur in the prolonged articulation of a target plosive+approximant cluster, such as *pram* [pΦw̥am]. Nor can it handle the idiosyncratic insertion of a 'non-English' sound before an initial vowel, a pattern which some children with severe speech problems use habitually: e.g. *owl* [xaʊ]; *eye* [ßaɪ].

With regard to omissions, the difficulty arises as a result of the various different interpretations that have been proposed for this type of error. The definition provided above initially appears very straightforward. However, some authorities, (e.g. Van Riper & Irwin 1958), include as omissions: glottal stops, unvoiced articulatory placements (i.e. 'silent articulations', see Appendix and PRDS 1983), and 'short exhalations'. The last-named type, judging by the description provided, appears to suggest the occurrence of an [h]-type sound (voiceless glottal fricative or approximant) in word-final or syllable-final position. Another type of omission could be the occurrence of a short period of silence equivalent in duration to the omitted segment; (see especially Bernthal & Bankson 1981: 177 for a discussion of these points). Thus apart from the category 'substitution', the traditional classifications of speech errors are extremely ill-defined and therefore provide an unreliable framework in which to analyse and assess speech disorders.

Most applications of this traditional framework of analysis, however, do not appear to have operated at the level of phonetic sophistication implied by the preceding discussion. Indeed, in many instances procedures using this classification system have not required an impressionistic phonetic transcription and the categories have thus been applied according to their simplest face-value definitions. Subsequent to such an analysis it has been customary for the severity of a speech disorder to be assessed in terms of the number and types of errors. The numerical measure employed is simply: the greater the number of errors the more severe the disorder. With regard to the 'quality' of the errors, the degree of severity from greatest to least is usually given as: omissions–substitutions–distortions (Van Riper & Irwin 1958: 12).

There is, however, little virtue in this simplicity. A measure of severity based on number of errors provides no indications whatsoever as to the nature of a person's speech disorder and no guidance as to the most appropriate intervention strategies. There is also no information as to the communicative implications of all or any one of the errors recorded. In particular the clinician has no knowledge of which phonemic contrasts, if any, are lost and what effect this has on the speaker's ability to signal meaning differences. The information provided by classification of the errors into three or four categories affords little further insight or guidelines for remediation. Without detailed recording and phonetic analysis of the mispronunciations the nature of a person's speech disorder cannot be fully or properly investigated. As a result the clinician is obliged to use the same framework in planning treatment as in assessment, that is to 'correct' the pronunciations that are deemed to be in 'error' and to treat each 'defective' sound individually.

The inadequacies of this framework have not gone unnoticed by clinicians (for example see Lund & Duchan 1978: especially

p. 120). A major failure is the inability of error analysis as traditionally applied to indicate whether there are any systematic patterns in the types of errors. An awareness of this possibility enables a clinician to appreciate the patterns in an individual's disordered speech and consequently to plan a potentially more efficient and effective intervention strategy. The following data provide a brief (but realistic, bearing in mind that only one example of each target is usually elicited) illustration of the inadequacies of the traditional procedure. The words are selected to elicit /s/ word initial and in initial clusters, word 'medial' and word final.

PAUL 6;11 (1975)

(1) *saw* [s̺ɔ]
(2) *sky* [taɪ]
(3) *slide* [s̺aɪ]
(4) *smoke* [foʊ]
(5) *snow* [s̺oʊ]
(6) *spade* [peɪ]
(7) *squirrel* ['tɪjʊ]
(8) *stove* [toʊ]
(9) *straw* [tɔ]
(10) *sweets* ['θʊ'θi] (= *some sweets*)
(11) *pussy* ['pʊʔs̺i]
(12) *ice cream* ['aɪʔ ti]
(13) *horse* [ʔɔ]
(14) *mouse* [maʊʔ]
(15) *bus* [bʊh]

All the pronunciations of /s/ would be assessed as 'wrong', but classified differently.

(1) [s̺] would probably be regarded as a 'distortion' of /s/, though phonetically it could just as plausibly be classified as a 'distortion' of /θ/, or even the use of an incorrect allophone of /s/, since normal speakers would tend to use [s̺], e.g. in '*we both saw it*'.
(2) [t] might be classified as an 'omission' of /s/, and a substitution error for /k/, though it could be regarded as a 'substitution' for /s/ as this realisation is known to occur in the speech of very young children.
(3) [s̺] would probably be regarded as a 'distortion' of /s/ (see (1) above) with /l/ being omitted.
(4) [f] would be classified as a 'substitution', but the decision as to whether /s/ or /m/ was omitted would be arbitrary as [f] is similar in manner to /s/ and in place to /m/.

(5) [s̪] would probably be regarded as a 'distortion' of /s/ (see (1) above) with /n/ being omitted.

(6) [p] would be classified as an /s/ 'omission'.

(7) [t] as with (2) above, the most obvious classification is an /s/ 'omission', though the 'substitution' classification is plausible here too.

(8)
(9) } [t] would be classified as an /s/ 'omission'.

(10) [θ] would be classified as a 'substitution' of [θ] for /s/ and 'omission' of /w/ in *sweets*. The pronunciation of *some* here would not be included in the assessment; it is, however, a 'substitution' which has an obvious phonetic similarity to the 'distortion' in (1).

(11) [ʔs̪] would probably be regarded as a distortion of /s/, (see (1) above); it is not clear whether the insertion of [ʔ] would be recorded at all since this segment is not a 'standard' English phoneme; in addition some authorities classify the glottal stop as an omission.

(12) [ʔ] might be classified as an omission, though it could be regarded as a 'distorted substitution' of /t/ perhaps.

Note: both (11) and (12) would be classified as word medial /s/ realisations, even though in (11) /s/ is syllable initial in the target and in (12) it is syllable final; Paul's realisations clearly differ according to the syllable position, another aspect of his pronunciation patterns which the traditional framework would not be able to handle.

(13) Ø undoubtedly an omission.

(14) [ʔ] might be classified as an omission, though the distortion classification (logically of /t/ given the definition of distortions) is arguable.

(15) [h] might be classified as an omission (as it is a 'short voiceless exhalation'), but it could be regarded as a substitution of [h] for /s/.

Clearly, this item-by-item assessment framework does not facilitate an analysis of the regularities in the data, which would be made obvious in other frameworks where, for example, the patterns in children's realisations of clusters are stated (see further Chapter Seven). In addition, the unclear definitions of 'distortions' and omissions results in uncertain classifications of certain segments. The substitution in (4), by the way, is probably an example of a context-sensitive realisation with a 'synthesis' of the fricative manner and labial place of the two constituents of the target cluster (see Chapter Seven).

As Lund & Duchan point out (1978: 121), particular types of errors are often attributable to context-sensitive effects. A particularly severe, though once again realistic, example of possible context sensitive patterns is provided by the following sample, which details the pronunciations of words selected to elicit /k/ and /g/.

DEREK 5;1 (1976)

(1)	*cup* [pʌp]	Initial
(2)	*gun* [dʌn]	
(3)	*pocket* [ˈpɒtɪt]	'Medial'
(4)	*dagger* [ˈdadə]	
(5)	*cake* [keɪk]	Final
(6)	*peg* [pɛb]	

Other words in the 'test sample' provide further examples of Derek's pronunciations of initial and final /k/:

(7) *back* [bap]
(8) *neck* [nɛt]
(9) *comb* [poʊm]
(10) *king* [kɪŋ]

Apart from (5) and (10), all of Derek's pronunciations of /k/ and /g/ would be assessed as 'wrong' and classified as 'substitutions'. According to the superficial classification of the traditional approach, there are both /p/ and /t/ substitutions for /k/, and /b/ and /d/ substitutions for /g/. If, however, the place of articulation of the other consonants in the words is taken into consideration it is clear that their presence influences the pronunciations of both /k/ and /g/ targets, and that the same patterns are found in (7), (8), and (9) (see Chapter Seven for further discussion of this type of pattern in children's speech).

These inadequacies could be circumvented by modifications and extensions to the framework of error analysis, such as those suggested by Lund & Duchan (1978: passim). But amendments of this kind are mere palliatives and do little to change the fundamental basis of the framework, which is inappropriate and misleading with regard to the description of most types of speech disorders to which it is applied. Analysing disordered speech as being made up of pronunciation errors implies that each target sound is regarded as an independent unit whose correct pronunciation has to be achieved. It is inevitable, given this framework of assessment, that the approach to treatment will involve mastery of the production of each individual sound that is mispronounced. The emphasis is on speech as a series of separate articulatory gestures. Although the term 'phoneme' occurs both in the definition of an 'error' and in the descriptions of the types of errors, it is used as if it were simply equivalent to the layman's concept of a 'speech sound'.

This is a serious misuse of the term. The phoneme is a phonological concept used in the analysis of speech as spoken language. Each phoneme is defined by its phonetic and functional relationships to all the other phonemes in the phonological system of a language. All the realisations of one phoneme must share certain phonetic characteristics; and to maintain its contrastive function they must be different from the realisations of other phonemes. In terms of its organisation as the spoken medium of language, speech is thus made up of a system of *interdependent* units. Disordered speech involves a disruption of this organisation which, more often than not, results in inadequacies in the system. The traditional error classifications fail to make these implications clear.

The term 'substitution' is non-technically defined as a 'replacement of one thing by another'; this definition would seem to imply the existence of both. Therefore when applied to a pronunciation error, the term 'substitution' should logically be taken to mean that the speaker used one sound instead of another when both were available to him. Occasionally 'substitution' is an appropriate designation for a speech error. For example, an otherwise normal speaker may make a 'slip of the tongue' involving substitutions, as did an unfortunate radio newsreader forecasting 'shattered scowers'. The pronunciation errors associated with some types of acquired dysphasia, usually termed *literal* or *phonemic paraphasias*, can be viewed as 'substitutions', since this disorder does not usually involve irretrievable loss of phonemes but disorganised use of the existing system. This is evidenced by the fact that a dysphasic speaker will pronounce a word incorrectly on one occasion and correctly on another, will often be aware of his 'error', or when made aware of it will attempt to correct himself.

The occurrence of so-called 'substitutions' in child speech disorders is a very different matter (for an early criticism of this usage see Grady 1966). Here the term is not only totally inappropriate, it is misleading. The following typical example illustrates the point at issue. A well-known 'substitution error' in child speech is the use of [t] where an adult would use [k] (e.g. Snow 1963: 279; Anthony *et al.* 1971: 33). This is usually described as substituting the phoneme /t/ for /k/. This is patently inaccurate, as the child does not have the phoneme /k/ in his pronunciation system. Nor, indeed, does his system contain the *adult* phoneme /t/, since part of the definition of this phonological unit (as against the phonetic segment), is that it is distinct from /k/. Thus the child says [ti], he could be 'meaning' *tea* or *key*, just as his pronunciation [bat] could be either *bat* or *back*. Since his system lacks the contrast between /t/ and /k/, he cannot signal these meaning differences. Therefore, systemically, he has neither /t/ nor /k/ *adult* phonemes; they are both 'wrong'. The child is not simply mispronouncing /k/ as [t], he is using an inadequate system of distinctive sounds. Any 'substitution' error in child speech usually has similar implications.

Paradoxically, an 'omission' error does not necessarily imply that the target is totally absent from a person's sound system. For example, a child may omit the initial /s/ before /p, t, k,/ in clusters, that is pronounce *spoon* [pun], *star* [tɑ], *sky* [kaɪ], but pronounce it correctly in initial position immediately prevocalic, that is *sun* [sʌn], *saw* [sɔ], *sea* [si]. However, as this example illustrates, 'omissions' always involve differences in the structural organisation of pronunciation by comparison with the target. In addition, omissions usually involve the loss of contrasts. For example, omission of /s/ from the /st/ cluster in *stop* [top] entails the loss of contrast between this word and *top*. 'Errors' of this type have a differential effect upon a person's ability to communicate depending on which targets are omitted, how many are subject to omission and which positions in the structure are affected. Word-final consonants are particularly vulnerable to omission (see Renfrew 1966, quoted in Ingram 1976: 29–30). This tends to result in a large number of contrasts being lost, for example [kɑ] could be *cop*, *cob*, *cough*, *cot*, *cod, cos, cosh, cock, cog.* The omission of one consonant in a target cluster, as in the example above, is another common error pattern which is in fact a characteristic of the early stages of speech development (see further Chapter Seven). While the potential failures to signal meaning differences here are also considerable, if only one consonant is omitted and the pattern conforms to the normal developmental trends it is usually not too difficult to guess the words the speaker is intending.

As already indicated, 'distortions' are an ill-defined type of 'error'. Furthermore, their systemic implications are rarely revealed by traditional analyses. A single 'distortion' error may have no effect whatsoever on the speaker's ability to signal meaning differences; and if it is 'mild', it will not be obtrusive. Therefore, it will presumably not cause listeners to focus attention on the person's pronunciation rather than on what he is saying, and the speaker will be able to communicate quite adequately. The pronunciation of /f/ as [Φ] would be such a 'distortion'; this is frequently encountered in elderly speakers without, and with, dentures. A 'severe distortion' is presumably a pronunciation that is obtrusive, for example /s/ pronounced as a voiceless alveolar nasal fricative [n̥ᶠ]. Yet, provided this 'distortion' was used for the one target phoneme only, the speaker's *system of contrasts* would be normal, even though his pronunciation was obviously 'defective'.

If the same 'distortion' is used for two (or more) target phonemes then the system of contrasts that the speaker is using is reduced. For example, if both /s/ and /ʃ/ are pronounced [s] (again a common immature pattern, see Anthony *et al.* 1971; 33,44), then [s̺i] might be *sea* or *she.* This 'distortion' is phonetically similar to both targets and therefore is presumably 'mild'; in addition, being developmentally normal, it would probably not be obtrusive. Yet it will tend to handicap effective communication quite considerably. Applying the error-analysis procedure as traditionally described, there is no method of indicating the loss of contrast that this type of distortion pattern implies since each target and each mispronunciation are analysed separately.

All the above criticisms of these traditional error categories can be attributed to one basic inadequacy in the analytical framework: the requirement that errors are classified in isolation from each other. The assessment procedure is phoneme-based but not phonemic. It assesses the realisation of phonemes but not the signalling of phonemic contrasts. A phonemic assessment, however, while being theoretically and technically feasible, is practically impossible in the strictest application of the concept. It would require a set of words selected to investigate a speaker's ability to signal the differences between minimal pairs for the target phoneme system at all places in word and syllable structure. Such an articulation test would be extremely lengthy and probably difficult to administer as a 'naming game' because of the problems that one would encounter finding picturable minimal pairs.

The articulation test as an assessment procedure and error analysis as an assessment framework are both inadequate as clinical tools for the investigation of a speaker's phonology. The data upon which a speech assessment is based should as far as possible be naturally occurring spontaneous speech, with the provisos that it must be representative and glossable; that is the analyst needs to know what words the speaker intended to say. The analysis should be as detailed as possible: it should identify the *patterns* in a speaker's pronunciation system. The traditional procedures are considered inadequate because they provide an incomplete data base and an unreliable assessment which fails to provide the information required to devise an explicitly principled treatment programme. Nevertheless, the articulation test is a useful method of obtaining a speech sample relatively rapidly for the purpose of a screening assessment. By using a standardised scoring technique individuals can be identified whose pronunciation performance on the test falls significantly below the norm or, in the instance of children, below the level of performance expected at a particular age, i.e. their peer group norm. In the final section of this chapter we will therefore consider two very different published articulation tests, in regard to their construction and as illustrations of specific applications of error analysis. Two procedures which apply error analysis in the phonological investigation of spontaneous speech samples are also reviewed.

REVIEWS OF FOUR CLINICAL ASSESSMENT PROCEDURES

In these reviews the focus is entirely upon the phonetic and phonological issues in the construction and scoring/analysis of the procedures. Other aspects of the procedures relating to the logistics of their clinical use (e.g. suitability of the materials, the picture stimuli, etc.) will not be discussed.

Goldman–Fristoe Test of Articulation (1972)

The Goldman–Fristoe Test of Articulation (Goldman & Fristoe 1972; hereafter GFTA) has been selected for review as it is in large part a typical example of the traditional articulation test procedure and it is widely available both in the UK and in the USA. Its procedures, however, do extend beyond those of the archetypal articulation test in that there is a section of the test which provides a means of examining a child's pronunciation of selected target sounds in connected speech. Thus the stated aims of the GFTA are:

(1) to examine all necessary phonemes;
(2) to obtain an adequate and accurate sample of speech production under several conditions;
(3) to provide a form for recording responses which facilitates comparison of patterns of errors under various test conditions (GFTA Manual: 5).

To achieve these aims there are three procedures:

Sounds in Words Subtest
Sounds in Sentences Subtest
Stimulability Subtest.

In the Sounds in Words Subtest we find the traditional articulation test format, with 44 single-word responses obtained using 35 pictures. These responses are selected to elicit 73 consonants, both singletons and clusters; therefore more than one target phoneme is frequently scored in a word. The words selected are intended to provide a representative sample of the target phoneme system but the authors indicate that there are several targets excluded on the grounds of infrequent occurrence: /ʒ/ completely; medial /h; w; j/ and /hw/ which is tested as an initial target in *wheel*; final /ð/. 'Eleven common consonant blends' (sic., op. cit.: 6) are included: /br; bl; dr; fl; kl; kr; pl; skw; sl; st; tr/. These are tested in word initial position only.

The Sounds in Sentences Subtest is intended to reveal any discrepancies between the pronunciations of single words and their pronunciations when they occur in connected speech. The procedures involve the tester reading two stories aloud, after which the child is required to retell the stories from memory with the assistance of pictures. The pictures are also intended to control the lexical content of the speech sample obtained. While the procedure has the potential to assess most of the target consonants, only a subset is scored. The selection of these, according to the authors, has been made on the criterion of including those consonants most likely to be defective (op. cit.: 6). The consonants included on these grounds are:

initial: /g; k; f; j; ʃ; tʃ; l; r; dʒ; θ; v; s; z; ð; bl; br; dr; fl; pl; skw; sl/
medial: /g; k; ʃ; l; r; dʒ; θ; v; s; z; ð/
final /g; k; f; ʃ; tʃ; l; r; dʒ; θ; v; s; z/

This subtest thus charts a total of 44 target consonants for scoring purposes.

The Stimulability Subtest is designed to satisfy the clinical requirement to establish whether a child can 'produce a previously misarticulated phoneme when given maximum stimulation'. If a positive response is obtained on a stimulability test then the stimulable sound(s) can be viewed as appropriate primary targets for therapy. The Stimulability Subtest only investigates those consonants which are misarticulated by a child in the responses to the two previously described subtests. The child is required to imitate the tester's pronunciation of the target sounds in increasingly complex contexts, ranging from initial in CV nonsense syllables through single-syllable real words to the same words in sentences.

The scoring procedures for the GFTA are designed to cater for testers with differing levels of knowledge and skill in assessing pronunciation errors. It is suggested that the test can be used by testers with minimum or no phonetic training. In this mode the scoring involves the simple judgement of presence *v.* absence of a pronunciation error; i.e. right/wrong pronunciation. On the basis of the error score obtained a decision can be reached as to whether a child should be referred to a speech therapist for further investigation. Testers with phonetic training and a knowledge of the nature of articulation disorders (op. cit.:

8), are required to judge the type of error produced when a mispronunciation is detected. The instructions for recording the error categories are:

substitution – record (in transcription) the sound (phoneme) that was used;
omission – mark with dash;
addition – record (in transcription) the added sound as well as the symbol for the correct sound;
distortion – mild distortion is marked 2, severe distortion is marked 3; or additional markings (diacritics) may be used for a more 'definitive' transcription.

A response matrix for the consonants tested is provided, in which scores are entered. The consonants are listed in this scoring matrix in developmental order, according to the authors, so that the phonemes that tend to be used earlier in speech sound development are at the top of the list, and later sounds are lower down. The order in which the sounds are listed (and numbered) is as follows:

/p m n w h b g k f d ŋ j t ʃ tʃ l r dʒ θ v s z ð bl br dr fl kl kr pl skw sl st tr hw/.

As well as comparing the responses to the different subtests the authors also suggest that certain types of patterns might be observed and that therefore the matrices should be examined along the following dimensions:

effect of word position (i.e. position of sound in word);
types of errors (substitutions, omissions, etc.);
effect of complexity (single words *v.* sentences);
effect of frequency of occurrence of target sounds;
occurrence of errors in different phonetic categories, such as manner, place, voicing;
developmental status of sound misarticulated.

Finally, tables of percentile rankings of error scores are provided based on a large population sample (*N*=38,884), between the ages of 6;0 and 16;0. The choice of age range is particularly surprising; all available evidence indicates that children's pronunciation development in terms of the skills tested on the GFTA, viz. the acquisition of the consonant system, is completed by the age of 6;0.

While the GFTA does extend the articulation test procedure beyond the single-word response stage, the innovative Sounds in Sentences Subtest does not realise its potential either systematically or consistently. Only a selected number of targets are examined in this subtest for consistency of response across different contexts, and no substantiated justification for this selection is provided. No evidence is cited to support the claim that the consonants selected are those which are most frequently in error. Given that variability in pronunciation typically involves correct pronunciations in one context (usually the least complex, i.e. one-word utterances), and incorrect pronunciations in other contexts, (usually the more complex), there are very strong grounds for testing the same comprehensive set of targets in the Sounds in Sentences Subtest as in the Sounds in Words Subtest. Another less than satisfactory aspect of the Sounds in Sentences Subtest is that certain targets are tested in the same words and others in different words; this adds another variable which may influence a child's production of a consonant.

With regard to the words selected for inclusion in the GFTA, there are a number of difficulties that may arise when using the test cross-culturally; i.e. in the UK, given that it is of American English origin. The specific lexical items are: *wagon, zipper, bathtub* and perhaps *vacuum.* There are also some minor problems scoring the test across accents with the inclusion of post-vocalic /r/, in *car,* and the virtually extinct initial /hw/, in *wheel.*

Of more significance phonologically is the apparent confusion over the definition of word medial consonants, which takes no account of the position of consonants in syllables (in spite of the authors' awareness of this controversy; op. cit.: 4–5). Examples of the inconsistent representation of 'medial' consonants include:

SIWW	/m/	*Christmas*	SFWW	/n/	*Santa*[5]
SFWW	/θ/	*bathtub*	SIWW	/ð/	*feather*

The somewhat random selection of initial consonant clusters is also unfortunate, and although it is claimed that those selected represent the most frequently occurring types, there are some surprising exclusions, such as:

/sp; sk; sm; sn; gr; pr; fr; spr; str; skr/.

It is, however, the scoring procedures that leave the most to be desired. The preceding sections of this chapter have comprehensively illustrated the inadequacies of the traditional error classifications and those arguments will therefore not be rehearsed again. We shall examine here the specific suggestions for evaluating the responses to the GFTA. The suggestion that the tester should look for patterning in errors is welcome, but there is no formal procedure for embarking on such an exercise and no specified framework of analysis. In any event the results of this type of examination of the data would only provide a more detailed analysis of errors, not a phonological analysis. There is also the proposal that a developmental assessment might be obtained as the targets are listed in order of development. There is no identified source of the developmental ordering; indeed certain orders appear rather unexpected, such as the late ranking of /t/ after /k/ and the ranking of /θ/ before both /v/ and /s/. No information therefore is provided as to the developmental status of common mispronunciations, and it is these which the user of the test is most interested in evaluating. In fact the authors state that:

> Percentile ranks do not provide a determination of what is normal and what is deviant, or what constitutes a mild, moderate or severe articulation disorder. That classification is an arbitrary judgment which must be made by the user of the test. (op. cit.: 16).

This is hardly a reliable basis upon which to take clinical decisions. The second assessment procedure to be examined in this review has the advantage of removing some of the arbitrariness from such judgements.

Edinburgh Articulation Test (1971)

The Edinburgh Articulation Test (Anthony, Bogle, Ingram & McIsaac 1971; hereafter EAT), is currently the only articulation test standardised on a British population that has become widely used by speech pathologists, at least in the UK. It is, moreover, unique amongst all published articulation tests known to the author in its construction and assessment procedures. It is therefore atypical in regard to the characteristics of the traditional assessment tools outlined in the preceding sections of this chapter. It does, however, employ the typical elicitation technique of a picture-naming game and involves an assessment primarily based on error analysis. It therefore provides an interesting example of an innovative approach to speech assessment within these traditional restrictions.

The EAT is a test of 'the maturation of articulatory skills' (op. cit.: 3). With this stated aim the devisors designed a procedure whereby children's progress in the development of mature pronunciations can be evaluated and monitored. The emphasis on articulatory skills is crucial to an understanding of the construction of the test. A test of articulation in this sense does not need to be phonologically exhaustive (or even to attempt to be). It must, however, test those phonological segments, sequences and structures which most reliably reveal the developmental status of a child's articulatory skills. The EAT does not therefore test every consonant phoneme and cluster in all possible places in word structure. The items tested are those which in an extensive pilot study were found to be:

(1) reliable discriminators between children at different ages in terms of their articulatory development;
(2) reliable representatives of classes of phonemes, sequences and/or structures which share a common pattern of development.

For example, both /ʃ/ and /s/, and clusters and sequences including /s/, are good discriminators; there are therefore a goodly number of items in the test containing these targets. Furthermore, it was found that a similar pattern of development occurs for all /s/+ plosive clusters at the same place in syllable structure; therefore only a selection of these needed to be included. Similarly, plosive+approximant clusters share a common developmental route and this can be investigated therefore through the inclusion of a selection of representatives of this type, including both voiced and voiceless plosives and all places of articulation. In selecting the words for the test the possible range of phonotactic structures was also considered. The EAT is therefore one of the few tests, perhaps the only test, to take this dimension of phonological organisation into account. The consequence of these criteria for the selection of items for the test is that the targets assessed bear little resemblance to the traditional targets of articulation tests; for example:

stamps; Christmas toothbrush; bottle; pencil

As is evident from these examples, more often than not several items are elicited using one word.

The instructions for recording the child's responses to the pictures, i.e. the test words, are quite simply:

> The test utterances should be recorded in the symbols of the International Phonetic Alphabet and the requisite diacritics to note such secondary features as palatalisation and labialisation. (op. cit.: 43)

As the authors emphasise, it is essential that the tester be trained to a high level in phonetic transcription. The type of transcription required is impressionistic, i.e. narrow rather than broad; the test certainly cannot be recorded and analysed effectively if the tester is only capable of making a broad (phonemic) transcription.

Like the test construction, the scoring and analysis of the EAT is unique. The first stage in scoring is the Quantitative Assessment which evaluates the child's pronunciations of the test items as Right/Wrong, having especial regard to the locally acceptable adult pronunciations, the authors warn. The total number of right items can be compared against those provided by the normal population used to standardise the test (N=510 children, age range: 3;0–6;0). This provides a standardised score and an articulation age for the child tested. If the standard score obtained is one standard deviation (= 15 points, or the equivalent of one year in articulation age), below the norm, the authors suggest that this is a 'danger level' score and that further investigations should be instigated. These will include the second stage in the scoring of the EAT: the Qualitative Assessment. Here the child's pronunciations of the test items are compared with those provided by the normal standardisation population. This is why a narrow phonetic transcription is essential. The normal child pronunciations are of course all 'errors' by comparison with the adult targets, until the child achieves the adult form. The EAT classifies the 'errors' into developmental categories:

Almost Mature; Immature; Very Immature; Atypical.

It is thus possible to gauge the articulatory maturity of a child's pronunciations and to monitor the changes that occur in these pronunciations over a period of time. Here are some examples of the developmental classifications provided on the EAT Qualitative Assessment:

Adult Form	Almost Mature	Immature	Very Immature	Atypical
SIWI				
/s/	s	θ	t	h
/ʃ/	ʃ̬	ç	c	f
/br/	βr	bw	b	kf
SFWF				
/dz/	dz	dlʒ	z	t

It has to be noted that the Atypical category provides some problems as, according to the authors, this includes both very very immature and idiosyncratic (i.e. atypical) realisations. For the other categories there are detailed descriptions of the characteristics of the realisations of each target type, and therefore as long as close attention is paid to these, entering realisations which are not included in the preprinted tables is not particularly difficult (op. cit.: 30–47).

Whilst in terms of its analytical procedures the EAT has many advantages over traditional approaches to articulation testing, it does share with these the major disadvantage of only sampling one occurrence of each target item and only in single-word utterances. It is difficult to apply the traditional criteria of sample construction to the items tested on the EAT because of its own very different and explicitly stated criteria for the inclusion of items. In its own terms it is representative. There are, however, a number of problematic items for certain English accents, since its Scottish origins lead to the inclusion of post vocalic /r/ in: soldie*r*; bi*r*thday. These items must be credited as correct for a child speaking a non-rhotic accent if a standard score is to be reliably calculated.

The Qualitative Assessment is the most valuable of the analytical tools provided by the EAT; indeed these tables furnish the clinician with comprehensive information about the patterns of normal articulatory development. There is, however, some initial difficulty in discerning these patterns as the authors, although they discuss in some detail the characteristics of the patterns at different maturational stages (op. cit.: 32–47), unfortunately do not make clear the organisation of the record forms. In fact the forms are organised into phonetic/phonological classes of sounds which follow a developmental sequence:

(1) plosives, nasals, early fricatives and approximants;
(2) /s/, /z/ and clusters including these consonants;
(3) /ʃ/, /tʃ/ and /dʒ/;
(4) plosive/fricative + approximant clusters;
(5) /r/ and clusters including /r/;
(6) /θ/, /ð/ and clusters including /θ/.

With this knowledge the tester can more easily discern the developmental status of a child's responses overall; and it is possible to arrive at a preliminary developmental assessment (see further Chapter Seven). It is no doubt clear from this description of the EAT Qualitative Assessment procedure that this is also a particularly useful tool for evaluating changes in children's pronunciations over time, and progress at a reassessment.

Notwithstanding all these advantages the EAT is limited by its very nature. It is not a phonological assessment and it does not seek to obtain a phonologically comprehensive or strictly representative sample. It must therefore be regarded as a screening procedure which, when employed sensitively and to its full potential, can identify children whose articulatory skills are developing slowly but normally, and to diagnose those children whose speech development is extremely delayed and/or disordered (Grunwell 1981b; Milloy 1985).

Profile of Phonology (1982)

The Profile of Phonology (Crystal 1982; hereafter PROPH), as its name suggests, is not an articulation test. It is included in this chapter because, as indicated earlier, its basic framework of analysis is the traditional classification of pronunciations into:

correct; omitted; substituted.

As one of the four profiling procedures devised by Crystal, PROPH is designed to satisfy the criteria laid down for clinical linguistic profiles (op. cit.: Chapter 1). In summary these are primarily that the profile should:

(1) provide a comprehensive framework for the exhaustive analysis of the data into categories which represent the structural contrasts available in a language;
(2) identify the linguistic level achieved by a person in relation to the expected norm;
(3) identify the goals for intervention and suggest strategies by which to achieve those goals.

Crystal regards the normal order of acquisition as the most preferable and principled way of grading the level of a person's linguistic performance (op. cit.: 7–8).

> PROPH ... is essentially a presentation of the English sound system on a 2-page chart. To facilitate the compilation of a profile a transcriptional page is added. To facilitate the interpretation of the profile a separate 3-page section provides various suggestions about ways of summarising the main patterns in the data. (op. cit.: 54)

The profile is constructed from an analysis of a transcribed data sample in 'broad phonetic' transcription; i.e. not broad phonemic, but not as detailed as a fully impressionistic transcription (op. cit.: 57). The data sample may be obtained through picture-naming or any other suitable elicitation procedure. A data base of up to 100 different words is recommended. Certain general quantitative indices are computed such as Total Word Types; Total Word Tokens; Type–Token Ratio; Repeated Forms, etc.; but as the author observes, the true clinical significance of such measures has yet to be established.

The primary analytical procedure in PROPH — the Profile — involves classifying the child's realisations of target phonemes according to the three traditional categories, classified with reference to positions in word structure and syllable structure. For consonants there are three positions in structure:

syllable initial; syllable final; within word.

The third category is invoked when the syllable division is unclear. Crystal's criteria for the division of words into syllables are different from those advocated earlier in this chapter, as they take account of morphological factors and phonological factors relating to stress placement. Indeed, consonants are also subclassified according to whether they occur in stressed or unstressed syllables. PROPH analyses all target singleton consonant phonemes and all target consonant clusters at these three places in structure. The tables upon which the consonant pronunciations are entered, are organised so that the consonants are grouped according to place and manner of articulation. Unlike most other procedures, PROPH also provides for an analysis of vowels, again subclassified into stressed and unstressed position. The target vowel system employed is RP (Received Pronunciation), but Crystal emphasises that these descriptive categories must always be checked against the local accent norms. The profile chart also provides tables on which to summarise the stress patterns used in polysyllabic words and the occurrence of connected speech phenomena (such as assimilations, elisions, liaison, etc.).

Crystal states that 'Having completed the transcriptional page and the accompanying profile chart, and allowed for the existence of awkward cases, the PROPH procedure is in a sense complete' (op. cit.: 73). It is further suggested that many speech pathologists will find this exercise sufficient basis for principled therapy. The additional procedures are thus offered as supplementary rather than necessary assessments, though Crystal does point out that they can be very illuminating and help to broaden one's view of a person's speech problems. There are several supplementary procedures. It is not intended that every one should be undertaken for each data sample analysed using PROPH. They are:

Inventory of Phones: a phonetic classification, irrespective of target type, of phones in the sample into place and manner categories, but not voicing; number of occurrences is recorded;

there is no indication of the range of manner types at each place of articulation, or vice-versa.

Target Analysis: an analysis in terms of place and manner of target articulations of the total correct, substituted and omitted phones in each articulatory category; error realisations are then analysed with regard to the type of error feature; but this is not strictly a feature analysis; for example a target bilabial error realisation can be bilabial, e.g. /b/ : [p], which is also an example of a target plosive error realisation which is also a plosive.

Feature Analysis: apart from suggestions that this procedure can be used to analyse voicing errors, as yet unanalysed in any of these procedures, the feature analysis framework is simply provided for the clinician to use to analyse whichever feature errors are of interest.

Process Analysis: this is a very minor section in PROPH and is primarily designed to capture syllable structure and assimilation processes (see Chapter Seven for detailed discussion of process analysis).

There are a number of other brief analyses primarily aimed at examining whether the correspondences between the child and adult phoneme realisations involve one-to-many ('functional overload' in the child's speech) or many-to-one (variability in the child's speech) relationships and which adult contrasts the child is signalling correctly.

As is evident from this summary, the PROPH procedures *in toto* provide for the type of comprehensive analysis which Crystal sees as the goal of clinical linguistic profiles. There is, however, the clear indication that the Profile of Phonology is essentially the 2-page chart summarising the English sound system. The clinician is given rather inadequate guidance on how to select and use the supplementary procedures, and indeed how to interpret the results. Thus PROPH is primarily an error analysis of the pronunciations of target phonemes. It has the advantage of being exhaustive of the potential target system, but it does not lead to an automatic and rapid identification of the *patterns* in the pronunciation errors. Indeed it tends to promote the phoneme-by-phoneme approach to analysis typical of the traditional articulation test procedures. There is no provision for analysing the system of contrasts being used by the child. Furthermore, notwithstanding Crystal's own criteria for clinical linguistic profiles PROPH does not have an acquisitional dimension. The author states that this is lacking because it would be a serious oversimplification to state age norms for the acquisition of sounds as there is such a wide range of individual differences between children. This is a most regrettable decision, as a developmental profile as well as being a necessary assessment measure would have provided a framework in which treatment goals could be more easily identified than is presently possible in PROPH.

In the chapter immediately following, and in Chapter Seven, a phonological assessment procedure is presented which more nearly meets Crystal's criteria for clinical linguistic profiles.

Substitution Analysis (1981)

In his set of four *Procedures for the Phonological Analysis of Children's Language* (1981), Ingram includes a substitution analysis. This is basically a straightforward procedure identifying matches and mismatches between the consonants produced by the child for the target consonants. As with PROPH the sample analysed is preferably spontaneous speech. Also as with PROPH the consonants are analysed separately according to their occurrence in three positions in word and syllable structure: initial (prevocalic); final (postvocalic) and ambisyllabic (intervocalic). The first two categories include both word and syllable positions in their definitions; the third is designed to cover a consonant or consonant cluster that 'functions both to end one syllable and to begin the next, e.g. [p] in *paper*'. It is unfortunately not entirely clear how one identifies such ambisyllabic consonants.

The main function of the analysis, however, is to analyse a child's substitutions — a category which in Ingram's procedure includes deletions, i.e. omissions. It probably also includes distortions; but as his data samples do not include non-English phones, it is not possible to make a definitive statement on this point. The analysis enters all the consonants in the sample on Consonant Inventory Sheets, which provide lists of target consonants for each place in structure. Consonants occurring in clusters are entered separately; i.e. treated in the same way as singletons and entered in the same box as the singletons, with no record being kept of which realistions were matched to target single consonants and which to target consonants in clusters. This is an unfortunate and inadvisable conflation of the two types of structure, which more often than not show different realisations of target consonants.

After entering realisations on the Consonant Inventory Sheets the number of substitutions for each target type, i.e. consonant, is calculated. These numbers together with each of the substitutions (in transcription) are then entered on an 'Item and Replica Sheet' (see Chapter Four for a similar tabular format). Where a child provides a match, i.e. a correct realisation of the target consonant, then this is indicated with a tick (or check (Amer.)).

As is evident from this description, Ingram's Substitution Analysis is precisely an error analysis procedure presented in a succinct tabular format. He also provides a Summary Table from which can be calculated the number of total correct matches across all three positions in structure, which is then set against the total number of target phonemes across all three positions. From these calculations one can estimate the proportion of matches and mismatches in the child's speech. Ingram also suggests that the analyst totals the number of 'Acquired Sounds'; i.e. sounds matched (i.e. correct) at all three positions in structure. While Ingram's Substitution Analysis is a very straightforward and relatively quick procedure it is very restricted. It is not a phonological analysis, but simply a clearly presented catalogue of the child's errors, which even so could unfortunately provide a somewhat misleading picture of the child's substitutions, given the conflation of clusters and singletons and the potential ambiguity in the division of words into syllables.

The following chapter describes a procedure which uses the same type of tabular presentation as Ingram's procedure, but to make a comparison between the child's own pronunciation *system* and the target pronunciation system.

EXERCISES

1. Make a phonemic transcription, marking the stressed syllables, of the following words as they would be pronounced by a normal adult English speaker (using a specified accent) in a fairly slow conversational style. If

you think that within the same accent there is more than one probable pronunciation, then transcribe and analyse all the variants. Analyse the phonotactic structure of each pronunciation in terms of C and V units and mark the syllable divisions; see above for discussion of the treatment of single intervocalic consonants. For each word, indicate the syllabic status of the 'medial' consonant(s). Note: all these words are frequently encountered in elicitation procedures.

1. chimney
2. feather
3. telephone
4. christmas
5. window
6. vegetables
7. postman
8. children
9. wellingtons
10. smarties
11. monkey
12. chicken
13. elephant
14. garage
15. engine
16. hospital
17. soldier
18. aeroplane
19. squirrel
20. sandwich
21. policeman
22. pencil
23. orange
24. indian
25. grasshopper
26. finger
27. December
28. picture
29. umbrella
30. whisker
31. valentine
32. biscuits
33. gingerbread
34. toothbrush
35. tractor
36. bubbles
37. chocolate
38. raincoat
39. raspberry
40. catastrophe

2. The following words are included in a hypothetical elicitation procedure in order to sample the pronunciation of English plosives in word-initial and word-final positions and in word-initial consonant clusters. Will this list elicit the whole range of possible plosives and clusters including plosives? If not, which possibilities are omitted? Suggest words that might be used to elicit them. Are any of the words in the list liable to elicit unrepresentative pronunciations of the items tested? Give reasons why you think they would do so.

1. pig
2. brick
3. stream
4. clock
5. boy
6. bread (bun)
7. spoon
8. truck
9. drawer
10. blade
11. fruit (pie)
12. pie
13. toe
14. goat
15. pram
16. cube (sugar)
17. squash (orange)
18. cow
19. splint
20. crown

3. Draw up a list of words which will provide a representative and comprehensive sample of a person's pronunciation of the English approximants. Provide two words for each approximant in each of the contexts you think you should test. Remember to include clusters in your sample. Classify the words according to context tested.

4. The following data present a sample of words elicited to test the pronunciation of /k/. Classify the child's realisations using the categories of error analysis, viz. 'substitutions', 'distortions', 'omissions'. Comment on any problems and/or inadequacies of this procedure as applied to this sample; in making your evaluation you should take into account all of the information provided in the data sample, not just the realisation of the items tested.

NICHOLAS 4;4 (1976)

1. *car* [dɑ]
2. *broken* [ˈwoʊtən]
3. *smoke* [fmoʊt]
4. *cloud* [laʊt]
5. *christmas* [ˈwɪfməfˈdeɪt] (= Christmas cake)
6. *queen* [ʍin]
7. *school* [ˈdoʊ ˈdu ˈduʊ] (= go to school)
8. *squash* [wɒf]
9. *monkey* [ˈmʊŋt̡i]
10. *boxes* [ˈbɒʔfɪv]

5. The following data present a sample of words elicited to test the pronunciation of /t/ and /d/. Classify the child's realisations using the categories of error analysis, viz. 'substitutions', 'distortions', 'omissions'. Comment on any problems and/or inadequacies of this procedure as applied to this sample; in making your evaluation you should take into account all of the information provided in the data sample, not just the realisations of the items tested.

JOANNE 5;0 (1974)

/t/	/d/
1. *teddy* [ˈtɛdi]	9. *dog* [gɒg]
2. *cotton* [ˈkɒxən]	10. *middle* [ˈmɪgʊɫ ˈlɛtə] (= middle letter]
3. *sitting* [ˈʃɪʔɪn daʊn] (= sitting down)	11. *seed* [sidʒ̥] (= seeds?)
4. *cat* [kak]	12. *dress* [dʒɛs]
5. *trumpet* [ˈʧʊmpət]	
6. *twelve* [fwɛɫb]	
7. *stop* [ˈdɒp ˈdɛd] (= stop dead)	
8. *strawberries* [ˈʧ̥ɔbiz̥]	

NOTES

1. Many of the factors outlined in the section that follows should also be taken into consideration in the construction of instruments for auditory assessments, especially auditory discrimination.

2. This is in contrast to the term ALLOPHONE (of a phoneme); allophones are the variant realisation of the phonological unit, the 'phoneme'. The types and groupings of allophones into phonemes are discovered by making a phonemic analysis (see Chapter Two).

3. Tests devised for and standardised on American populations are also inappropriate and invalid in a British context from other sociolinguistic and non-linguistic points of view. For a full discussion see Grunwell (1980b).

4. Her evaluation of the currently-available published tests, however, is far from enthusiastic. Her main criticisms relate to phonetic, sociophonetic and sociolinguistic factors, most of which are also dealt with in this chapter. The second part of her paper evaluates the analytical techniques of articulation tests; here, as in this chapter, the conclusions are negative.

5. Of course it must be acknowledged that this criticism only holds good for a British English speaking population; in American English *Santa* would almost invariably be pronounced /sanə/, and the /n/ here is in the same position in structure as the /m/ in *Christmas*, viz. SIWW.

4

Analysing and Comparing Phonological Systems: Contrastive Assessment

In Chapter Three we have highlighted the need for an adequate and appropriate framework in which to describe and analyse disordered speech. This framework is required to replace the traditional speech pathological framework which we have seen in the preceding chapter has severe limitations. There are two major shortcomings of the traditional framework:

(1) it fails to identify patterns in the pronunciations (or more precisely mispronunciations) of disordered speakers since it analyses the 'defects' of individual speech sound production;

(2) it fails to take account of the linguistic function of speech sound differences, that is to signal meaning differences, and therefore it does not assess the communicative implications of mispronunciations.

It will be evident from the discussion in Chapters One and Two that these shortcomings can be overcome by developing assessment procedures within a phonological framework. Phonology describes and analyses the organisation of speech, the *sound patterns*, with regard to their *contrastive function* in spoken language. As the 'meeting point' of phonetics and linguistics it thus provides an eminently suitable approach to the assessment of speech disorders. By applying a phonological approach the patterns that recur across several individual mispronounced segments/phones can be identified; this can facilitate more economical and effective treatment. In addition, and more importantly, the loss of phonological contrasts resulting from mispronunciations can be identified; this information facilitates the assessment of the speech disorder from a functional point of view and enables the clinician to specify precisely the treatment goals that will enhance the client's language abilities and communicative potential. Indeed, many speech disorders can in consequence be defined as involving a linguistic disability resulting from the aberrant pronunciation patterns in spoken language.

As we have already seen, especially in Chapter Three, phonological studies of normal pronunciation patterns are essential in clinical practice. Descriptions of the pronunciation systems used by normal speakers are a prerequisite for the identification of disordered usage. They are the 'normative model' (in a sense the 'ideal'), against which to compare the disordered patterns. As such the normal pronunciation system also constitutes the goal of remediation. The essential clinical procedure is therefore a comparison of the disordered patterns with the normal patterns in order to assess the deficiencies of the disordered patterns and to specify the treatment goals. Logically therefore one should compare like with like. A description of the pronunciation system of a disordered speaker should be couched in the same analytical framework as the description of the pronunciation system of normal speakers which provides the basis for assessment.

In this chapter we shall examine how such an analysis and assessment can be carried out. A selection of analytical procedures are presented which attempt to analyse a disordered speaker's pronunciation system in the same framework as is most commonly used in clinical contexts to describe the normal pronunciation system. A number of approaches to clinical assessment will then be discussed based on this type of analysis. In recent years this approach to clinical analysis and assessment has grown in popularity. There are several published clinical assessment procedures which adopt this approach. In the final section of this chapter three procedures which apply some of the phonological concepts illustrated in this chapter will be reviewed. Throughout the chapter the analytical techniques which are described and illustrated are based on those employed in one of the procedures summarised in the final section: the Contrastive Analysis and Assessment of the PACS set of phonological procedures (Grunwell 1985c).

The pronunciation system of an individual speaker (or of a community of like speakers, i.e. an accent or language) is observable as regularities in speech behaviour (or 'sound patterns in spoken language'). These regularities or patterns therefore are often described in terms of 'rules' of pronunciation which govern the speech behaviour. This description of the pronunciation system is made up of a series of statements which specify the patterns observed by the analyst-phonologist, clinical linguist or clinician. The concept of 'phonological system' has thus come to refer to both the pronunciation patterns used in speech and the description of these patterns. The definition of a 'phonological system' is:

> a description of the sound patterns in spoken language in terms of a finite inventory of sound elements, which are dependent upon each other in functioning contrastively and which combine with each other in forming larger linguistic units. (cf. Grunwell 1981b: 12)

Like all definitions of theoretical concepts this compresses a great deal of information into a few carefully chosen words. The implications of these terms, as used in this definition, must be understood if the concept is to be correctly applied.

First of all, the definition indicates that the sound elements function contrastively. In other words, the prime phonological function (cf. above ref. the 'phoneme', in Chapter Two) is implied in the definition, viz. distinctive sound differences signal meaning differences and thus phonological patterns encode patterns at other levels of linguistic organisation. Secondly, there is the implication that there are patterns in the combination of units as well as units that contrast with each other. This requires the already familiar descriptive framework of a *hierarchy of organisation* in which smaller units (e.g. phones) are combined in specified ways to form larger units (e.g. syllables). It is useful to extend this hierarchy to include (a) units smaller than the phone, viz. *features*, which combine simultaneously to compose phones (see Chapter Five); and (2) units larger than the syllable, viz. *words*, which are composed of successive combinations of syllables (see Chapter Three). The definition of 'phonological system' thus covers both the paradigmatic and syntagmatic dimensions of description; it indicates that spoken language involves patterns in both system and structure.

This definition of the concept of a 'phonological system' thus presents us with a terminological problem. On the one hand we routinely employ the term 'system' to refer to the overall patterns in a person's spoken language; in this sense 'phonological system' refers to the pronunciation system as a whole. On the other hand, we equally routinely use the term 'system' to refer more narrowly to the system of segments that are distinctive: in this sense 'phonological system' refers to the systems of contrasts (perhaps at different positions in structure) within the pronunciation system as a whole. In order to obviate the potential confusion that results from these two uses of the term, we shall consistently distinguish between the two applications of the concept, by referring to the overall patterns as the 'pronunciation system' and the more specific descriptive statements of contrastive phones as the 'system(s) of contrasts'.

Although the definition quoted above emphasises the equality of the two types of phonological patterning, structural and systemic, in the pronunciation system as a whole, it is custom and practice in phonological analysis to regard the contrastive function, which is seen to reside in the systemic patterning, as primary. Thus the narrower concept of a system of contrasts provides the basis for defining the characteristics of *systemic* pronunciation patterns.[1] An understanding of these characteristics, i.e. of *the criteria for establishing systemicity in phonological patterning*, is essential for the applications of this type of phonological analysis to clinical data. We shall therefore examine these criteria in some detail in this opening section of the chapter.

Each individual contrastive phonological unit depends for its identification and function upon its being different from all the other units in the system of contrasts. This is its 'systemic value'. This idea has already been encountered in discussing the inappropriateness of the term 'substitution' (see Chapter Three). If the number of units in a system is changed, then the value of each individual unit changes. Thus, if there is a two-term system of contrasts, for example [p] *v.* [t], there is only one contrast or distinctive sound difference, which could be described as *labial v. lingual.* If there is a three-term system, for example [p] *v.* [t] *v.* [k], there are three contrasts or distinctive sound differences: [p] *v.* [t], [p] *v.* [k], [t] *v.* [k], or labial *v.* alveolar *v.* velar; and consequently the contrastive values of both [p] and [t] are changed by the addition of [k]. The terms in a system are therefore described as '*mutually defining*'.

The second characteristic of systemic phonological patterning follows logically from the first. In addition to being mutually defining, terms in a system of contrasts are '*mutually exclusive*'. Obviously if a term, for example [p], is identified and defined by its being different from other terms, for example [t], it cannot occasionally be realised as identical to [t]; all occurrences of [p] must be exclusive of and different from all occurrences of [t]. Otherwise the two units would 'overlap', and in such instances could not be contrastive.[2] The following data provide an example of overlapping:

PAMELA 7;2 (1975)

train [deɪʂ]	*race* [weɪʂ]
shells [dɛʝ]	*well* [wɛʝ]
go [doʊ]	*rope* [woʊp]
cabbage ['dabɪ]	*rabbit* ['waʔbɪ]
donkey ['dɒnti]	*swan* [wɒn]
trees [diʂ, wiʂ]	
grass [daɕ, waʔʂ]	
ground [dɑʊ, wɑʊ]	

The first five (almost) minimal pairs indicate that [d] and [w] are contrastive in Pamela's speech. It would appear, however, that they 'overlap' in certain instances as indicated by the two pronunciations recorded for each of the last three words. If there was considerable overlapping in speech it would be difficult for the analyst to describe the system of contrasts, since contrastive units could not be identified and defined as being consistently different from each other. Overlapping also results in difficulties for the listener in establishing which words were intended by the speaker. Therefore an important criterion for establishing sound patterns as systemic is that the contrastive units should be mutually exclusive. Another way of defining this characteristic of systemicity is to describe systemic patterns as being internally consistent.

Another dimension of consistency is involved in the definition of systemicity. This is the requirement that the system of contrasts is in a 'state of equilibrium' or 'homeostasis'. If a system were in a state of change then some contrastive units would be disappearing from and/or coming into the system; therefore it would be difficult to define the value of each unit in the system. The following data exemplify such a situation:

TANYA 8;0 (1975)

baby ['beɪbi]	*painting* ['peɪʔɪn]
butterfly ['bəʔəfaɪ]	*purple* ['pɜʔpʊ]
book [bʊʔ]	*put* [pʊʔ]
bat [baʔ]	*park* [pɑʔ]
box [bɒʔ]	*pop* [pɒʔ]

big [bɪʔ, pɪʔ], *pig* [pɪʔ]
bees [piɕ], *peas* [piɕ, bɪɕ]
boy [pɒɪ, bɒɪ]
blue [plu, blu]
pan [pan, ban]
pencil ['pɛntʊ, 'bɛntʊ]

The first five (almost) minimal pairs suggest that [b] and [p] are contrastive in Tanya's speech; however these represent a minority of consistent pronunciations. The rest of the data illustrates that there is much free variation (see Chapter Two) between these two phonetically different segments. There is apparently a potential contrast between them, which has not yet stabilised in the system.

As Tanya's data illustrate, a system of contrasts cannot function efficiently if it is unstable in terms of the numbers of distinctive units it contains. For example, having established that [b] and [p] are probably contrastive on the basis of the first ten words (or more importantly five pairs of words), an analyst and a listener might reasonably assume on encountering [pɪʔ] that Tanya was likely to be referring to a *pig* and when hearing [biç] that she was talking about *bees*. As we can see, these assumptions might indeed be correct; but they might equally be incorrect. Hence the requirement that normal systemic patterns be homeostatic; i.e. that the system of contrasts be in a stable state. Otherwise analysts and listeners alike cannot make reliable predictions.

In the clinical applications of the concept of a system of phonological contrasts, however, this particular requirement has to be interpreted flexibly. The development of speech in children has often been described as the 'creation' of the child's own phonology; i.e. the child is building up his own pronunciation system (see for example Elbert 1983; Elbert & Gierut 1986; Ferguson 1976; Grunwell 1981a, 1985a; Stoel-Gammon & Dunn 1985).

This is a clinically applicable interpretation of speech

development and change, whether developmentally natural or facilitated by intervention. In this interpretation speech development is viewed as a gradual expansion of the system of contrasts and patterns of combination of sound used by the child. The problem with this interpretation is that child speech is seen to be in an almost constant state of change, 'a state of flux'. This, according to at least one authority (Cruttenden 1972: 33), renders analysis of the child's own system inappropriate, if not impossible, because the patterns do not conform to the strict requirement of homeostasis.[3] As has been demonstrated in the examples from Pamela and Tanya, developing systems in states of change can be analysed by using the concepts of 'overlapping' and 'free variation'. Therefore, unless the instability of the pronunciations is extreme, it is usually possible to analyse the child's speech patterns as the child's own phonology, albeit made up of a somewhat variable system of contrasts.

Of course, in a relatively short space of time this system should change and new contrasts stabilise. Changes may begin to occur within one day; and in normal development they may be completed in the space of a few days (e.g. Waterson 1970: 15) and certainly over a period of a few weeks. Unfortunately, children with speech disorders do not undergo such rapid changes (Grunwell 1981b). When describing a child's speech development the child's system of both contrasts and structures will have to be analysed at frequent intervals to chart the changes in the system as they occur. This description is therefore a 'micro-diachronic' study of the ontogenesis of the phonological system of a language, or the 'natural history' of speech development in an individual (e.g. Smith 1973: 37–51, 103–31).

Another important factor in the analysis of a child's pronunciation system is that it is not developing, and indeed could not develop, in isolation. The child's speech is being continually influenced by the speech of those around him; it is a 'system in contact' (Weinreich 1964). It is therefore to be expected that the variability in the child's system will be related to the patterns in the system(s) of adult speakers; their system is the 'dominant system'. Furthermore, the adult system is the *model* and *target* for the child; his patterns are based on the adult pronunciation system and his ultimate system will be isomorphic with it. Any variability showing the influence of the adult system is therefore progressive and indicative of a potential expansion of the system, a positive developmental change towards the target. As will be demonstrated below, using these concepts an analysis of a child's own phonology is a particularly appropriate framework for clinical assessment.

It is important to appreciate from the outset that this approach to the analysis is very different from the traditional approach, and also most other types of clinical phonological analysis (to be described in subsequent chapters). This analysis attempts to establish and describe the child's pronunciation system independently of the adult target system. Of course one cannot operate in total ignorance of the target pronunciations. The analyst will inevitably use these to identify the lexical items and thus the contrasts the child is required to signal. This knowledge therefore defines our expectations. We do not, however, at this stage of analysis compare the child and adult pronunciations directly; that is an assessment procedure which is employed after the analysis of the child's own pronunciation system is complete (see Grunwell 1981b: Chapter 5, esp. pp. 136–7; Stoel-Gammon & Dunn 1985: Chapter 4, esp. p. 92).

In the author's experience, however, this approach is not easily applied to acquired phonological disorders encountered in adult patients with dysphasic and/or dyspraxic speech impairments. In such disorders the pronunciation patterns are usually extremely unpredictable and inconsistent: unpredictable as to whether a particular word will be pronounced normally or not; inconsistent in regard to the type of pronunciation 'error' that will occur if a word is mispronounced. In addition, the treatment implications derived from an analysis of a person's system, viz. guidelines as to how to change the system, are not particularly appropriate in most cases of acquired speech disorders in the adult population, since it appears that the system is often in fact intact, but unreliably accessed.

The discussion in the rest of this chapter is therefore confined to the analysis and assessment of the speech of children with phonological disorders. Data from one such child will be used to exemplify the framework of analysis. The two exercises at the end of the chapter use data from one other child. Here two large samples are provided so that the reader can make realistic analyses and contrastive assessments. The same words are presented in each sample so that comparisons can be made between the two children and between the speech patterns of the same child at different stages. The sample has been selected to be as representative as possible within the constraints of space (and the reader's time and endurance!).[4]

In clinical practice, the speech sample for this type of analysis and assessment should conform to the criteria set out in the preceding chapter. The *minimum* size recommended is 250 words, provided that the child has achieved this level linguistically.

ANALYSIS OF THE CHILD'S OWN PHONOLOGICAL SYSTEM

Analysis of the phonological system in a child's speech patterns (the child's overall pronunciation system, according to the distinction adopted in the preceding section) involves descriptions of the phonotactic structures of syllables and words and the system of contrasts. For clinical assessment the most appropriate framework is to analyse the systems of contrastive segments separately for each place in the structure, that is to employ a *polysystemic approach* (see Chapter Two). Therefore, the segment-sized distinctive sound units are referred to here as *contrastive phones*, not phonemes, since this latter term is used conventionally in a monosystemic framework. In addition to analysing the contrastive phones, it is also useful to describe the phonetic 'content' of the phones. This requires the concept of phonetic *features*, which co-occur simultaneously in 'bundles' to compose the contrastive phones. This feature analysis can be made using the traditional phonetic categories of voice and place and manner of articulation; these generally prove to be entirely adequate for clinical assessment (cf. Chapter Five). The aim of this feature analysis is to state the contrastive features that maintain the distinctions between the contrastive phones.

The analysis of the child's phonological system is therefore made up of the following:

(1) a statement of the sets of contrastive phones at each place in the structure, together with details of the non-contrastive variants of each contrastive phone;
(2) a statement of the feature compositions of the contrastive phones;
(3) a statement of the phonotactic possibilities.

Table 4.1: *MARTIN* 6;3 (1975)

1. aeroplane ['ɛəɹəpeɪn, 'ɛəwəbeɪ]
2. black [baʔ]
3. boat [boʊʔ]
4. box [bɒt̪]
5. bridge [bɪv]
6. butterflies ['bʊʔəfaɪ]
7. cabbage ['gabɪ]
8. cage [geɪv]
9. cake [keɪʔ, keɪ]
10. cap [gap, gaʔ]
11. cart [gɑʔ]
12. cheese [fi]
13. chimney ['fɪmni]
14. chip [fɪʔ, fɪʔ͡p]
15. chopper ['fɒpə]
16. claws (M) [kɔɹɭ]; [gɔ]
17. colour ['kʊvə]
18. cotton ['kɒʔən]
19. cough [kɒʔ, gɒʔ]
20. crab (M) [kjab˺]
21. dish [dɪʔ]
22. dog [dɒg]
23. drinking ['fɪnʔɪn]
24. farm [fɑm]
25. feather ['fɛvə]
26. finger ['fɪnvə]
27. fish [fɪʔ]
28. five [faɪ]
29. flag [fav, faʋ]
30. flower ['fɑʊə]
31. garage ['gaɹɪʔ, 'gaʋɪ]
32. glove [gʊ, gʊʋ]
33. grapes [geɪʔ͡p]
34. juice [fuʔ]
35. lip [wɪʔ͡p, ʋɪʔ]
36. lock [ʋɒʔ]
37. mat [maʔ]
38. match [maʔ]
39. mirror ['mɪɹə, 'mɪwə]
40. needle ['nigʊ]

(Note: nobody ['noʊbɒdi])

41. paint [beɪnʔ]
42. pan [ban]
43. pig [bɪv]
44. plate [beɪʔ]
45. pram (M) [pə'lam]
46. queen [kin, kim]
47. race [weɪ]
48. rain [weɪn]
49. red [ɹɛ, ʋɛv]
50. rock [ʋɒʔ͜k]
51. sandwiches ['famwɪʔɪ]
52. scissors ['fɪvə, 'fɪʋə]
53. ship [fɪp, fɪʔ]
54. sleeping ['fiʔɪn]
55. slide [fɑʊw]
56. smoke [moʊʔ]
57. snow [noʊ]
58. soldier ['foʊwə,'foʊʋə]
59. spade [peɪʋ]
60. spoon [pum, bun]
61. stamps [tamp˺]
62. stove [toʊw]
63. strawberries ['fɔbɛɹi]
64. string [fɪn, fɪm]
65. sugar ['fʊʋə, 'fʊvə]
66. swimming ['fɪmɪn]
67. tap [dap˺]
68. tea [ti]
69. teeth [tiʔ, di]
70. thread[fɛv]
71. three [fi]
72. thumb [fʊm]
73. tractor ['faʔtə]
74. train [feɪm]
75. tree, sea [fi]
76. van [ʋan]
77. watch, yacht [ʋɒʔ]
78. wool [wʊɟ]
79. yellow ['lɛloʊ]
80. yes [ʋɛʔ]

Phonetic Inventory and Distribution

As a preliminary to analysing the systems of contrastive phones, the total phonetic inventory and the distribution of all these phonetically-different segments should be stated. The phonetic inventory lists, under phonetic feature classification, all the different segment types that occur in the data sample. Any phones that occur only once or twice in a large and representative sample can usually be treated as 'marginal' to the child's pronunciation system. Nevertheless, it is often useful to include them in further analyses as they constitute indicators of incipient changes in the child's pronunciation patterns.

MARTIN Phonetic Inventory

	Labial	Labio-dent.	Alve-olar	Post-alv.	Velar	Glottal
Nasal	m		n			
Plosive	p b		t d		k g	ʔ
Fric.		f v				
Approx.	w	ʋ		ɹ		

Marginal Phones: [ţ, l, ʝ, ɭ, j].
(Note: several occur in repeated words.)

In all analyses of phone distribution, four positions in word structure are examined:

Onsets:
syllable initial word initial;
syllable initial within word;

Terminations
syllable final word final;
syllable final within word.

A table can be drawn up as follows:

Syllable Initial Word Initial (SIWI)	Syllable Initial Within Word (SIWW)	Syllable Final Within Word (SFWW)	Syllable Final Word Final (SFWF)

Thus, the analysis of phone distribution in Martin's data is as given below. It is evident from an examination of Martin's data that his pronunciation patterns of modelled words tend to be different in structure and phonetic constituents from spontaneously produced words. Therefore any occurrence of a phone that is restricted to a modelled word (e.g. final [b] in (20)) is excluded from the analysis of his system. This is not necessarily routine practice; other children's pronunciation patterns may not be so easily influenced by 'models' as Martin's appeared to be.

SIWI	SIWW	SFWW	SFWF
m	m	m	m
n	n	n	n
p	p		p
b	b		
t	t		
d	d		
k			k
g	g		g
	ʔ	ʔ	ʔ
f	f		
	v		v
ʋ	ʋ		ʋ
w	w		w
ɹ	ɹ		

From this phonetic analysis we can already draw some conclusions as to the characteristics of Martin's pronunciation system and its restrictions. The phonetic inventory indicates a paucity of fricative phones, while the table of phonetic distribution reveals a very imbalanced occurrence of the phones across the different places in structure, with a striking restriction on phones in terminations.

Analysis of Contrastive Phones

Although the framework of analysis to be used here is polysystemic, the criteria of phonemic analysis are employed in discovering the contrastive phones at each place in structure and in grouping the different segments together as variants of contrastive phones (see Chapter Two). In particular the concepts of complementary distribution and free variation are applicable. Where there is no positive evidence to indicate that a phone is a non-contrastive variant, then it should be analysed as a contrastive phone. In other words, every phonetically different segment should be regarded as potentially contrastive, unless there are clearly statable grounds for including it as a variant of an already identified contrastive phone. Furthermore, when there is evidence (e.g. several consistently contrasted minimal pairs) that two phonetically different segments are contrastive, then they are to be regarded as remaining distinct even if there is variability between them in the pronunciation of some words. The variability in such instances is analysed as 'overlapping' (see above).

Applying these criteria to Martin's data sample the statement of contrastive phones at each place in structure is as follows:

MARTIN Contrastive Phones

SIWI	SIWW	SFWW	SFWF
m	m	m	m
n	n	n	n
	p		(p)
b	b		
	t		
d	d		
			(k)
g	g		
	ʔ	ʔ	ʔ
f	f		
ʋ	ʋ		ʋ

The occurrences of phones within words in this small data sample are so few that it is, in fact, inadvisable to assume that all the phones stated here for the SIWW position are definitely contrastive; but as there is no evidence to prove otherwise they should be regarded as potentially contrastive. The range of possible within-word terminations (SFWW) is also very small in this sample; it is therefore not surprising that only a few phones are found to be contrastive here. Indeed, in most clinical samples, this position in structure usually has a rather restricted range of possible targets.

With reference to SFWF terminations, however, the small set of contrastive phones here is a characteristic of Martin's system, not an artefact of data sampling. Here, it is unlikely that [p] and [k] are regularly contrastive in Martin's speech, especially as in many realisations they are 'supported' by [ʔ]. Furthermore, depending on one's interpretation, [p] and [k] frequently 'overlap' or are in 'free variation' with [ʔ]; examples include for [p], (10) and (14), and for [k] (50) only.

In SIWI onsets, the fortis and lenis plosives have been analysed as non-contrastive variants at each place of articulation, on the basis of occurrences of free variation: for example [t,d] (69), [k,g] (19). In onsets SIWW, however, [pb] and [td] appear to be potentially contrastive. In both word-initial and within-word onsets, the phones [v,ʋ,w,ɹ] appear to be variants of one contrastive unit, stated here as |ʋ| (vertical brackets being employed to indicate a child's contrastive phone; see Chapter Two). While there are no examples of free variation between all four phones, there are several words where two realisations occur for example: (31), (49), (52), (58), (65). Similarly in word-final position [v,ʋ,w] are analysed as variants of one unit, although in this sample only (29) provides definite evidence in support of this analysis.

The variability between |m| and |n| in word-final position, for example (46), (60), (64), is an instance of overlapping. There are also instances of overlapping in word-final position between |n| and zero phone in (1); |ʔ| and zero phone in (9), (69); and |ʋ| and zero phone in (49), (32).

The contrastive analysis of this sample confirms the first impressions suggested by the phonetic analysis and reveals even greater restrictions on the systems of contrastive phones. It is apparent that all the phonetically different segments are not functionally different, in regard to their contrastive value in the child's pronunciation system. It is very important that this aspect of a child's pronunciation patterns is appreciated in making a clinical assessment. It has major implications in planning a treatment programme and strategies for intervention, since it reveals that while a child is able to produce a sound adequately from the phonetic point of view, he is not using it systemically, that is to signal meaning differences consistently.

Analysis of Martin's data sample illustrates the applications of the concepts of phonemic analysis to child speech. In particular it shows how we apply the concepts of free variation and overlapping. It is not, however, necessary to employ the concept of complementary distribution in the analysis of Martin's sample. This is mainly the result of having adopted a polysystemic approach to the analysis. In this framework occurrences of complementary distribution are rare and are almost entirely restricted to contextually conditioned variants in clusters (see Chapter Two, Exercise 9, for an example), and variants whose occurrence is determined by the features of the other segments in the word, especially the vowels (see Chapter Two, Darren 6;3 and Exercise 8 for examples). Other approaches to the analysis of the child's phonological system, in particular that of Elbert & Gierut (1986), do employ the concept of complementary distribution, as they use a monosystemic framework. These authors cite as examples of this type of patterning: the occurrence of consonants at different places of articulation determined by the quality of the following vowel (see also Camarata & Gandour 1984) and the occurrence of voiced and voiceless consonants determined by word position, specifically [dʒ] always and only in word-initial position and [tʃ] always and only in word-final position (Elbert & Gierut 1986: 80–1). These examples are exactly analogous to those presented in Chapter Two.

Elbert & Gierut also employ another concept from phonemic analysis which is not strictly speaking applicable in a polysystemic framework. This is the concept of *neutralisation* of contrasts. In a monosystemic framework a contrast between two phonemes may be established at one position in structure, but be found not to operate at another position in structure. For example in the analysis of Martin's data we found that there is probably a contrast between the voiced and voiceless plosives ([p b] and [t d]) in onsets SIWW. In SIWI position, however, we established that there is no such contrast; the voiced and voiceless plosives are in free variation. Therefore the contrast that operates in SIWW position is said to be neutralised in SIWI position. This is a particular instance of neutralisation, since the phones that are contrastive in one position are neutralised as non-contrastive free variants in the other position. The examples that are cited by Elbert & Gierut (op. cit.: 82–7) are more clear-cut than the patterns in Martin's data. For example they present the data from a child who used [f] and [s] contrastively in onsets, both SIWI and SIWW, and who only used [s] in SFWF position:

	SIWI		SIWW		SFWF
fat	[fat]	*laughing*	['jafɪn]	*laugh*	[jas]
soup	[sup]	*mousey*	['maʊsi]	*mouse*	[maʊs]

(NB: The fact that this neutralisation involves the loss of a 'correct' phonemic contrast is significant in Elbert & Gierut's application of this concept; see further below.)

Although neutralisation is not applicable in a polysystemic framework, since this establishes the system of contrasts at each position in structure separately, the basic concept encapsulated in the idea of neutralisation can of course be employed when the different systems of contrasts at each position in structure are compared. Indeed one would tend to highlight an instance where a contrast operates in one position but not in another; as we have done in our analysis of Martin's data.

In case there is any potential for confusion, it must be emphasised once again that neutralisation, overlapping and free variation are three very different concepts. *Neutralisation* occurs where a contrast established at one position in structure does not operate at another position. *Overlapping* occurs when a pair of established contrastive phones are used at the same position in structure in the pronunciation of the same word on two separate occasions; for example Martin's two pronunciations of *queen* (46), *spoon* (60) and *string* (64). *Free variation* occurs where a pair of phonetically different phones occur at the same position in structure in repeated pronunciations of a substantial number of words; in such circumstances these phones cannot be established as contrastive and are analysed as variants of one contrastive phone (see also Elbert & Gierut op. cit.: 78–9). These three concepts are very important for understanding the different 'systemic values' (i.e. contrastive *v.* non-contrastive function) of the phonetically different phones in the child's pronunciation system.

Analysis of Feature Contrasts

After analysing the systems of contrastive phones, tables of the feature compositions of the contrastive phones can be drawn up. This, following the framework of previous analyses, should be stated separately for each position in structure. In making separate statements for Martin's sample, those for terminations would provide little more information than is available from the statement of contrastive phones; and the feature contrasts in this position are in fact a subset of the contrasts in onset positions. The statement for within-word onsets (SIWW) on the basis of this data sample would be extremely tentative; it would, however, suggest a potential fortis-lenis contrast for the plosive phones, which would warrant further investigation in the clinical context, since this contrast is absent from word-initial onsets. Thus the only definite statement of feature contrasts that can be made on the basis of this sample is that for SIWI. This is given in full here, to exemplify this aspect of the analysis.

MARTIN Feature Contrasts — SIWI

	Labial	Alveolar	Velar	Glottal
Nasal	m	n		
Plosive	b	d	g	ʔ
Fricative	f			
Approx.	ʋ			

This statement indicates the range of phonetic differences that are used contrastively in the child's system. In Martin's instance it reveals an extremely small range of feature contrast and possible combinations to form the 'content' of contrastive phones.

Phonotactic Analysis

Finally in the analysis of the child's pronunciation system, the statement of phonotactic structures is made, in terms of the C (consonant) and V (vowel) structure of syllables in words. Monosyllabic words are analysed separately from multisyllabic words, and in the latter group it is advisable to examine disyllabic words separately from polysyllabic words. This is because disyllables have a much higher frequency, especially in clinical data, than polysyllabic words. Thus, the phonotactic analysis of Martin's data sample is as follows:

MARTIN Phonotactic Possibilities
Monosyllables
CV
CVC
(CVCC)
Disyllables
CVCV
CVCVC
CVC, CV
CVC, CVC
Polysyllables
CVCVCV
CVCVCVC
CVC, CVCV

These phonotactic possibilities can be summarised in formulaic statements as follows:

Monosyllables:	$C_1V\ C_{0-1}$
Disyllables:	$C_1V\ C_{0-1}, C_1V\ C_{0-1}$
Polysyllables:	$C_1V\ C_{0-1}, C_1V\ C_1V\ C_{0-1}$

This analysis makes it quite clear that in Martin's data words are made up of strings of syllables with the simplest CV structure. There is only one word with an initial cluster (20) and as this is a repetition of a modelled word (indicated by (M)) it can obviously be regarded as an exceptional form. There are, in this sample, only two words (41 and 61) with final clusters ((16) being a repetition of a modelled word and thus probably exceptional); this low frequency of occurrence suggests that this structure should not be regarded as an established pattern in the child's system. In fact, in the total sample from which these data are taken, there were 275 monosyllabic words, of which only five were CVCC structures, that is under 2 per cent (Grunwell 1977 Vol. II: 704). Therefore, in this regard at least, the sample given here reflects this child's habitual patterns.

In analysing a speech sample for clinical assessment, the percentage occurrence of each type of word and of each type of structural pattern provides an indication of the relative dominance of the different types in the child's system. The most frequently occurring syllabic structures can be regarded as the child's '*canonical forms*', that is the structures that are central to the child's system. These percentages have not been calculated for Martin's sample, as this has been selected from a larger sample and is biased in favour of illustrating the characteristics of the segmental patterning rather than the structural. Nevertheless, the predominance of monosyllables (which were 60 per cent of the larger sample) and of simple structures does represent an accurate reflection of Martin's system (see Grunwell 1981b: Table 17).

Assessment of the Child's Own Phonological System

There are two basic approaches to the assessment of a child's pronunciation system:

(1) it can be assessed as a phonological system *per se*;
(2) it can be assessed by comparison with other systems with which a clinically relevant comparison can be made.

In the first instance, one is posing the question: is this a normal adequate phonological system according to our expectations of the organisation and operation of such systems? In the second, one is addressing the question: in what ways is the child's pronunciation system different and/or deficient by comparison with the other system(s) with which it is being compared? In actual practice, information about other phonological systems enters into the evaluation of the phonological system *per se.*

In these assessments of the child's pronunciation system a number of dimensions of the system are evaluated. In the assessment of the phonological system *per se,* we are examining in particular the organisational characteristics and the operating potential, that is its functional adequacy. In comparing the child's system with other systems, these two dimensions are also considered, but the focus is on the differences between the two systems. As we shall see, two types of comparison are clinically relevant: we can use as our 'normative yardstick' the adult pronunciation system, or we can compare the child's system with a descriptive profile of the normal development of children's pronunciation systems.

Assessment of the Child's Phonological System as a Phonological System

The definition and discussion of the nature of phonological systems at the beginning of this chapter provide the criteria for an assessment of the normality of the child's own phonological system. For sound patterns to be analysed as systemic, contrasts should be consistently maintained and should not overlap. Variability in the realisations of contrastive phones contravenes, to a greater or lesser extent, this criterion of systemicity. It is possible to assess this dimension of systemicity without reference to any other factors. Since, however, the child is attempting to speak a language that is normally encoded via an adequate, adult pronunciation system, from the practical point of view it is useful to take account of the normal patterns of contrasts. It would be unrealistic to ignore the fact that the analyst possesses information relevant to the assessment of the child's speech that is not in fact in the data. This enables us to make a more appropriate and applicable assessment of the variability, and the adequacy (see below), of the child's system.

It must be emphasised, however, that even though reference is made to the normal adult system, we are not at this point evaluating the child's pronunciation system by comparison with that system. The variability and adequacy that is being assessed here is *internal* to the child's own system *per se*. In a subsequent section the comparative assessment with the adult system is to be described. Here another type of variability is discussed: that of variable relationships between the child and adult systems.

There are two types of variability in the child's pronunciation system that are indications of a lack of normal systemicity. The first is occurrences of overlapping between apparently contrastive phones. The clinical relevance of this variability is particularly significant where the overlapping in the child's system involves phones that are consistently contrastive (i.e. realisations of different phonemes) in the adult system. The overlapping of |m| and |n| in word-final terminations in Martin's system is an example of this type of variability. The clinical implications in such instances are that the variant realisations should be suppressed and the correct pronunciations stabilised.

The second type of variability involves free variation between phonetically different phones that do not appear to operate contrastively in the child's system. It is unusual to find unpredictable free variation (i.e. variation that is not rule-governed by contextual factors) occurring very frequently in normal phonological systems. Also 'normal' non-contrastive variation does not usually involve a wide range of different segments; furthermore, the variants tend to be phonetically similar (but see Chapter Two). Non-contrastive variability is particularly significant when it involves free variation in the child's speech between phones that are consistently contrastive (i.e. realisations of different phonemes) in the adult system. The free variation between [t, d] and between [k, g] in word-initial onsets are obvious examples of this in Martin's system. The clinical implications here are very different from those applicable to the first type of variability resulting from overlapping. In such instances of non-contrastive variability the contrastivity of the different phones must be established; that is this variability is a potential starting point for the expansion of the child's system.

Another example of free variation in Martin's system is the variant realisations of |ʊ|. In this pattern, however, the relationship to the adult system is not so straightforward, either phonetically or phonologically, and the potential for establishing new contrasts is therefore not so directly available. It is only in SIWI position that the variant realisations could form the starting point for an expansion of the system. Within words and in word-final positions this variability is clinically unproductive.

It is evident from the foregoing discussion that certain types of variability have positive implications. There are instances of *progressive variability* where the occurrence of variation in the child's system indicates the potential for establishing a new contrast. As was pointed out at the beginning of the chapter, variability is not abnormal in child speech; it is a necessary condition, indicative that the child's system is still developing and is being influenced by the systems with which it is 'in contact'. The absence of any signs of variability is therefore also clinically significant, as it indicates that there are no incipient changes inherent in the child's system; that is it appears *stable*. Where there is an apparently stable, but inadequate, system the primary aim for clinical intervention is to introduce *new* contrasts (see further below as to the guidelines for deciding which new contrasts to start with).

Equally, *extremely variable* pronunciation patterns are indicative of disordered speech patterns in a child's system. They suggest that few if any phonetically-different segments have been stabilised as contrastive phones. The following data exemplify extreme variability.

JOANNE 5;0 (1974)
cage [keɪg, seɪz]
children [ˈt̺ɹʊʤɪn, ˈkʊɹʊdən]
Karen [ˈtawən, ˈʃ̺awən]
shop [ʃɒp, ʧɒp]
some [sʊm, s̺ʊm, ʧʊm, tʊm]
strangers [ˈʤeɪnʤəz, ˈkʊeɪnʤəz]
teeth [tif, sif]
tent [tɛnt, kɛnt]
tidy [ˈtaɪdi, ˈʃaɪdi]
tree [tʃi, ʃi, kɰi]

Here there seem to be no stabilised contrasts between [t, s̺, s, ʃ, ʃ̺, tʃ, k] and also possibly [dʒ]. Speech behaviour of this kind could be regarded as *asystemic*. This type of variability must be suppressed (cf. Ingram 1976: 141) and consistent contrasts established.

In the assessment of the child's system therefore, the two diametrically opposite organisational characteristics of (1) a stable system and (2) extreme variability are therefore both indicative of phonologically disordered speech patterns. Moreover, variability, although it is often an indicator of potential progress, does not always warrant a positive assessment. Often the child's system is found to be variable; it therefore contains the indices of change, though it may not be changing. That is, over a period of time during which spontaneous progress might be expected to take place, there is no evidence of any developmental changes occurring. In such instances, the child's pronunciation patterns are described as a *static variable phonological system*. This type of disordered phonological system is frequently encountered when assessing the speech of children referred for speech therapy; Martin, in fact, was just such a case (for further discussion see Grunwell 1981b). In such instances, as has been already pointed out, intervention should usually aim at capitalising on the inherent variability in the system.

The second aspect of the child's system which is relevant to clinical assessment is its functional *adequacy.* The function of any pronunciation system is to signal the meaning differences required by the other levels of linguistic structure. Where different meanings are not being signalled in pronunciation, it is clear that the pronunciation patterns are functionally inadequate. The occurrence of *homophones* (i.e. two or more different words with the same pronunciation) is evidence of inadequacies in the system. Examples of homophones in Martin's data sample include (5) and (43); (14), (27) and (53); (12), (71) and (75). The communicative significance of actual homophones is in fact difficult to assess.[5] After all, homophones occur in normal pronunciation patterns, for example *meat, meet* and *mete* /mit/, *see* and *sea* /si/, etc. Also contextual factors may reduce or almost entirely eliminate the possibility of conflict between homophones. For example, linguistic factors such as grammatical class will delimit the potential structural collocations, so that Martin's pronunciation of the verb *try* as [faɪ] is unlikely to be confused with the numeral *five* [faɪ]. Sense relations and other contextual information will also help to resolve many ambiguities; for example, *tree* and *cheese,* both of which Martin pronounced as [fi], are unlikely to occur in the same conversational context. The homophony of *tree* and *field* [fi], however, resulted in very real problems when Martin tried to inform his therapist where he thought butterflies lived. Evidence of actual or potential homophony, often supported by repeated experience of serious difficulty in understanding the child, is almost always indicative of a communicatively as well as functionally inadequate system (cf. Ingram 1981). We shall explore this functional dimension further in the Contrastive Assessment, in which the child's system is compared with the normal adult system (see below).

The two assessment criteria that have been considered so far are concerned with evaluating the operational normality and adequacy of the system. As indicated above the assessment should also consider the organisational characteristics, that is the structural potential and the contrastive potential (as indicated by the phonetic content) of the child's pronunciation system. Once again, Martin's system provides a typical example of the *characteristics of the phonological systems of children with developmental phonological disorders.* These are:

(1) limited phonotactic resources: very few, if any, consonant clusters occur; words are constituted of strings of simple syllabic structures; open syllables predominate;
(2) limited phonetic resources: place and/or manner of articulation feature contrasts are restricted; the fortis/lenis distinction between obstruents is often lacking;
(3) different sets of contrastive phones operate at different positions in structure.

These characteristics usually imply that the child's system is, to a greater or lesser extent, deviant by comparison with organisational patterns found in normal phonological systems. Normal pronunciation systems tend to be 'economical'; they 'exploit' the contrastive potential of their phonetic resources. For example, if there is a plosive:fricative feature contrast at one place of articulation (e.g. /p/ contrasts with /f/), and the plosive contrasts with another plosive at another place of articulation (e.g. /p/:/t/), then it is very likely that there will also be a plosive:fricative contrast at the second place of articulation as well (i.e. /t/:/s/). Thus systems of contrasts tend to be *symmetrical,* or show *pattern congruity*:

	Labial	Alveolar
Plosive	p	t
Fricative	f	s

Similarly, if one pair of plosives is contrasted by the fortis:lenis feature, then other pairs are likely to occur for other plosives, and often for the whole class of obstruents too; thus in normal adult English we have:

/p/:/b/ /t/:/d/ /ʧ/:/ʤ/
/f/:/v/ /s/:/z/ /ʃ/:/ʒ/

Where different pairs of contrastive phones are distinguished by the same feature contrast, as in this example, they are called *correlative pairs* or *correlations*; for example, /p/ is to /b/ as

/t/ is to /d/; /f/ is to /v/ as /s/ is to /z/; etc. It is evident from the analysis presented above that Martin's pronunciation system is 'uneconomical' in the use of potential feature contrasts. It is only at the labial place of articulation that all the manner contrasts are exploited. In addition, the analysis of contrastive phones indicated that there is possibly a fortis:lenis contrast between [p] and [b], and between [t] and [d], at the onset position within words (SIWW). There is no evidence for a distinction at this or any other position in the structure between [k] and [g], even though both phones occur in the data sample. Furthermore, the fortis:lenis difference is clearly *not* distinctive in SIWI position, a further sign of an uneconomical system.

Another characteristic that results in uneconomical organisation of the pronunciation system is the occurrence of different sets of contrastive phones at different positions in the structure. This means that phone contrasts are not exploited for their distributional possibilities. Thus the paradigmatic and syntagmatic dimensions of the system are both limited in organisation as well as resources.

There are direct clinical guidelines to be derived from a descriptive assessment which pinpoints these characteristics. As appropriate (i.e. to the model and target system), contrasts evidenced at one position in structure must be established at all positions in structure; that is the maximum set of contrastive phones should have maximum distributional possibilities. It is very often more appropriate to remediate this aspect of the child's pronunciation system first, that is to facilitate the development of structural combinations within the contrastive resources of the existing system, before expanding the system of contrasts. When it comes to expanding the contrastive resources of the pronunciation system, potential correlative pairs and the asymmetrical use of phonetic feature contrasts are logical starting points. Where appropriate, newly introduced contrasts should, of course, be established at all positions in the structure. Decisions as to the order of facilitation of new contrasts cannot, however, be made on a purely (phono)logical basis. Patterns in normal phonological development also provide relevant guidelines for clinical intervention. Sometimes these two sources conflict; for example, the fortis:lenis contrast appears to enter children's systems in a somewhat piecemeal fashion (see below and Chapter Seven). As always, clinical decisions must be taken in the light of what is appropriate to each individual child. The above guidelines are designed to provide general principles; these are applicable to particular instances only when the child's speech patterns have been exhaustively described using this framework of analysis and assessment.

Contrastive Assessment

The basic principle of contrastive assessment is very different from the framework of error analysis. In contrastive assessment the comparison is *not* between the pronunciations of individual speech sounds in certain words; it *is* the comparison of the patterns of organisation in two pronunciation *systems.* If the child's pronunciations are analysed according to the procedures described in the preceding sections of this chapter, the patterns in his pronunciation system are stated using the same framework of description that is employed in the analysis of normal adult phonological systems. One is therefore able to compare like with like.

Three dimensions of phonological organisation are examined in this comparison:

(1) the structural patterns, or phonotactic possibilities;
(2) the system of contrasts;
(3) the distributional restrictions on the contrastive phones.

In practice it is more appropriate to work in the polysystemic framework that has been adopted throughout the analysis, and conflate (2) and (3) above into one basic comparative procedure, making *comparisons of the sets of contrastive phones at each position in syllable and word structure.* The most relevant contrastive assessment for clinical purposes is a *comparison with the adult phonological system*, which is the model and target for the child's pronunciation system. From now onwards this will be designated the *Contrastive Assessment.*

The phonotactic assessment here is very straightforward. The structural possibilities of the adult English system are monosyllables in the range of $C_{0-3}V\ C_{0-4}$, and combinations thereof in multisyllabic words (see Chapter Two). By comparison with the phonotactic possibilities of the child's pronunciation system (for example, see Martin's system above) one can gauge the differences between the two. Martin, as before, provides a typical example of an extremely restricted range of phonotactic possibilities by comparison with the adult. If required a more detailed phonotactic assessment can be carried out examining the child's syllabic structures which correspond to each type of adult target syllabic structure (see further below in the review of the Contrastive Assessment in PACS (Grunwell 1985c)).

Contrastive Assessment of the systems of contrastive phones at each position in the structure involves 'mapping' the child's system of contrasts on to the adult system; i.e. stating the relationships or correspondences between the two systems. The following chapters examine three other phonological frameworks that have been used in clinical assessment to state the relationships between the child and adult pronunciation patterns. The Contrastive Assessment that is proposed here is very different from these (see also Grunwell 1985c). It is a simple, but graphic, statement in a tabular format, of the relationships between the two systems *in toto* (see also Ferguson 1968 for the original formulation of this format, and Grunwell 1975 for the first known clinical application). The adult systems of contrastive phones (phonemes) in SIWI and SFWF positions are displayed in Tables 4.2 and 4.4. The child's system of contrastive phones at each of these positions in structure is superimposed on these by entering the child's realisations of the adult phonemes in the appropriate box. It is essential that this comparison is between the child's contrastive phones, as established in an analysis of his system of contrasts, *not* his phonetic realisations of the adult phonemes. These latter, as the preceding analysis has demonstrated, may be non-contrastive variants which are not being used systemically to signal meaning differences. Where one contrastive phone in the child's system is equivalent to several adult phonemes, it is often possible on the table to enclose the adult phonemes in a single 'box', thus indicating that there is only one unit in the child's system by comparison with two or more in the adult. Where two contrastive phones in the child's system map on to one adult phoneme, both should be entered in to the appropriate box.

The Contrastive Assessment of Martin's system is presented in Tables 4.3 and 4.5. These reveal in a succinct and at the same time comprehensive format the inadequacies and restrictions of the child's system by comparison with the adult. It is clear that even in SIWI position, where the child's largest set of contrastive phones occurs, the system is considerably reduced and

Table 4.2: Adult System SIWI Consonants

m		n					
p	b	t	d	ʧ	ʤ	k	g
f	v	θ	ð	ʃ	ʒ		
		s	z				
w		r		j		h	
		l					

Table 4.3: Martin (6;3) Contrastive Assessment: SIWI

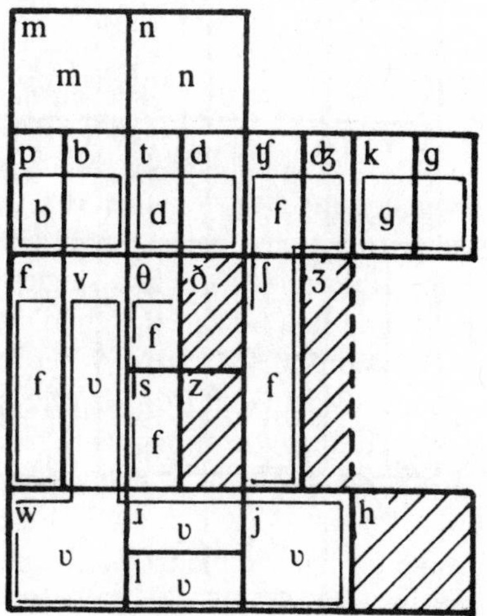

Table 4.4: Adult System SFWF Consonants

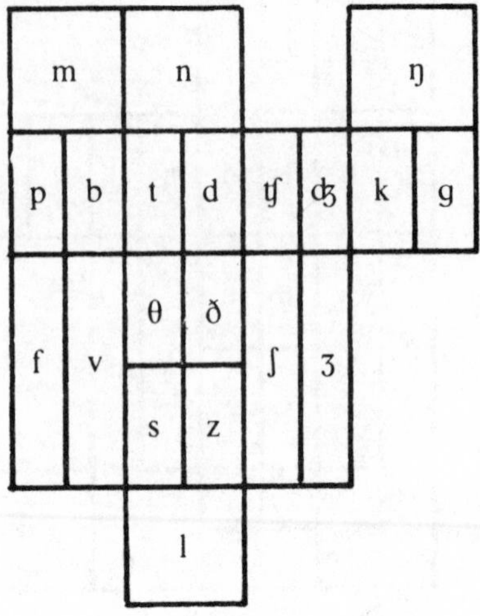

m		n				ŋ	
p	b	t	d	ʧ	ʤ	k	g
f	v	θ	ð	ʃ	ʒ		
		s	z				
		l					

Table 4.5: Martin (6;3) Contrastive Assessments: SFWF

m m		n n ø				ŋ n m	
p ? (p)	b (b)	t ?	d ø (ʋ)	ʧ ?	ʤ ?ø (ʋ)	kø ? (k)	g (g) (ʋ)
f ?	v ø (ʋ)	θ ø ?	ð (hatched)	ʃ ?	ʒ (hatched)		
		s ø ?	z ø				
		l l ~ ʋ					

All Obstruents →[?] or ø

cannot possibly function adequately to signal the meaning differences required in the adult language. By comparing the assessments at both positions in the structure, one can identify the even greater inadequacy of the child's contrastive system in syllable terminations word-final. Because of the small data sample and the consequent tentative analysis for within-word positions, only the two places in structure are assessed here. In clinical practice, analysis of the contrasts at SIWW position should be attempted; terminations within words are usually too restricted to attempt a valid assessment. It must again be emphasised that Martin's assessment is typical in demonstrating how this format highlights the inadequacies of the system of a child with a phonological disorder (see Grunwell 1975: 38; 1980a: 150–1 for further examples).

By mapping the child's system of contrasts on to the adult's system, different types of relationships are revealed between the two systems. Ideally there should be an isomorphic relationship; i.e. one-to-one correspondence between the units in the two systems. If this were so then the child would be using the same system of contrasts as in the adult pronunciation system and he would therefore be able to signal all the meaning differences normally signalled in his language. Such a situation is rarely found of course in clinical assessments, as there would be no need for a phonological analysis of the child's speech if it were so. More often than not there is a lack of contrasts in the child's system by comparison with the adult system; i.e. one child contrastive phone corresponds to many adult phonemes. An example of this in Martin's sample is the correspondence between his |f| and the adult phonemes /tʃ dʒ f θ s ʃ/ in SIWI position. This type of relationship entails a multiple loss of adult phonemic contrasts.

Frequently there are several child contrastive phones corresponding to one adult phoneme. This type of relationship involves variable correspondences between the child and adult system of contrasts. There are many examples of this in the Contrastive Assessment of Martin's system in SFWF position; e.g. both his |n| and |m| (and ø) map on to adult /n/; both his /ʋ/ and /ʔ/ (and ø) correspond to adult /dʒ/. It should be noted that variable correspondences between the child and adult system of contrasts do not necessarily result from internal variability in the child's system. Overlapping of course does entail variable correspondences, as illustrated in examples of the correspondences for the adult phoneme /n/ in *spoon* (60). Variable correspondences more often than not result from different child contrastive phones occurring as realisations of the same adult phoneme in different words; e.g. in Martin's pronunciation system the adult phoneme /s/ is invariably realised as |ʔ| and ø in SFWF position (see *race* (47) and *yes* (80)). Variable correspondences thus entail inconsistent signalling of *adult* contrasts. Although this variability may not be internal to the child's system it may nevertheless be progressive in the sense discussed above, in that one of the child's variable realisations of an adult target phoneme may be a newly emerging correspondence that is closer phonetically to the target. In Martin's data the occurrence of |p| (as [ʔ͡p]) variably with |ʔ| as realisations of adult /p/ in SFWF position provides an example of precisely such a situation.

The clinical (treatment) implications of the Contrastive Assessment are usually quite clear. The general principle is that the child's system should be expanded where it is most different or inadequate by comparison with the adult system. In Martin's case, the assessment indicates that treatment should first aim at distributional expansion of the set of contrastive phones in onsets to all positions in the structure, and subsequently at a systemic expansion by the introduction of new contrasts, specifically in the fricative system.

Other types of contrastive analysis and assessment are possible and can provide information about a child's speech patterns that is particularly relevant in clinical practice. The child's system can be compared with a profile of the normal development of the phonological system. An example of this type of profile is given in Table 4.6. Patterns in phonological development are discussed in detail in Chapter Seven. The profile provides an outline of the developing system of contrastive phones in a format which is comparable with that of the Contrastive Assessment tables. The ages for the stages indicated on the left of the table are those proposed by Crystal, Fletcher & Garman for grammatical development (1976: 85). Thus, by using this profile to make a Developmental Assessment, a child's phonological development can be compared with his development of other levels of linguistic structure.

This profile of phonological development is based on the findings of a variety of studies of child speech (for details see Grunwell 1981a). At Stage I there is a great deal of individual

Table 4.6: Profile of Phonological Development: Phonological System

Stage				Labial		Lingual
Stage I (0;9–1;6)	Nasal					
	Plosive					
	Fricative					
	Approximant					
Stage II (1;6–2;0)		m		n		
		p b		t d		
		w				
Stage III (2;0–2;6)		m		n		(ŋ)
		p b		t d		(k g)
		w				h
Stage IV (2;6–3;0) / Stage V (3;0–3;6)		m		n		ŋ
		p b		t d		k g
		f		s		
		w		(l)	j	h
Stage VI (3;6–4;0) (4;0–4;6)		m		n		ŋ
		p b		t d	ʧ ʤ	k g
		f v		s z	ʃ	
		w		l (r)	j	h
Stage VII (4;6<)		m		n		ŋ
		p b		t d	ʧ ʤ	k g
		f v	θ ð	s z	ʃ ʒ	
		w		l r	j	h

variation in the types of phones used in speech. Most children, however, appear to use a minimum of one phone from at least three of the four manner-of-articulation categories, and to have both labial and lingual consonants. The outline of the development of the system in the later stages must be interpreted equally flexibly, both in regard to the chronology (Crystal *et al.* 1976: 84 suggest that ± six months is a safe margin for the age ranges specified), and as to the contrasts that are present. Children tend to follow somewhat idiosyncratic routes in developing their phonological systems; Table 4.6 represents a 'composite norm'.

With these provisos in mind, a developmental contrastive assessment can be made. This will indicate whether a child's system is comparable with a normally developing child system or appears to have deviated from the normal route. If the former, the stage of normal development can be specified. This assessment thus provides the possibility of differentiating between delayed, but normal, versus deviant development and of calculating the degree of delay in the development of the child's *system of contrasts* (see Grunwell 1985c, especially Chapter Five).

One major drawback of this developmental profile is the absence of information about the structural dimension of the phonological system. There is some evidence that certain sound types develop in one position in the structure before others; for example, fricatives often emerge first in word final terminations (see Ferguson 1978: 111). Unfortunately, this profile based on a 'composite norm', cannot specify these details, as compatible results on this aspect of sound usage in child speech are not available in all the studies from which the information was compiled.[6]

With regard to the development of the range of phonotactic possibilities in child speech, there is little direct information provided by any published studies. A tentative profile can be proposed, based on currently available descriptions of children's use of consonant clusters and multisyllabic words. Phonotactic structures appear to develop in the following sequence:

Stage I }
Stage II } CV; CVCV; (CVC)

Stage III } CV; CVCV(CV); CVC;
Stage IV } (CVCCV; CVCCVC)

Stage V	CV; CVCV; CVC;
Stage VI	CVCCV; CVCCVC; CVCVCV; etc.
Stage VII	CCV; CCVC; CVCC; CCVCC; etc.

It must be emphasised that, even more than with the norms for the emergence of the system of contrasts, this information must be interpreted flexibly.

Comparison of Martin's system with the profile shows that, in terms of a developing system of contrasts, Martin's speech patterns have not yet achieved the range of contrasts used in the speech of a 2;6–3;0-year-old child (Stage IV). Furthermore, his system is not strictly comparable with any stage of normal development.

There are two other types of contrastive analysis and assessment that are useful in clinical practice. One child's phonological system can be compared at two different times to chart developmental progress or to assess the efficacy of a period of speech therapy or special education. Alternatively, the systems of two different children can be compared to assess the relative severity of the speech disorder or the similarity of their problems. This might serve a variety of purposes in clinical practice, such as whether two children might benefit from treatment together or in a larger group of children with similar difficulties. It could also form part of an attempt to sub-categorise developmental phonological disorders on the basis of their contrastive and developmental characteristics. Although an academic exercise here, the reader can make these types of contrastive assessments for himself, using the data sample of Martin at 6;3 and the exercise samples of Simon at 4;7 and 5;2.

REVIEWS OF THREE APPROACHES TO CLINICAL ASSESSMENT

In this final section three approaches to clinical assessment based on the concept of analysing the child's own pronunciation system are examined. None of the three approaches are test procedures; rather they are frameworks within which to present an analysis of a child's pronunciation system, derived for a representative sample of the child's (preferably spontaneous) speech. Only one of the approaches, however, presents the framework as part of a set of formal assessment procedures (Grunwell (1985c) *PACS*).

'Independent Analysis' of Children's Speech Productions (Stoel-Gammon & Dunn 1985)

In Chapters 4 and 6 of their book *Normal and Disordered Phonology in Children*, Stoel-Gammon & Dunn present an *independent analysis* of children's speech productions as one of two approaches to the analysis of child speech, both normal and disordered. The second approach they call a *relational analysis*, which involves comparing the adult forms and the child's pronunciations, mainly in terms of phonological processes (see further Chapter Seven). In the independent analysis the child's speech production is analysed as 'a self-contained system' without reference to the adult model (op. cit.: 87). Their type of analysis includes three descriptive statements:

(1) A phonetic inventory of consonant phones classified into manner of articulation categories and grouped according to their occurrence in three positions in word structure: initial, medial and final. Phones occurring only once or twice are marked in parentheses, and it is said that they should be considered marginal.
(2) An inventory of syllable and word structures stated as strings of CV structures, with numbers of occurrences of each word shape.
(3) Statements regarding sequential constraints on phones; this part of the analysis appears to provide for the occurrence of constraints on combinations of different consonants in clusters, and/or in discontinuous sequences, such as the pattern where if the second consonant in a CVC sequence is velar, then the first consonant must also be velar (i.e. consonant harmony; op. cit.: 91; see further below Chapter Seven). Stoel-Gammon & Dunn do not always include this third statement in their own exemplificatory analyses (op. cit.: 147, 157).

Stoel-Gammon & Dunn's examples of this approach to analysis are given in a textbook about normal and disordered child phonology. It is not surprising, therefore, to find that they do not provide step-by-step instructions in the applications of their analytical approach. Nevertheless sufficient information is provided to build up an overall picture of the type of analysis they suggest should be undertaken. From their description and examples it is difficult to establish how the outcome of these procedures can be regarded as an analysis of the child's own pronunciation system in the sense understood in this chapter. Their independent analysis is simply a statement of the phonetic inventory and distribution of the consonants in the child's speech production. No attempt appears to be made to establish whether these phonetically different segments have phonological functions; i.e. serve to signal meaning differences. At a subsequent stage Stoel-Gammon & Dunn present a similar 'model and replica' table to that presented for the Contrastive Assessment described in this chapter. This they use to compare the adult and child 'phonemic systems' (op. cit.: 102–3). It is not clear how the child's phonemic system differs from his phonetic inventory, or even if it does. However, they do use the concept of complementary distribution to analyse contextually conditioned variants of one child phoneme.

Stoel-Gammon & Dunn's approach to the independent analysis of the child's system is therefore only a partial attempt at a description of the child's own self-contained pronunciation system. What it lacks is a thorough investigation, based on the concepts of phonological analysis, into the contrastive functions of the phones in the child's phonetic inventory.

Contrastive Analysis and Assessment (Grunwell 1985c)

In contrast to Stoel-Gammon & Dunn's book, *Phonological Assessment of Child Speech* (Grunwell 1985c; henceforward PACS) is written as an instruction manual in the clinical applications of phonological assessment procedures. Contrastive Analysis and Assessment is one of these procedures; it is described in Chapter Four of PACS. This approach to analysis is preceded by an analysis of the child's phonetic inventory and distribution, which is exactly comparable with the approach to this type of analysis described by Stoel-Gammon & Dunn. The Contrastive Analysis then continues the analysis at the point where their procedure is apparently complete.

The Contrastive Analysis procedure employs the concepts of phonological analysis outlined in this chapter, and analyses the child's systems of consonant phones at three positions in syllable and word structure: SIWI; SIWW and SFWF. SFWW is not analysed because of the observed paucity of data for this position in structure in most clinical data samples. After this polysystemic analysis of the child's systems of consonant contrasts has been completed, the Contrastive Assessment can be undertaken. This involves the same type of mapping procedures on to a 'model and replica' table and on to a Developmental Profile has have been described in the preceding section of this chapter. Thus far, therefore, the procedures in PACS follow the framework of analysis established in the preceding discussion.

The procedures in PACS, however, go beyond the confines of this framework: firstly with regard to the inclusion of a Contrastive Assessment of Clusters. This is acknowledged to be essentially a straightforward statement of the child's realisations of the target clusters; it is in effect a list of the correspondences arranged in a tabular format to facilitate the identification of patterns in the child's pronunciations. It is suggested that by carrying out this analysis in close proximity to the Contrastive Analysis and Assessment an important additional dimension is added to the assessment of the functional adequacy of the child's pronunciation patterns. When, as is frequently the case, the child's clusters are reduced to single consonants, it is also more often than not found that these consonants are already occurring as realisations of more than one singleton target consonant phonemes. The Contrastive Assessment of Clusters facilitates the identification of such a situation.

The second aspect of the PACS Contrastive Analysis and Assessment procedures which extends beyond the framework presented in this chapter is a comprehensive analysis and assessment of the Phonotactic Possibilities in the child's pronunciation patterns. This involves a detailed comparison of the child's syllable and word structures with the target structures in a matrix format. The information obtained by this comparison is then summarised in order to carry out a Contrastive Assessment of the syllabic structures used by the child and the adult, and to identify the child's canonical word and syllable structures. While the Phonotactic Analysis follows the guidelines outlined in this chapter it additionally involves adopting a radically different approach to the analysis since it is based on a matrix analysis of child and adult structures. Once again while this approach is not strictly speaking at the outset an analysis of the child's own pronunciation system, when viewed in its entirety it does produce an analysis and assessment of the child's phonotactic structures.

Having regard to other possible aspects of phonotactic patterning in the child's system, further analytical procedures are presented in Chapter Six of PACS. In particular a procedure is outlined for carrying out a Polysystemic Phonotactic Analysis. Using this analysis sequential constraints on discontinuous sequences of consonants can be identified (op. cit.: 76–7, 83–5).

As is evident from the foregoing, PACS attempts to provide a comprehensive framework for analysis and assessment based, in the instances of the Contrastive Analysis and Assessment procedures, on the principles of phonological analysis applied to the child's own pronunciations system as outlined in this chapter.

Assessing Productive Phonological Knowledge (Elbert & Gierut 1986)

Elbert & Gierut present their own approach to phonological analysis and assessment in Chapters Three and Four of their *Handbook of Clinical Phonology*. They explain that this approach is designed to enable the clinician to assess a child's productive phonological knowledge; i.e. the knowledge the child possesses in regard to the pronunciation of spoken language, no account being taken of his perceptual knowledge or skills. They state that their analytical procedures are drawn from 'standard generative phonology' (op. cit.: 49). However, the concepts that are employed in making the analysis are those which have been introduced in the preceding sections of this chapter. Their analyses bear little resemblance to those based on the generative phonological principles and procedures described in Chapter Six below. It is therefore more appropriate to discuss Elbert & Gierut's approach in the context of the type of analytical framework examined in the present chapter.

As with the two preceding approaches Elbert & Gierut focus on describing 'a child's sound system as a unique phonology' (op. cit.: 50). They state that a child's phonology must first be described independently of the adult target sound system and then comparisons can be made between the two systems. As with Stoel-Gammon & Dunn, it is a little difficult to establish precisely what procedures are included in Elbert & Gierut's approach, as they describe their analysis in the context of a textbook about disordered child phonology.

However, it appears that they require a phonetic inventory to be drawn up which also includes information about the phonetic distribution of consonants. The next step in their analysis is to determine the child's phonemic inventory. In order to establish which consonants are used to signal meaning differences, the analyst should examine the data for the occurrence of minimal pairs. In addition two types of 'phonological rules' may be found to operate in a child's sound system: static rules and dynamic rules (op. cit.: 56–8, 74–81). Static rules describe the phonotactic constraints operating in the child system, of which there are three types:

(1) inventory constraints – certain sounds do not occur in either the phonetic or phonemic inventories;
(2) positional constraints – certain sounds occur only in certain positions but not in others;
(3) sequence constraints – certain sound combinations do not occur.

Dynamic rules are of two types:

(1) allophonic rules – which describe the allophonic variants of child phonemes by invoking the concepts of free variation and complementary distribution;
(2) neutralisation rules – which describe the merging of two otherwise contrastive phonemes at one position in word and syllable structure (see above).

As is evident from this summary this approach employs precisely those basic concepts of phonological analysis outlined in Chapter Two and illustrated further in the present chapter.

There is, however, a perplexing restriction to Elbert & Gierut's approach to phonological assessment, and this is in their comparison of a child's phonology with the adult target sound system (op. cit.: 65–7). It appears from the descriptive statements in this comparison that if a child accurately produces and matches a target consonant then it is assumed that the child has acquired phonological knowledge of the target. No account is taken, however, of the fact that the child may be using the same phonetic unit as the realisation(s) of other targets. In the example provided by Elbert & Gierut this must be the case, since they state that their subject, Ryan, never produced [s z θ ð] in any position; i.e. these targets were subject to an 'inventory constraint'. Unfortunately no transcribed data are provided to verify which of Ryan's consonants he did use to realise these absent targets. We do know for certain that words with these targets were attempted by Ryan, since the authors state that 'For these sounds Ryan ... maintain(ed) non-adult-like lexical representations for all morphemes in all word positions' (op. cit.: 67).

There is another example of an ambivalent interpretation of the nature of this type of independent analysis of the child's phonology in the application of the concept of neutralisation. This is only exemplified where a child signals a *target* phonemic contrast correctly in one position in structure and loses that contrast in another position in structure (see example of neutralisation above).

From these comments one must conclude that Elbert & Gierut's approach to analysis and assessment is in fact a compromise between analysing the child's phonology as a completely independent pronunciation system and viewing it as an emerging adult system. It would appear that the latter perspective does determine, and indeed dominate, their approach to the task of describing the child's own system.

EXERCISES

Analyse these two samples using all the procedures outlined in this chapter for the analysis of the child's own phonological system. You should produce four descriptive statements:

(1) Phonotactic Possibilities;
(2) Phonetic Inventory and Distribution;
(3) Sets of Contrastive Phones at Each Place in Structure;
(4) System of Feature Contrasts (at each place in structure, if appropriate).

In analysing Simon at 5;2, the description of the patterns in onset clusters should be stated as outlined in Chapter Two.

Make Contrastive Assessments of Simon's system with the

adult system at both stages in development. Also compare Simon's two systems with each other. (During this six-month period, Simon was receiving special education in a language unit staffed by a qualified 'first school' teacher and a full-time speech therapist.)

Simon's systems can also be compared with Martin's.

Write a clinical report on each of these assessments, detailing your findings and conclusions, including their clinical implications. Specifically, the reports should:

(a) — indicate the treatment guidelines to be derived from the Phonological Analysis and Contrastive Assessment of Simon at 4;7;
— assess the developmental status of Simon at 4;7.

(b) — evaluate the progress Simon made by 5;2;
— assess the developmental status of Simon at 5;2;
— indicate any further treatment aims you consider appropriate.

(c) — compare the Phonological Analyses and Contrastive Assessments of Martin and Simon;
— compare the developmental status of Martin at 6;3 with Simon at 4;7 and 5;2;
— attempt to assess the relative severity of Martin's and Simon's phonological disorders, on the basis of their Phonological Systems, Contrastive Assessments and the developmental status of their systems.

(i) *SIMON* 4;7 (1979)

1. aeroplane ['ɛəwəbeɪn]
2. black [ba]
3. boat [boʊt]
4. box [bɒt, bɒ]
5. bridge [bɪd]
6. butterflies ['bəʔə'waɪd]
7. cabbage ['dabɪd]
8. cage [deɪd]
9. cake [teɪʔ, teɪ, deɪ]
10. cap [tap, dap]
11. cart (M) [dɑt]
12. cheese [did]
13. chimney ['tɪməni]
14. chip [tɪp]
15. chopper ['tɒpə]
16. claws (M) [dɔd]
17. colour ['dʊlə]
18. cotton ['dɒʔən]
19. cough [dɒ]
20. crab [wab]
21. dish [dɪ]
22. dog [dɒd]
23. drinking ['wɪnʔɪn]
24. farm [wɑm]
25. feather ['wɛdə]
26. finger ['wɪndə]

27. fish [wɪ]
28. five [waɪd]
29. flag [wad]
30. flower ['waʊwə]
31. garage ['dawɑd]
32. glove [dəd]
33. grapes (M) [weɪpt]
34. juice [du]
35. lip [lɪp]
36. lock [lɒʔ]
37. mat [mat]
38. match [mat]
39. mirror ['mɪwə]
40. needle ['nidʊɫ]
41. paint [beɪnt]
42. pan [ban, pan]
43. pig [bɪd]
44. plate [beɪt]
45. pram [bam]
46. queen [win]
47. race [weɪ]
48. rain [weɪn]
49. red [wɛd]
50. rock [wɒʔ]
51. sandwiches ['jamwɪdɪ]
52. scissors ['jɪdəd]
53. ship [jɪp]
54. sleeping ['lipɪn]
55. slide [laɪd]
56. smoke [moʊʔ]
57. snow [noʊ]
58. soldier ['joʊdə]
59. spade [beɪd]
60. spoon [bun]
61. stamps [dampt]
62. stove (M) [doʊd]
63. strawberries ['wɔbɪd]
64. string [wɪn]
65. sugar ['jʊdə]
66. swimming ['wɪmɪn]
67. tap [tap]
68. tea [ti]
69. teeth [di]
70. thread [wɛd]
71. three [wi]
72. thumb [jəm]
73. tractor ['waʔdə]
74. train [weɪn]
75. tree [wi]
76. van [wan]
77. watch [wɒt]
78. wool [wʊʊ]
79. yellow ['lɛloʊ]
80. yes [jɛ]

(ii) *SIMON* 5;2 (1980)

1. aeroplane ['ɛəwə'pleɪn]
2. black [blak]
3. boat [boʊt]
4. box [bɒt]
5. bridge [bə'wɪd]
6. butterflies ['bətə'flaɪd]
7. cabbage ['kabɪd]
8. cage [keɪd]
9. cake [keɪk]
10. cap [kap]
11. cart [kɑt]
12. cheese [tid]
13. chimney ['tɪmni]
14. chip [tɪp]
15. chopper ['tɒpə]
16. claws [klɔd]
17. colour ['kʊlə]
18. cotton ['kɒʔən]
19. cough [kɒf]
20. crab [kwab]
21. dish [dɪ]
22. dog [dɒg]
23. drinking ['dwɪŋkɪn]
24. farm [fɑm]
25. feather ['fɛdə]
26. finger ['fɪŋgə]

27. fish [fɪ]
28. five [faɪv]
29. flag [flag]
30. flower ['flɑʊə]
31. garage ['gawɑd]
32. glove [gə'ləv]
33. grapes (M) [gweɪpt]
34. juice [du]
35. lip [lɪp]
36. lock [lɒk]
37. mat [mat]
38. match [mat]
39. mirror ['mɪwə]
40. needle ['nidʊɫ̩]
41. paint [peɪnt]
42. pan [pan]
43. pig [pɪg]
44. plate [pleɪt]
45. pram [pwam]
46. queen [kwin]
47. race [weɪ]
48. rain [weɪn]
49. red [wɛd]
50. rock [wɒk]
51. sandwiches ['s͓amwɪdɪd]
52. scissors ['s͓ɪdəd]
53. ship [s͓ɪp]
54. sleeping ['tlipɪn]
55. slide ['tlaɪd]
56. smoke [m̥mooʊk]
57. snow [n̥noʊ]
58. soldier ['s͓oʊdə]
59. spade [peɪd]
60. spoon [pun]
61. stamps [tampt]
62. stove [toʊv]
63. strawberries ['twɔbɪd]
64. string [twɪn]
65. sugar ['s͓ʊdə]
66. swimming ['twɪmɪn]
67. tap [tap]
68. tea [ti]
69. teeth [ti]
70. thread [twɛd]
71. three [twi]
72. thumb [t̯θəm]
73. tractor ['twaʔdə]
74. train [tweɪn]
75. tree [twi]
76. van [van]
77. watch [wɒt]
78. wool [wʊɫ]
79. yellow ['lɛloʊ]
80. yes [jɛ]

NOTES

1. The term *SYSTEMIC* must not be confused with *SYSTEMATIC*. Speech patterns in child speakers and speech disorders are described as 'systematic' when a regular pattern of correspondence can be established between the deviant pronunciations and normal pronunciations, i.e. there are systematic relationships between the two systems (see further Chapter Six). As is evident from the following discussion 'systemic' has an entirely different meaning.

2. For example, in the normal pronunciation of English, /n/ and /m/ could be described as 'overlapping' in that both have [m̪] as a possible allophone; if, that is, one follows the orthography in a phonemic transcription of *emphatic* [ɛm̪'fætɪk] as /ɛm'fætɪk/ and *enforce* [ɛm̪'fɔs] as /ɛn'fɔs/. It is usually claimed, however, that there is relatively little overlapping in normal systems (see Sommerstein 1977:

esp. 24–5). It occurs quite frequently in phonological disorders in children (Grunwell 1981b: 153–5).

3. Smith (1973: 181) takes an even more extreme position. In his view analysing the child's speech as an internally-consistent system is an exercise in mythology. He alleges that the child has the complete adult system virtually from the onset of speech development, and uses a gradually diminishing set of 'realisation rules' to determine his actual pronunciations. One of the main pieces of evidence that Smith cites in support of his position is that changes in the child's pronunciation patterns occur 'across-the-board', i.e. all, and only, the appropriate sounds undergo a change. Most other researchers and Smith's own data demonstrate that this is not so; children seem to establish new contrasts gradually and with 'coexistence of success and error' (Olmsted 1971). For further discussion of Smith's position see Grunwell 1981b: 60–1, 133.

4. Another sample of a similar size and representative of a child with the same type of speech disorder is analysed using the same analytical framework in Grunwell 1980a.

5. The definition of homophony here is based on the phonetic realisations of the words as recorded by a phonetically-trained observer (the author, for Martin's data). This is, however, a rather superficial approach to instances of apparent homophony in child speech. For a stimulating discussion of the different factors underlying apparent child homophony see Priestly (1980).

6. For example, in one study 'initial, medial and final' refer to the positions of sounds in 'utterances' (Olmsted 1971), while in others these terms have their more usual reference to sounds in words (see further Grunwell 1981a).

5

Distinctive Feature Analysis Applied to Disordered Speech

In the preceding chapters there has been no discussion of the historical perspective of the phonological framework of analysis. It must not be thought that the analytical procedures presented there were instantly formulated, uncontroversial techniques, agreed and adhered to by all phonologists. The development and refinement of the 'phonemic principle' and phonemic analysis were hotly debated topics, indeed for many years apparently the major issues, in the historical evolution of modern linguistics in the first half of this century.[1] The theoretical arguments which formed the focus of these debates, and others like them with reference to different phonological theories, are not of immediate relevance to the practitioner applying the framework in a clinical or other context. As long as the method of analysis and its implications are fully understood and applied appropriately, knowledge of much of the theoretical controversy is unnecessary, though it cannot be denied that it often provides an interesting, insightful background. With regard to the subject of this chapter, however, the historical dimension must be considered, as the theoretical development of distinctive feature analysis has been reflected in its clinical applications.

DISTINCTIVE FEATURE ANALYSIS: BASIC PRINCIPLES

The concept of feature analysis has already been introduced in the statement of contrastive phones in phonological systems (see Chapter Four). In its most traditional and transparent form the concept of the 'feature' can be seen in the voice, place, manner articulatory labels for phones. From these phonetic descriptions it is obvious that many phones share certain phonetic features in common:

e.g. voiceless [p t k f θ s ʃ x q] etc.;
velar [k g x ɣ ŋ ɰ] etc.;
fricative [f s ɬ x v z ʒ ɣ] etc.

These feature descriptions, however, are phonetic; they specify the articulatory characteristics of the phones, irrespective of their phonological function. The basic phonological function, as has been seen in Chapters Two and Four, is contrastivity. Phonemic contrasts depend on phonetic differences between phonemes – differences in their PHONEMIC CONTENT, that is their features. Distinctive feature theory and analysis thus grew originally out of phonemic analysis; and like the 'phoneme', the 'distinctive feature' is an abstraction, a theoretical concept used in the phonological analysis of pronunciation patterns.

The concept of 'distinctive feature' implies the concept of non-distinctive feature; i.e. phonetic differences that do not function contrastively to signal meaning differences. Thus in the phonological system of English the feature fortis/lenis is distinctive for plosives but the feature aspirated/unaspirated is not. In distinctive feature analysis only the distinctive features of the phonemes of the language are described.

Phonemes are analysed as being constituted of bundles of simultaneously-occurring distinctive features. Each phoneme is distinguished from all other phonemes in the language by its unique combination of features, or its feature specification (cf. above Chapter Two). In preceding chapters it has been demonstrated that phonological systems operate with a set of contrastive segment-size units, viz. phonemes or contrastive phones. The set of features which constitutes the phonemes and maintains the contrasts between them is smaller in number than the set of phonemes. A brief example using the traditional articulatory features will illustrate this point. Five 'features' are required to differentiate/distinguish the nine 'stop' consonants of English:

		Labial	Alveolar	Velar
Nasal		m	n	ŋ
Oral	Fortis	p	t	k
	Lenis	b	d	g

Thus, using + to indicate that a feature is present in the composition of a phoneme, and − to indicate that it is not, the 'stop' consonants can be described in a matrix format:

	m	n	ŋ	p	t	k	b	d	g
Labial	+	−	−	+	−	−	+	−	−
Alveolar	−	+	−	−	+	−	−	+	−
Velar	−	−	+	−	−	+	−	−	+
Nasal	+	+	+	−	−	−	−	−	−
Fortis	−	−	−	+	+	+	−	−	−

It is therefore features, not phonemes, that are the ultimate or minimal distinctive sound units in phonological analysis and in the sound patterns of languages. The distinctive feature is the *phonological prime.*

Since the set of distinctive features is smaller than the set of phonemes, phonemes can be grouped together according to the features they have in common. A group of phonemes that can be described, or to use the more usual term 'specified', as sharing one, or more, features is called a *natural class.*[2] It is frequently found that phonemes so grouped, that is natural classes, operate in similar patterns in the phonological system of a language. For example, English voiceless fortis plosives /p, t, k/ are all aspirated initial in a stressed syllable. Feature description and analysis therefore facilitate a more economical description of phonological patterns by providing for more general statements. As will be seen below, it is this aspect of feature analysis which has been most usefully applied and is most applicable in the description and assessment of patterns in disordered speech.

If the foregoing points were the only claims of distinctive feature theory and its applications, then the approach would be entirely uncontroversial and its clinical relevance an equally straightforward matter. Unfortunately for the practitioner, this is not so; furthermore, the controversial theoretical issues have implications for the practical applications of the approach.

One issue that is now to all intents and purposes dead is the phonetic nature of the optimal distinctive feature system. The first theoretically consistent distinctive feature system was proposed by Jakobson, Fant & Halle (1952) and was constituted of 12 *acoustic* distinctive features. More recent systems (Chomsky & Halle 1968; Ladefoged 1971, 1982 – both outlined below) are based, for the most part, on articulatory dimensions of description. The arguments for and against acoustic and articulatory features are now no longer relevant to the clinical applications of the approach. Few authors have used the acoustic feature system in a clinical context.[3] An articulatory feature system is much to be preferred as it is closer to the phonetic dimensions that a clinician can work with in intervention procedures. Indeed, several researchers have even found the articulatory systems proposed by phonologists too distant from phonetic reality and have devised feature systems of their own, for use in the clinical context.[4]

The acoustic feature system of Jakobson, Fant & Halle does have a continuing significance in distinctive feature theory as it introduced two concepts that are critical to the theory: UNIVERSALITY and BINARISM. In regard to the first of these the aim of most devisers of distinctive feature systems is to construct a universal feature system which will be capable of describing the phonemic contrasts in all human languages. Such a system could be regarded as a statement of the universal primes from which all phonological systems are constructed. If, following Chomsky, one accepts the premise that linguistic theory provides insights into the organisation of the human brain, then the universal distinctive features are part of man's innate, species-specific facility for language. The corollary of this premise is that these universals will be apparent in the development of language. As has been pointed out,[3] Jakobson's feature system is closely linked to his theory of phonological development.

It cannot be too clearly emphasised that Jakobson's description of the development of phonemic contrasts as an orderly universal expansion of the distinctive feature system is a working hypothesis, not a proven theory. The results of many subsequent research studies fail to provide support for many of the detailed proposals in Jakobson's original conception.[5] The basis of his hypothesis is that the presence of a certain feature contrast in a phonological system implies the presence of certain other contrasts in that system. For example, if affricates occur as contrastive phones, then both plosives and fricatives at the same place of articulation will also be contrastive. Thus, if there is a /tʃ/ phoneme in a language, then there will also be /t/ and /ʃ/ phonemes. Jakobson claims that such a hierarchy accounts not only for the universal organisation of phonological systems, but also the order of acquisition of sound contrasts; that is a child develops /t/ *v.* /ʃ/ before /tʃ/. In fact, this particular claim has been subjected to considerable dispute (e.g. Cruttenden 1979: 18). Yet despite many serious doubts about the Jakobsonian model of phonological development, it continues to receive considerable attention in accounts of children's language development.

Apart from the developmental implications of universal distinctive features, this aspect of the theory has rarely been alluded to in applied clinical studies. Only one study has explicitly considered the possibility that disordered speech might contravene the postulated universal feature patterns and this investigation produced a largely negative result (Grunwell 1981b: 160).

The second aspect of distinctive feature theory originally proposed by Jakobson, Fant & Halle, and subsequently upheld by Chomsky & Halle, is that distinctive features are always *binary.* This implies that for any phoneme the specification of its distinctive feature content can be stated in terms of one of two values for every distinctive feature in the phonological system. The two values are usually termed 'plus' and 'minus', and represented [± feature]. A 'plus' value or specification might imply the presence of a phonetic property versus its absence: for example [+ voice] specifies a voiced sound in contrast to [− voice], specifying a voiceless sound. A 'plus' value might also indicate the extreme value of a phonetic dimension, in which instance a 'minus' value does not necessarily imply the opposite extreme: for example [+ low] specifies a vowel produced with the tongue in an open or low position in the mouth; [− low] describes a vowel that does not have a low tongue position — it may be high but it could also be mid, that is between the extremes of tongue height for vowels (see further below).

It must be pointed out that there is no satisfactory logical justification for the hypothesis that the sound patterns of all languages operate on the binary principle (see especially Sommerstein 1977: 109). As will become evident from the description of the Chomsky-Halle feature system below, it leads to rather complex and indirect categorisations of place of articulation of consonants and not entirely satisfactory specifications of its equivalent in the description of vowels, viz. tongue height. These phonetic dimensions, at least in terms of speech production, do not readily lend themselves to two-way contrasts.

The counter-phonetic aspects of certain distinctive feature systems have led other phonologists, most notably Ladefoged, to reject the strict binarity principle for distinctive features. His feature system (see further below) consists of both binary features, for example [± nasal], and *multi-valued* features, for example [place], [stricture]. Multi-valued features are used to describe contrasts in a single articulatory dimension which has more than two values. Thus, place of articulation, for example, is a single feature with several contrastive values.

The majority of clinical studies using distinctive feature analysis employ the binary system of Chomsky & Halle. This system does not handle the articulatory dimensions in a particularly straightforward way. In the author's opinion, for clinical applications it is advisable to use a distinctive feature system which reflects phonetic reality as closely and directly as possible. Therefore, a system such as Ladefoged's is much to be preferred to that of Chomsky & Halle (see Grunwell 1981b for an illustration of the use of a similar system).

One concept in phonological theory that originated in the first exposition of distinctive features (Trubetzkoy 1939; see Hyman 1975: 27, 143–5) is '*markedness*'. This concept is now closely associated with Chomsky & Halle's framework (see esp. 1968: Chapter 9; Hyman 1975: 1436ff; Sommerstein 1977: 168–9). It is generally acknowledged by both phoneticians and phonologists that certain feature combinations are more 'natural' than others; for example, voiceless plosives are claimed to be more 'natural' than voiced plosives, lip-rounding tends to occur much more frequently with back vowels like [u] than with front vowels. To capture this phenomenon, Chomsky & Halle proposed a 'theory of markedness', whereby certain feature values (i.e. plus or minus) would be classified as 'marked' or 'unmarked' (m/u) in combination with other features with specified plus or minus values. Thus [− voice] is 'unmarked' for plosives (in fact this markedness value holds for all obstruents, i.e. [− sonorant], see further below); [+ round] is 'unmarked' for back vowels, but 'marked' for front vowels. It should be noted from these examples that both 'marked' and 'unmarked' features may have either plus or minus values. Markedness is determined by the combination of feature values. Markedness has also been extended to segment sequences, in particular to clusters, where one segment in the cluster is claimed to be more 'natural' than the other(s). This segment is designated the 'unmarked' member of the cluster, the other, 'less natural' member(s) being termed the 'marked' member(s) (see especially Ingram 1976: 32ff). For example, /r/ is the 'marked' member in the cluster /pr/.

The concept of markedness and its use in theoretical studies of phonological analysis are extremely controversial and complex issues in distinctive feature theory. Suffice to say here, that the criteria invoked to determine the markedness value of any one feature value in combination with others involve a complex of factors including 'articulatory complexity' and 'phonetic naturalness' (often based on the analyst's own intuitions), relative perceptual saliency, statistical frequency in known human languages, and the apparently universal characteristics of phonological patterning. Given such a diverse range of criteria, it is not surprising that 'marking conventions', as the rules for alloting m/u values to features for specified segments are called, are always put forward as tentative proposals by their devisers, and are therefore subject to continual amendment by other authorities. In such a situation, the clinical applications of this concept must be equally circumspect (see below).

It will be evident from the foregoing discussion that there is still much controversy in theoretical circles about distinctive features and distinctive feature analysis. The only aspect of distinctive feature theory that emerges as non-controversial is the undeniable fact that such a phonetic and/or phonological framework of analysis allows one to group segments together into categories, or 'natural classes', which share properties or features in common. This, fortunately, is also the aspect of the theory which is most readily applicable to disordered speech data and most clinically relevant. However, it hardly requires the complexities of an entirely new framework of description to arrive at the clinical insights afforded by this concept.

DISTINCTIVE FEATURE SYSTEMS

The aim of this section is to explain as briefly and succinctly as possible two distinctive feature systems. The two systems are (1)

Chomsky & Halle (1968) – used frequently in recent clinical studies; and (2) Ladefoged (1971, 1982) – to illustrate a system which could be considered more useful in clinical work. The theoretical status of the individual features in either system is not discussed (see Hyman 1975: 42–55; Sommerstein 1977: 98–108), nor are the two systems compared (see Ladefoged 1971: 91–111, 1982: 241–69). One final restriction must be pointed out. While both systems aim to be 'universal', that is to describe the sound patterns in all human languages, the description and examples given here concentrate upon the features required to specify the sound patterns of English, especially English consonants. In view of the majority of readers' experience, the clinical motivation of this will be obvious.

Chomsky–Halle Distinctive Features (1968: 293–329)

These features are designed to reflect the articulatory possibilities of the human speech production mechanism that can be controlled and therefore are potentially available to serve a linguistic, contrastive function (ibid.: 294, 297). As indicated above, features not relevant to the analysis of English, such as 'Suction' (clicks and implosives) and 'Pressure' (ejectives), are not included in this summary. It should be noted that while the features are all binary at the phonological level, at the phonetic level they would be given a numerical value, indicating the 'degree' of phonetic feature realised in any specified context. Clinical applications of the features have only used them in their binary mode, as phonological features.

In the definition of many of the features, the 'point of departure' is crucial; this is called the '*neutral position*', which Chomsky & Halle claim is the position of the organs of speech immediately prior to the commencement of utterance.

In the neutral position:

- the glottis is narrowed; the vocal folds are adducted so that with unimpeded air flow, voicing will take place;
- the velum is raised;
- the front of the tongue is raised to the position for [ɛ]; the blade of the tongue is lowered.

The first three features of the Chomsky–Halle system are

those which distinguish between vowels and consonants. These provide potentially useful subclassifications of sound types, indicating for example the vowel-like properties of certain consonants such as laterals, which on occasions may fulfil the function of vowels and be syllabic (see further Hyman 1975: 42; Sommerstein 1977: 98).

Sonorant — Non-sonorant

[+ son]; the organs of articulation are in a position such that unimpeded air flow occurs through the oral and/or nasal cavities and therefore spontaneous voicing is possible: vowels, nasals, glides, liquids can be collectively classified as *sonorants.*[6]

[− son]; the organs of articulation are in a position such that air flow is impeded and spontaneous voicing is impossible; i.e. a stop or fricative oral stricture: plosives, fricatives, affricates collectively form the class of *obstruents.*

Vocalic — Non-vocalic

[+ voc]: the stricture in the oral cavity is one of open approximation, no greater than that for close vowels [i] and [u], and the vocal folds are in the position for spontaneous voicing; only voiced vowels and liquids are [+ voc].

[− voc]: the oral stricture is closer than for [i] and [u] and/or the vocal folds are not loosely adducted; one or both of these conditions are required: obstruents, nasals, and, according to Chomsky & Halle, glides [j, w] have a closer stricture; [h, ʔ], also designated 'glides' and voiceless vowels have vocal fold positions that do not allow spontaneous voicing.

Consonantal — Non-consonantal

[+ cons]: there is a 'radical' oral obstruction, i.e. at least a fricative stricture; 'liquids' are [+ cons] as they involve a 'radical' obstruction; this is obviously applicable to [l] with its central closure, but is questionable for [ɹ].

[− cons]: there is no 'radical' oral obstruction: vowels and both types of 'glides', I [j, w] and II [h, ʔ], have an open oral stricture.

The classification of speech sounds into the basic categories is therefore as shown below:

	Sonorant	*Consonantal*	*Vocalic*
Voiced Vowels	+	−	+
Voiceless Vowels	+	−	−
Glides I [j, w]	+	−	−
Glides II [h, ʔ]	+	−	−
Liquids	+	+	+
Nasals	+	+	−
Non-Nasal Consonants (Obstruents)	−	+	−

Place of Articulation Features

The Chomsky–Halle system specifies the place of articulation of both consonants and vowels in a way that is only indirectly related to traditional descriptions. The specifications are to a certain extent more logical and phonetically transparent since they indicate some of the articulatory similarities between some consonants and vowels.

Anterior — Non-anterior

[+ ant]: a stricture in front of the palato-alveolar region: labials, dentals, alveolars.

[− ant]: there is no stricture in front of the palato-alveolar region: palato-alveolar, retroflex, palatal, velar, uvular, pharyngeal consonants and all vowels.

Coronal — Non-coronal

[+ cor]: the blade of the tongue is raised from the neutral position: dental, alveolar, palato-alveolar, retroflex consonants (and vowels with retroflexion/'r-colouring').

[− cor]: the blade of the tongue is lowered as in the neutral position: labial, palatal, velar, etc. consonants and all vowels (except retroflex).

The classification of consonants using these two features is:

	Labial	*Dent/Alv*	*Pal-Al*	*Palatal*
Coronal	–	+	+	–
Anterior	+	+	–	–

	Velar	*Uvular*	*Phar.*
Coronal	–	–	–
Anterior	–	–	–

All vowels are: $\begin{bmatrix} -\text{ant} \\ -\text{cor} \end{bmatrix}$

Features describing 'body of the tongue configurations', that is tongue height and placement, further specify the place of articulation of consonants and vowels.

High – Non-high

[+ high]: body of the tongue raised above the neutral position.

[– high]: no raising of the body of the tongue.

Low – Non-low

[+ low]: body of the tongue lowered from the neutral position.

[– low]: no lowering of the body of the tongue.

These definitions imply that while [+ high, + low] is impossible, [– high, – low] is possible; it specifies the neutral position. It should, however, be noted that using these classifications only three degrees of vowel height are specifiable as functioning contrastively.

Back – Non-back

[+ back]: body of the tongue retracted from the neutral position.

[– back]: body of the tongue not retracted.

Using these features, the specification of vowels is traditional, though limited:

	High	*Low*	*Back*
Close Front	+	−	−
Close Back	+	−	+
'Mid' Front (Neutral Position)	−	−	−
'Mid' Back	−	−	+
Open Front	−	+	−
Open Back	−	+	+

The specification of [−ant, −cor] consonants is straightforward, though somewhat unfamiliar:

	High	*Low*	*Back*
Palatals	+	−	−
Velars	+	−	+
Uvulars	−	−	+
Pharyngeals	−	+	+

Thus, the phonetic similarity between close front 'palatal' vowels and palatal consonants is made explicit, and also that between close back 'velar' vowels and velar consonants.

Secondary articulations of palatalisation and velarisation are also specified using the 'body of the tongue' features. For example:

	Coronal	*Anterior*	*High*	*Low*	*Back*
Palatalised Alveolars	+	+	+	−	−
Velarised Alveolars	+	+	+	−	+

Thus the phonetic similarity between, for example, palatal consonants, close front vowels and palatalisation is made explicit. Also, it is implicit in the system that palatalisation and velarisation are mutually exclusive, and that palatals and velars cannot be palatalised or velarised.

The feature system also indicates the phonetic independence of the third traditional secondary articulation of labialisation (lip-rounding). This is specified by an obvious feature:

Rounded – Non-rounded
All classes of sounds, including labials, may be [+ round], that is have co-occurring lip-rounding.

Manner of Articulation Features

The features that specify the manner of articulation of English consonants are a mixture of traditional and novel phonetic categories.

Nasal — Non-nasal

[+ nas]: the velum is lowered allowing nasal air flow; there may be simultaneous oral airflow; this feature thus specifies nasals and nasalisation.

[− nas]: the velum is raised, so that air can only escape through the mouth.

Lateral — Non-lateral

[+ lat]: one or both sides of the tongue are lowered, allowing lateral passage of the air stream, which may be unimpeded, i.e. [+ voc]: lateral approximants/liquids, or constricted, i.e. [− voc]: lateral fricatives.

[− lat]: there is no lateral passage of the air stream.

This feature is not in fact required to contrast the two English liquids /l/ and /r/, which also contrast in being [+ ant] and [− ant] respectively.

Continuant — Non-continuant

[+ cont]: the primary oral stricture allows continuous though restricted passage of the air stream: fricatives, liquids.

[− cont]: the air stream through the mouth is stopped: plosives, affricates and, according to Chomsky & Halle's definition, nasals.

Delayed — Non-delayed (Instantaneous) Release

[+ del rel]: a stop closure is released slowly so that friction occurs at the place of primary stricture: affricates.

[− del rel]: a stop closure is released rapidly ('instantaneously') so that there is little or no local 'turbulence' of the air flow: plosives.

Strident — Non-strident

[+ strid]: sounds which have greater noisiness, usually

resulting from a faster air flow over a 'rougher' surface.

[− strid]: sounds which have less noisy friction.

As is evident from the definitions, this feature is restricted to contrasts between obstruents that are [+ cont] or [− cont, + del rel], that is fricatives and affricates. It is also the only feature that is defined acoustically. This feature is used to distinguish the following fricatives.

	Strident
Bilabial e.g. [ɸ, β]	−
v. Labiodental e.g. [f, v]	+
Dental e.g. [θ, ð] and affricates [t̪θ d̪ð]	−
v. Alveolar e.g. [s, z] and affricates [ts dz]	+
Palato-Alveolar e.g. [ʃ, ʒ] and affricates [ʧ ʤ]	+
v. Palatal e.g. [ç, j].	−

The classification [+ strid] is therefore very similar to the traditional category of 'sibilants' [s, z, ts, dz, ʃ, ʒ, tʃ, dʒ]; it is not, however, identical, as labiodental fricatives are [+ strid] but are definitely not 'sibilants'.

Voiced — Non-voiced (Voiceless)

[+ voice]: the vocal folds are approximated so that vibration results, given sufficient air flow.

[− voice]: the vocal folds are apart so that no vibration is possible.

The definition of the [+ voice] specification is carefully worded to allow for devoiced lenis consonants (which are phonetically voiceless, but phonologically 'voiced' in contrast to voiceless fortis consonants) to be classified as [+ voice] at the binary phonological level.

The distinctive feature specifications of phonemes are usually presented in a matrix. Table 5.1 is the matrix of features required to minimally specify the consonant phonemes of English, with the three additional features of Lateral, Delayed Release and Round also included for full specification of the characteristics of /l; tʃ; dʒ; w/. Except for these last three features all the consonant phonemes are fully specified in this matrix (cf. McReynolds & Engmann 1976: 34). In fact it is not

Table 5.1: Specification English Consonant Phonemes According to Chomsky–Halle Distinctive Feature System

	p	b	m	f	v	t	d	n	θ	ð	s	z	ʧ	ʤ	ʃ	ʒ	k	g	ŋ	r	l	h	w	j
Sonorant	–	–	+	–	–	–	–	+	–	–	–	–	–	–	–	–	–	–	+	+	+	+	+	+
Vocalic	–	–	–	–	–	–	–	–	–	–	–	–	–	–	–	–	–	–	–	+	+	–	–	–
Consonantal	+	+	+	+	+	+	+	+	+	+	+	+	+	+	+	+	+	+	+	+	+	–	–	–
Anterior	+	+	+	+	+	+	+	+	+	+	+	+	–	–	–	–	–	–	–	–	+	–	–	–
Coronal	–	–	–	–	–	+	+	+	+	+	+	+	+	+	+	+	–	–	–	+	+	–	–	–
High	–	–	–	–	–	–	–	–	–	–	–	–	+	+	+	+	+	+	+	–	–	–	+	+
Low	–	–	–	–	–	–	–	–	–	–	–	–	–	–	–	–	–	–	–	–	–	+	–	–
Back	–	–	–	–	–	–	–	–	–	–	–	–	–	–	–	–	+	+	+	–	–	–	+	–
Nasal	–	–	+	–	–	–	–	+	–	–	–	–	–	–	–	–	–	–	+	–	–	–	–	–
Continuant	–	–	–	+	+	–	–	–	+	+	+	+	–	–	+	+	–	–	–	+	+	+	+	+
Strident	–	–	–	+	+	–	–	–	–	–	+	+	+	+	+	+	–	–	–	–	–	–	–	–
Voice	–	+	+	–	+	–	+	+	–	+	–	+	–	+	–	+	–	+	+	+	+	–	+	+
Lateral																				–	+			
Del Release	–	–				–	–						+	+			–	–						
Round																							+	

(Based on McReynolds, L.V. & Engmann, D.L., *Distinctive Feature Analysis of Misarticulations* (1975), pp. 31–4)

necessary to enter all the feature values for the consonants as for certain phonemes the value of a particular feature is entirely predictable. For example for nasal consonants as a class the value of the [Voice] feature in English (and indeed in almost all known languages) can only be [+ Voice]. Entering the specification on this matrix is therefore superfluous; the [Voice] feature is *redundant* in nasals as it does not serve to signal a contrast. It should be noted that redundant features are different from non-distinctive features. Redundant features serve to signal a distinction between certain groups of phonemes but not others. Thus [Voice] is distinctive for plosives but not for nasals.

It will be evident, from the introduction to the Chomsky–Halle system above, that there are many more features available in the system to specify the phonetic characteristics of the allophonic variants of these phonemes and, if required, phonetically 'deviant' realisations (or a 'distortion' type of speech error, see Chapter Three), such as for example palatal or velar fricatives. However, the phonetic potential of this system has not been exploited in the clinical applications of distinctive feature analysis; the features used, and their definitions, have been restricted to the phoneme inventory of English (see further below).

Ladefoged Distinctive Features (1971: passim; 1982: 254–69)

This is a non-binary set of 'Prime Features', defined as measurable parameters of articulation which produce appreciable changes in sound quality. Some of the features, however, have a primary acoustic definition, for example Vowel Height; these features are also correlated with particular articulatory changes. Some of the features are binary and some are multivalued. As with the Chomsky–Halle system, several features are not required for the classification of English consonants, for example:

Velaric: [± click];
Trill: [± trill].

The following discussion will concentrate on the features relevant to the description of English. The definition of the features indicates the articulatory parameter involved.

Sonorant :	amount of acoustic energy.	[+son] [−son]
Syllabic :	syllabic nucleus.	[+syll] [−syll]
Place :	place of articulation of primary constriction (consonants).	[bilabial] [labiodental] [dental] [alveolar] [retroflex] [palatoalveolar] [palatal] [velar] [uvular] [pharyngeal] [glottal]
Height :	height of vowel as inverse of F1 frequency; equivalent to traditional vertical axis of tongue height (for vowels).[7]	[4 height] (close) ↑ [3 height] [2 height] [1 height] (open) ↓
Back :	horizontal axis of vowel articulation.	[+back] [−back]
Nasal :	degree of lowering of the velum.	[+nasal] [−nasal]
Lateral :	amount of airstream flowing over side(s) of tongue.	[+lateral] [−lateral]
Stop :	degree of approximation of the articulators, i.e. stricture.	[stop] [fricative] [approximant]
Sibilant :	amount of high frequency energy (i.e. over 3000 Hz); only used to specify fricatives.	[+sibilant] [−sibilant]
Voice :	degree of approximation of the arytenoid cartilages; with this definition, five glottal positions (states of the glottis) can be specified.	[glottal stop] [laryngealised] [voice] [murmur] [voiceless]

Using some of the features described above Ladefoged specifies the consonant phonemes of English as shown in Table 5.2 (1982: 267). Notably absent from his discussion here are the affricates /tʃ, dʒ/; in his previous work (1971: 55) he suggests that affricates should be classified as both [stop] and [fricative]. This is rather unsatisfactory, as it exceptionally describes these segments as having two specifications on a single feature dimension; in spite of this it is the solution adopted here.

Table 5.2: Classification of English Consonants According to Ladefoged's Prime Feature System

Sonorant	[+sonorant]	/m n ŋ r l/ and all vowels
	[−sonorant]	/p b t d k g f v θ ð s z ʃ ʒ ʧ ʤ w j/
Syllabic	[+syllabic]	(all vowels)
	[−syllabic]	(all consonants)
Place	[Labial]	/p b m f v/
	[Dental]	/θ ð/
	[Alveolar]	/t d n s z l r/
	[Palatal]	/ʧ ʤ ʃ ʒ j/
	[Velar]	/k g ŋ w/
Nasal	[+nasal]	/m n ŋ/
	[−nasal]	(all other consonants)
Lateral	[+lateral]	/l/
	[−lateral]	(all other consonants)
Stop	[Stop]	/p b m t d n k g ŋ ʧ ʤ/
	[Fricative]	/f v θ ð s z ʃ ʒ ʧ ʤ/
	[Approximant]	/w r l j/
Sibilant	[+sibilant]	/s z ʃ ʒ ʧ ʤ/
	[−sibilant]	/f v θ ð/
Voice	[+voice]	/b d g m n ŋ v ð z ʒ ʤ w r l j/
	[−voice]	/p t k f θ s ʃ ʧ/

CLINICAL APPLICATIONS OF DISTINCTIVE FEATURE ANALYSIS

Just as distinctive feature theory originally developed from the theoretical concept of the phoneme, the application of distinctive feature analysis in the clinical context is closely related to the phoneme-based assessment procedure of error analysis (see Chapter Three). The differences/deviations in the segmental aspects of the speech of a person with a speech disorder are described as errors in the feature content of the intended phonemes by comparison with the target pronunciations realised by a normal speaker. The following examples illustrate the basic principles of the procedure; although it is not the most appropriate system, the Chomsky–Halle features are used here as this is the system advocated in the most widely-known clinical assessment in a distinctive feature framework (McReynolds & Engmann 1975; see Table 5.1 for full specification of targets).

	Target	Realisation	Feature Analysis	
			Target Features	Feature Errors
(1)	/s/	[t]	[+cont +strid]	[−cont −strid]
(2)	/z/	[d]	[+cont +strid]	[−cont −strid]
(3)	/ʃ/	[t]	[−ant +high +cont +strid]	[+ant −high −cont −strid]
(4)	/p/	[b]	[−voice]	[+voice]
(5)	/f/	[b]	[+cont +strid −voice]	[−cont −strid +voice]

It should be readily appreciated from the critical discussion in Chapter Three that this analytical framework is phonetically far more sophisticated than the traditional error analysis procedure. In order to specify the feature errors, the phonetic characteristics of the incorrect pronunciation must be recorded and analysed. In other words, the clinician has to make a phonetic transcription.

The feature specifications of the target phoneme and the error realisation are then compiled and compared in order to identify the feature(s) in error. The clinician thus analyses the qualitative nature of the error pronunciation in terms of the phonemic properties that have a different value from the target.

Some studies suggest that it is not essential to develop this potential of distinctive feature analysis to the full, and advocate a quantitative assessment of feature errors (e.g. Blumstein 1973: 49; Pollack & Rees 1972: 454). This involves a simple calculation of the number of features in error. For most clinical purposes this type of measure is lacking in essential information, as it does not provide a description of the types of errors which occurred.

For the most part, however, distinctive feature analysis has been applied to clinical data in order to obtain a qualitative descriptive assessment of pronunciation errors. In this mode the major advantage of distinctive feature analysis over the traditional analysis of misarticulations is that it facilitates the identification of error *patterns* in a person's speech production. As the examples above illustrate different segmental errors involve the same feature error: (1), (2), (3) and (5) all involve errors in the realisations of the Continuant and Strident features; (4) and (5) both involve an error in the Voice feature. Patterns of mispronunciations can thus be discerned which occur across the members of a natural class of phonemes. In other words target phonemes that share features in common are likely to show the same type of feature errors. The advent of distinctive feature assessments thus introduced the concept of regularity in speech errors when compared with their intended targets. The following data sample provides a further illustration of this.

DARREN 6;3 (1975)

(1) *mat* [bat] — *nest* [dɛɬ]
more [bɔ] — *nose* [doʊɬ]
mummy [ˈbʌhə] — *new* [du]

Segmental Errors
/m/ → [b] — /n/ → [d]

Feature Error
[+nasal] → [−nasal]

(2) *chest* [tɛɬ] — *jar* [dɑ]
chocolate [ˈtɒʔɪʔɪ] — *jug* [dʌk]
deckchair [ˈdɛʔˈtɛə] — *juice* [duɬ]

Segmental Errors
/ʧ/ → [t] — /ʤ/ → [d]

Feature Errors

$$\begin{bmatrix} -\text{ant} \\ +\text{high} \\ +\text{strid} \\ +\text{delrel} \end{bmatrix} \rightarrow \begin{bmatrix} +\text{ant} \\ -\text{high} \\ -\text{strid} \\ -\text{delrel} \end{bmatrix}$$

(3) *leg* [ðɛk] *red* [ðɛ]
lip [ðɪp] *race* [ðeɪɬ]
letter [ˈðɛhə] *read* [ði]

Segmental Errors

/l/ → [ð] /r/ → [ð]

Feature Errors

$$\begin{bmatrix} +\text{son} \\ +\text{voc} \end{bmatrix} \rightarrow \begin{bmatrix} -\text{son} \\ -\text{voc} \end{bmatrix}$$

Note also /r/ : [−ant] → [+ant]
/l/ : [+lat] → [−lat]

It is evident from these examples that in fact two types of regular patterning are revealed by distinctive feature analysis. Firstly, there are patterns of errors across classes of phonemes. This allows the clinician to group together target phonemes which are mispronounced in the same way. This type of patterning has been interpreted as having major clinical relevance for planning the remediation programme (see below). The second type of patterning is revealed when the feature characteristics of the target phoneme and error segment are compared. This comparison indicates that more often than not targets and errors share many feature values in common. This in turn suggests that there is a relatively close phonetic relationship between them. This is another insight afforded by distinctive feature analysis which has been explored further with regard to its clinical relevance.

The main practical application of distinctive feature assessment is in the philosophy and implementation of treatment planning. As pointed out above, distinctive feature theory was originally closely linked to Jakobson's theory of phonological acquisition. In its clinical applications, it is apparent that Jakobson's basic hypothesis that children acquire features, not sounds, is assumed also to apply to facilitated acquisition in a remedial context. A feature contrast that is absent from a class of phones is introducted and 'trained' in therapy on one contrastive pair of phonemes only; it is expected, however, that generalisation will occur on the other pairs of phonemes in which the same feature contrast is in error. This generalisation, or transfer, of 'corrections' in feature values will result in economies of time and effort and can therefore be regarded as a more effective and efficient method of treatment. It is important to appreciate that in no sense is a 'feature' *per se* being trained; the treatment concentrates on one pair of phonemes whose contrastivity is dependent upon a particular feature, for example /m/ *v.* /b/ are contrastive due to [± nasal]. It would be anticipated that with an error pattern such as that exemplified in Darren's data, if this new contrast was introduced in /m/ *v.* /b/ it would be spontaneously generalised to /n/ *v.* /d/, and both contrasts would not have to be 'trained'.

The most enthusiastic advocates of distinctive-feature-based treatment programmes are McReynolds and colleagues (see especially McReynolds & Engmann 1975). The effectiveness of the approach has been tested in carefully controlled clinical experiments (McReynolds & Bennett 1972). This study reports the results of treatment programmes with three children, all of whom gave evidence of spontaneous feature generalisation to a greater or lesser extent. Compton (1970, 1975, 1976) also claims that feature generalisation occurs. However, the evidence of all these studies indicates rather limited success for the approach. Only small numbers of children have been investigated using the procedure, and there have been no comparative studies evaluating the effectiveness of this method of treatment against any other method on a similar clinical population. Generalisation is only reported on clinically-elicited samples, which are often apparently obtained by the same artificial behaviour-modification strategies used in the treatment procedures; there is no reference to the effects on the child's spontaneous speech. In such circumstances, it would be wise to await stronger confirmation of the procedure and to apply 'distinctive feature therapy' in the treatment of speech 'errors' cautiously and without at present unwarranted optimism.

The following two data samples lend support to this counsel of prudence. They illustrate the very different developmental paths children may follow from very similar starting points.

CLIVE (1979–80)

5;8	5;10	6;0
finger [ˈfɪnnə]	*finger* [ˈfɪnnə]	*finger* [ˈfɪŋgə]
scissors [ˈhɪz̪͆əz̪͆]	*scissors* [ˈs̪͆ɪs̪͆əz̪͆]	*scissors* [ˈs̪͆ɪz̪͆əs̪͆]
sugar [ˈhʊdə]	*shovel* [ˈhʌvʊ]	*ship* [s̪͆ɪp]
chopper [ˈhɒpə]	*chicken* [ˈtɪʔɪn]	*chicken* [ˈtsɪkɪn]
juice [hus̪͆]	*ˈjamas* [ˈhaməs̪͆]	*ˈjamas* [ˈdjɑməz̪͆]

The changes that occur in Clive's pronunciation patterns appear to be introduced 'sound-by-sound' and at different rates. They do not support the generalisation hypothesis; cf. McReynolds & Bennett's study where the feature value common to all the above target phonemes [+ strid] was apparently generalised.

ANTHONY (1979–80)

4;6	4;7	4;9
finger [ˈhɪnnə]	*finger* [ˈsɪnnə]	*finger* [ˈfɪndə]
scissors [ˈhɪjəs]	*scissors* [ˈsɪjəs]	*scissors* [ˈsɪdəz̥]
sugar [ˈhʊjə]	*shovel* [ˈsʊvəɫ]	*sugar* [ˈsʊjə]
chocolate [ˈdɒʔsət]	*chicken* [ˈdɪʔɪn]	*chocolate* [ˈkɒʔtət]
juice [dus]	*ˈjamas* [ˈdɑməs]	*juice* [dus]

There is some evidence for generalisation in Anthony's data at 4;7; but again the feature contrast Strident is not introduced simultaneously or regularly in all the appropriate contexts. In addition, the change introduces a different error pattern. These changes were occurring more or less spontaneously in both children's speech.[8] These data, therefore, throw further doubts on the feature learning theory of speech development and by extension the assumption that feature generalisation should be 'an expected occurrence' (McReynolds & Engmann 1975: 25) in the clinical context.

The second aspect of distinctive feature analysis and assessment that is considered to have clinical relevance is the relationship between the feature specifications of target and error segments. It has been suggested that the number of feature errors co-occurring in the incorrect realisation of a target provides an index of severity of the error (e.g. see Pollack & Rees 1972: 454; Blumstein 1973: 48–9 appears to apply a similar measure in distinguishing one feature error from more than one). Pollack & Rees (1972: 455) extend their application of such an index and speculate on its potential as a measure of intelligibility. As they point out, this is a much more difficult concept to quantify. However, even simple judgements of error-severity, are not necessarily a straightforward matter. Certain common, developmentally normal and therefore arguably 'non-severe' segmental errors involve a large number of feature errors. The most obvious example is:

/r/	→	[w]	
+son		+son	
+voc		−voc	x
+cons		−cons	x
−ant		−ant	
+cor		−cor	x
−high		+high	x
−low		−low	
−back		+back	x
−nasal		−nasal	
+cont		+cont	
−strid		−strid	
+voice		+voice	
−lat			?
		+round	?

This error involves five, or even six or seven, feature errors (cf. Walsh 1974: 39). Of course, many familiar segmental errors entail few feature errors, thus indicating the close phonetic relationship between the target and error and suggesting the implication that the error is not particularly severe. For example,

(1) /s/ → [θ] involves only one feature error: [+strid]→[−strid]

(2) /s/ → [t] involves two

$$\begin{bmatrix}+\text{cont}\\+\text{strid}\end{bmatrix}\rightarrow\begin{bmatrix}-\text{cont}\\-\text{strid}\end{bmatrix}$$

(3) /θ/ → f also involves two:

$$\begin{bmatrix}+\text{cor}\\-\text{strid}\end{bmatrix}\rightarrow\begin{bmatrix}-\text{cor}\\+\text{strid}\end{bmatrix}$$

Of course, the same number of feature errors would also occur if these error patterns were reversed, that is /t/ → [s] etc. But these errors are relatively uncommon in normal speech development and would therefore probably be judged as more severe types. Other much less common segmental errors also may involve few feature errors, for example:

(1) /t/ → [θ] involves only one feature error: [−cont] → [+cont]

(2) /m/ → [d] involves two.

$$\begin{bmatrix}-\text{cor}\\+\text{nasal}\end{bmatrix} \rightarrow \begin{bmatrix}+\text{cor}\\-\text{nasal}\end{bmatrix}$$

Clearly, a simple count of the number of feature errors is at best a crude measure of severity, and at times misleading. This is partly because the features used are somewhat distant from articulatory phonetic reality. The main reason for the inadequacy of straightforward error counts is that the type of feature error or value change *per se*, and the co-occurring context of other feature values, are not taken into consideration. The importance of evaluating one feature value in regard to the values of the other simultaneous features is incorporated in the concept of 'markedness' (see above). There have been several studies investigating the relevance of markedness not only in evaluating speech errors but also in explaining them. Unmarked 'bundles' of features are claimed to be phonetically more natural, and therefore a change to an unmarked feature value, it could be argued, involves a natural simplification of speech production.

The theory of markedness which is applied in these studies is not fully developed, and this must be borne in mind in evaluating the findings. The results of one study of children's articulation errors, for example, are extremely equivocal; indeed the authors conclude that many of the feature changes are contrary to the direction predicted by the theory (McReynolds *et al.* 1974: 101).

In contrast an earlier study of normal school-age children (Williams *et al.* 1970) revealed a clear tendency for mispronunciations to involve a change from marked to unmarked feature values. A similar finding is reported in a more recent study of the articulatory substitutions of 3–7-year-old children with articulation disorders or linguistic delay (Toombs *et al.* 1981). This last study emphasises the value of markedness analysis as providing a basis for making generalisations about children's pronunciation errors, in particular by highlighting the simplifications that are involved in the errors by comparison with the targets. For example the results of this study revealed that Sibilant, Continuant and Place of Articulation features exhibited more marked to unmarked substitutions than any other feature. This finding of course reflects the well-known tendencies in children's speech to mispronounce fricatives, especially the sibilants /s z ʃ ʒ/ and to produce errors in the selection of the place of articulation of consonants.

Analyses of speech errors in adult speech disorders have also applied the concept of markedness (e.g. Blumstein 1973: 53; Marquardt *et al.* 1979; Klich *et al.* 1979; Wolk 1986). In all of these studies it is reported that the occurrence of changes from marked to unmarked feature values occurred more frequently than vice-versa in consonant substitutions. It appears that there were appreciable numbers of errors that were contrary to this trend, i.e. resulted in more marked consonants. However, all these studies emphasise the trend of reduced markedness of the error segments produced by aphasic/apraxic speakers. On the basis of this finding it is concluded that these speakers are effecting a systematic reduction in the complexity of their phonological output and thus simplifying their speech production. For a number of reasons these conclusions need to be examined circumspectly. The methodologies adopted in the studies involve restricted data bases and often the data are modelled utterances. The major provisos, however, are intrinsic to the nature of distinctive feature analysis itself and its suitability for investigations of these types of speech disorders. Specifically the analysis is in terms of abstract phonological features and can only handle phonemic substitutions. It is these constraints of the distinctive feature framework that we must now examine critically with regard to the clinical applications of this approach in the assessment and explanation of speech disorders.

Several authorities have raised fundamental questions as to the clinical applicability of distinctive feature theory and analysis (for example Walsh 1974; Parker 1976; Foster *et al.* 1985). Central to these criticisms is the fact that distinctive feature theory is a phonological theory which accounts for the contrastive function and systemic organisation in the phonologies of spoken languages. Distinctive features, like phonemes, do not 'exist'. They are abstract concepts postulated by linguists to account for the patterns in language. As a result, Walsh argues, the distinctive feature systems most widely used (Jakobson, Fant & Halle; Chomsky & Halle) are remote from articulatory reality and produce counter-intuitive measures of speech errors such as /r/ → [w], exemplified above. Walsh advocates complete abandonment of the phonologists' distinctive features; he suggests that these be replaced by a feature analysis of articulatory dimensions selected to handle the data of each individual patient. The apparent consequence of this approach would be not only to abandon the published distinctive feature systems but also the phonological concept that phonemic contrastivity is dependent on feature contrasts. This would be a most regrettable retrograde step, since it is specifically through the introduction of the concept of distinctive features that the descriptions of speech sound errors have potentially taken account of the fact that sound differences signal meaning differences. We have to acknowledge, unfortunately, that this is only a potential breakthrough; in clinical practice the implications of the phonological concept often appear not to be fully appreciated or exploited.

This is in part the basis of the criticisms levelled by Parker (1976, and in a later note with other colleagues in Foster *et al.* 1985). The main thrust of both these papers is to highlight the difference between an abstract phonological feature analysis and an articulatory phonetic feature analysis. The point is made most clearly in the following quotation:

> Speech production cannot logically be described in terms of DFs ... because these constructs are part of a theory of psychological (i.e. mental) organisation.

Consequently it is a contradiction in terms — and in theory — to talk about the

> production of a DF. ... At best one can talk about properties of the physical speech signal (i.e. acoustic cues) that lead to the perception (a psychological phenomenon) of a segment (a psychological construct). Likewise, one can talk about properties of the speech production mechanism in physiological terms (e.g. lip and jaw movement, tongue movement, etc.) but not in psychological terms. (Foster *et al.* op. cit.: 296)

As is apparent from this quotation, the criticisms that Parker and his colleagues level at the clinical applications of distinctive features do not imply abandoning the approach entirely. They are seeking a more insightful awareness of the use of phonological concepts in the description of speech sound errors. An example of this awareness can be found in the case study reported by Harris & Cottam (1985) where the distinction and relationship between phonetic and phonological features are clearly illustrated. We shall return to this issue in Chapter Eight.

The critical evaluation of the clinical applications of distinctive feature theory most relevant to the immediate concerns of this chapter is that of Carney (1979). Carney, like Walsh and Parker, points out that distinctive feature analysis is an abstract phonological representation of speech. He goes on, however, to illustrate how the type of distinctive feature analysis and assessment which has been illustrated above, and which is based on the phonemic concept, compels the clinician/analyst to ignore phonetic aspects of speech and consequently to classify errors ambiguously and/or misleadingly, or not at all. He demonstrates that a distinctive feature analysis is exactly analogous to making a phonemic transcription of disordered speech, (cf. Chapter Two). For example [s͓] might 'phonemicised' as /s/ or /θ/; its feature content is ambiguous and as a result it could happen that realisations of /s/ as [s͓] and of /θ/ as [s͓] might be scored as correct in a feature analysis; thus important information will be inconsistently analysed or even overlooked. In fact segmental errors that are not 'phonemic substitutions' cannot be handled by a distinctive feature assessment procedure, and we are therefore faced with the same types of problems as those which resulted from the traditional segmental error analysis procedure (see Chapter Three).

For example in the following data Lucy's realisations of /s z/ and /ʃ tʃ dʒ/ would all be classified as 'distortions', probably of /s/ and /z/. As such they could not be described and more importantly distinguished in a distinctive feature analysis of misarticulations.

LUCY 5;10 (1972)

soldier [ˈs͓oʊd̠ʐ̠ə]	*watch* [wɒt̠ʂ̠]
horse [hɔs͓]	*juice* [d̠ʐ̠us͓]
scissors [ˈs͓ɪz͓əz͓]	*matches* [ˈmat̠ʂɪz͓]
chips [t̠ʂ̠ɪps͓]	*hedge* [hɛd̠ʐ̠]
fish [fɪʂ̠]	*sugar* [ˈʂ̠ʊgə]

The detailed phonetic transcription reveals that there is a regular pattern in the data, with the contrasts between /s/ *v.* /ʃ/ etc., consistently signalled, albeit incorrectly in terms of the adult pronunciation. Target apico-alveolar strident fricatives are 'fronted' to the dental place of articulation, but retain a grooved stricture [s̪, z̪]; target palato-alveolar strident fricatives and affricates are articulated correctly in terms of place, that is in the post-alveolar region, with the blade of the tongue (indicated by the diacritic [s̠ z̠]); the fricative stricture, however, appears to involve a narrower grooved shape than for [ʃ ʒ], indicated by the symbols [s̠, z̠]; there is also a secondary articulation of palatalisation, indicated by [s̠ z̠]. These realisations are all characteristic of normal immature articulation patterns (cf. Anthony *et al.* 1971: 43–4; Carney 1979: 133). Phonetic transcription and analysis are essential to distinguish this type of 'distortion' from 'error' patterns which entail failures to signal phonological contrasts and/or developmentally unusual patterns (see further Chapter Seven).

It must not be thought that Chomsky–Halle's distinctive feature system could not specify the strident fricatives in Lucy's data. A feature which they call 'Distributed' would probably serve to specify the phonetic characteristics of her pronunciations together with the feature High to indicate presence/absence of palatalisation; this feature is used to specify palato–alveolar consonants in English. Thus the analysis would indicate that she is signalling the contrast required to differentiate the two types of adult target phonemes. *Distributed* sounds are produced with a 'long' stricture extending along the direction of the air flow; this often, though not always, correlates with laminal articulations, thus [s̠, z̠]: [+ dist]. Non Distributed sounds have a shorter stricture, often correlating with apical articulations, thus [s̪, z̪]: [− dist] (see Chomsky & Halle 1968: 312–14 for further details). This feature is not, however, needed in the specification of English consonant phonemes.

Another clinical inadequacy of distinctive feature analysis ably demonstrated by Carney is the inappropriate and potentially misleading feature specifications and definitions. For example, for clinical purposes the classification of /f, v/ with /s, z, ʃ, z, tʃ, dʒ/ as all sharing the specification [+ strid] is of no particular assistance, and contradicts empirical evidence: the two most natural classes of fricatives in English are /f, v, θ, ð/ with a 'slit'-shaped articulatory stricture, and /s, z, ʃ, ʒ, tʃ, dʒ/ with a 'grooved'-shaped stricture, that is the traditional sibilants. There are two further outstanding examples of misleading feature specifications. These are (1) the specification of

/b, d, g, v. ð, z, ʒ, dʒ/ as [+ voice] if the feature label is taken at its face value — these lenis obstruents are very frequently devoiced or even completely voiceless; (2) the specification of /m, n, ŋ/ as [− cont], that is 'stops' — nasals are so obviously 'continuable' consonants, and often syllabic, thus suggesting that it may on occasion be useful to consider them as 'vowel-like'.[9]

The last few paragraphs have seriously thrown into question the clinical value of a formalised distinctive feature analysis procedure. This implication is intentional. None the less, the CONCEPTS of distinctive feature contrasts and natural classes are of major importance and considerable clinical applicability. The concept that phonemes are differentiated by their 'content' of contrastive features enables the clinician to focus on the contrastive/distinctive feature that is in 'error' and also to recognise similar 'errors' in different phonemes, that is patterns in disordered speech. It is, however, very important that the functional 'value' of features as contrastive elements is borne in mind both in assessment and treatment procedures. Thus, it is incorrect to state that a child does not use [+ cont], but 'has the feature [− cont]', if he pronounces, for example, /θ, s, ʃ/ as [t]. The feature Continuant is absent from the feature specification of his [t] as there are no occurrences of both its values; that is: it is not contrastive. Applying the concept of distinctive features means that assessment and treatment will concentrate on the contrastive function of both segments and features, and therefore on evaluating and facilitating the development and expansion of the *phonological system of contrasts.* To this end, it is not necessary for all the features to be binary, and it is preferable that they are as close as possible to 'phonetic reality'.

The second concept in distinctive feature theory of clinical significance is the recognition of natural classes of segments. Applying this to clinical data leads to the identification of patterns in the incorrect realisations. As a result treatment may be better principled and perhaps more efficient, especially if generalisation of learning is promoted. It must be acknowledged, of course, that this is by no means an innovation; the traditional articulatory labels for segments were used to identify sound classes for many years prior to the advent of the concept of distinctive feature analysis.

REVIEW OF TWO CLINICAL ASSESSMENT PROCEDURES

There are two formalised assessment procedures available which employ the concept of distinctive features in the analysis of speech sound errors. One is based on the traditional articulation test procedure; the other is designed for use in the analysis of spontaneous speech samples.

Fisher–Logemann Test of Articulation Competence (1971)

The Fisher–Logemann Test of Articulation Competence (Fisher & Logemann 1971; henceforward FLTAC) is procedurally a traditional articulation test. The 25 English consonant phonemes (i.e. including /hw/) are elicited in single-word utterances using a set of pictures. The test also includes consonant clusters of three types: /s/+consonant; consonant+/r/ and consonant+/l/ and 16 vowels. The singleton consonants are elicited in three positions in syllabic structure: prevocalic, intervocalic and postvocalic. The ambiguous category of word medial is thus avoided; for example the authors point out that the medial /h/ in *dog-house* is prevocalic; and the medial /θ/ in *toothbrush* is postvocalic. They define intervocalic as follows: 'The consonant stands between two vowel phonemes, so that it serves the dual function of ending the preceding syllable and initiating the following syllable' (op. cit.: 3). All the consonant clusters except /tl/ in *bottle* are tested in prevocalic word initial position. The construction of the test is thus that of a phonemic assessment procedure. Furthermore the three realisations of each target phoneme are elicited sequentially since the three pictures are on the same page in the picture book. In the author's opinion this is not a particularly wise procedure since the mispronunciation of one target phoneme in one position may contaminate its realisation in other positions where it might be pronounced differently and may be correctly if the two occurrences were not juxtaposed. The FLTAC also includes a Sentence Test which consists of a set of 15 sentences which the child is asked to read aloud. Here again phonetically similar consonants are tested in the same sentence; for example sentence (1) tests /p; b/ and sentence (6) tests /s; z/, etc. Furthermore this procedure has severe practical limitations: the child has to be able to read, and read fluently. In addition it rests on the questionable assumption that in reading aloud the child's pronunciation patterns are representative of the patterns habitually used in speech.

Our main concern here, however, is the procedure for analysing the child's pronunciation of consonant phonemes. This employs a distinctive feature analysis which, according to the authors, uses categories that are 'traditional' in linguistic phonetics' (op. cit.: 24). These categories are:

Manner of Formation: stop, fricative, affricate, glide, lateral, nasal.
Place of Articulation: bilabial; labiodental, tip-dental, tip-alveolar, blade-alveolar, blade-prepalatal, front-palatal, central-palatal, back-velar, glottal.
Voicing: voiced, voiceless.

The place of articulation features in fact involve both active and passive articulators and some of the classifications are not traditional: /s z/ are classified as blade-alveolar; /ʃ ʒ tʃ dʒ/ as blade-prepalatal; /r/ as central-palatal. /s z/ may be blade-alveolar, but they may also be articulated using the tip of the tongue. The blade-prepalatal description for traditional palato-alveolars is in fact more accurate, though post-alveolar would have been better than prepalatal (see Ladefoged 1985: 147). Central-palatal is a most unusual description of /r/; the closest point of the tongue to the roof of the mouth involves the tip articulating with the post-alveolar region. According to Fisher & Logemann other published feature systems (they cite Jakobson, Fant & Halle) are too complex for routine use by speech therapists.

Fisher & Logemann advocate a fairly narrow phonetic transcription of the child's pronunciations, providing a system of diacritics for recording what they term 'consonant allophones' (op. cit.: 17–18). These include familiar IPA diacritics for dental, retroflex and nasalised consonants for example, alongside some less familiar conventions for the use of symbols. For example [⊥̣] is defined as modified production of both /ð/ and /z/ involving a tip-alveolar fricative and [ʈ] as a modified production of /t/ involving a tip-lowered instead of tip-raised articulation. It is clear from the presentation of all these 'consonant allophones' that they are to be viewed as modified productions of the target phoneme: 'an atypical allophone of the phoneme intended' (op. cit.: 25). The authors are, however, aware that this view may lead to some difficulties in classification: 'the modification of a distinctive feature for one phoneme may produce an ambiguous allophone which is not clearly identified with either of two possible phonemes' (ibid.). They cite the example of [β] being classified as either /b/ or /v/, (cf. Carney 1979). They do not, unfortunately, resolve this problem for the user of the test. Nor do they appear to be aware of the phonological implications of this phenomenon, i.e. that the phonemic contrast is thereby obliterated.

The pronunciations of the consonant phonemes are recorded on a form which has a matrix format enabling easy identification of the feature classes to which each phoneme belongs. The purpose of the FLTAC distinctive feature analysis procedure is said to be two-fold — to enable:

(1) an identification of the nature of the faulty production of a phoneme;
(2) an identification of feature violations common to several phonemes.

The first aim provides a focus for treatment, i.e. concentration on the specific aspect of the production of the phoneme which is faulty. The second aim facilitates generalisation of learning across phonemes which share feature errors in common (op. cit.: 24). It is clear from these aims that the philosophy underlying FLTAC is essentially the same as that underlying traditional error analysis procedures. The aim is to correct the misarticulation of individual consonant phonemes. There is an occasional reference to the fact that a feature error results in two phonemes not being distinguished. For the most part, however, feature errors are viewed as articulation, i.e. production, errors. Thus FLTAC represents an advance over the traditional error classifications in terms of the phonetic detail in which misarticulations are described. However, the phonological functional basis of distinctive feature analysis is not taken into consideration at all.

Distinctive Feature Analysis of Misarticulations (1976)

McReynolds & Engmann (1976) present a formalised procedure for analysing misarticulations in terms of distinctive features (henceforward DFA). This procedure is for use with spontaneous samples of children's speech, and the authors advise that each phoneme should be sampled a number of times in order to ensure that a reliable and representative analysis is obtained. They refer specifically to the necessity of establishing whether or not a child's pronunciation of a target phoneme is consistent or variable. To carry out DFA the sample must be transcribed employing the IPA or a similar symbol system to record the child's pronunciations as 'a correct phoneme, a substituted phoneme or an omission' (op. cit.: 37).

The child's pronunciations of every consonant and vowel phoneme are then analysed using the Chomsky–Halle set of distinctive features. The purpose of this analysis is to compute how many times the child used each feature correctly and incorrectly, and subsequently to calculate the percentage correct occurrences of each feature (as against the number of possible occurrences). This involves an extremely lengthy analysis procedure. Given the major shortcomings of the DFA one queries, with Carney (1979), whether the time spent can be justified, or indeed whether such a procedure is valid, never mind necessary.

As has already been pointed out above, and as is evident from the instructions quoted above with reference to recording the child's mispronunciations, DFA cannot handle 'distortions'. With regard to the occurrence of segments outside the English phonemic inventory, McReynolds & Engmann advise:

> If a production is a distortion whose features cannot be specified it is necessary to delete the production from the analysis, score it as an omission or use another feature system in the analysis. (op. cit.: 38)

This is a gross travesty of all the principles of clinical linguistic analysis and assessment. The clinician is being instructed here to discard or knowingly misclassify data which are vitally relevant to the evaluation and understanding of the nature of the child's pronunciation problems.

In carrying out DFA no account is taken of the position in

word or syllable structure in which the target phoneme and mispronunciations occur; nor indeed of whether consonants occur as singletons or in clusters. As we have seen in several examples in the preceding chapters this information is also essential for discerning the patterns of mispronunciation and the nature of the pronunciations problems.

The eventual outcome of DFA is intended to be a list of percentages of incorrect occurrences of each + and − value for each feature. It is impossible to derive from this information what a clinician really needs to know, which is how the distinctive features are used by the child to signal the segmental phonemic contrasts which are dependent upon them. One gains little insight from the statement that [+continuant] has an error rate of 90 per cent. This could involve mispronunciations of /rl/ and/or all or any subset of the fricatives. It should be noted that, as pointed out above, Nasals are classified as stops, i.e. [−Continuant] and /wj/ are not specified for the feature Continuant. This latter, as Carney points out, is another serious flaw in DFA; it entails the non-recording of redundant features. Therefore once again information about the child's pronunciations is discarded.

The DFA procedure does not provide the clinician with any new or additional clinically relevant information that could not be obtained by examining a child's mispronunciations using the more familiar set of articulatory features that describe the place and manner of articulation and voicing of consonants. Because it concentrates on features to the apparent exclusion of their function in phonemes, it produces an inappropriate assessment of a child's pronunciation at a level of abstraction which obscures and indeed ignores the phonetic data and conceals the phonological patterns and their functional consequences.

EXERCISES

1.1 Give the feature specifications of the following English consonant phonemes according to the Chomsky–Halle system. Try to do so without reference to Table 5.1. Present your answer in the form of a matrix.

/m/, /v/, /θ/, /ʤ/, /k/

1.2 Give the feature specifications of the following English consonant phonemes according to Ladefoged's system. Try to do so without reference to Table 5.2.

/b/, /s/, /ʒ/, /ŋ/, /r/

1.3 What features could be used to specify the phonetic characteristics of the following consonants? Try to provide two specifications for each: one in terms of the Chomsky–Halle system, the other using Ladefoged's features. Are all your specifications different from those provided for the English consonant phonemes in Tables 5.1 and 5.2?

[ʋ], [ɻ], [ts], [ɲ], [x]

2. Identify the feature errors in the following segmental 'substitutions' and 'distortions'. First, specify both the target and the realisation using the Chomsky–Halle system and indicate which features are in error. Then describe the feature errors in more traditional terms, based on Ladefoged's features.

	Target	Realisation
1.	/ŋ/	[n]
2.	/k/	[ɡ]
3.	/ʒ/	[d]
4.	/r/	[j]
5.	/f/	[w]
6.	/ʃ/	[θ]
7.	/ʤ/	[ɟ]
8.	/p/	[pɸ]
9.	/l/	[ɣ]
10.	/z/	[d̥ð]

3. Identify the error patterns in the following data, using the concept of *natural class* to characterise the feature similarities of the phonemes incorrectly realised and their realisations.

JANE 5;4 (1973)

1. *brush* [bʌɬ]
2. *pillows* ['pɪwoʊɮ]
3. *watch* [wɒtɬ]
4. *horse* [wɔɬ]
5. *garage* ['dawɑɮ]
6. *desk* [dɛɬ]
7. *rose* [woʊɮ]
8. *bridge* [bɪdɮ]
9. *yes* [wɛɬ]
10. *pens* [pɛnɮ]
11. *lettuce* ['wɛtəɬ]
12. *dish* [dɪɬ]
13. *lion cage* ['waɪjən deɪdɮ]
14. *rabbit's hutch* ['wabɪtɬ 'wʌtɬ]

4. The following data can be analysed in terms of distinctive feature errors as all the 'misarticulations' involve phonemic 'substitutions'. Analyse the feature errors in terms of Chomsky–Halle features and/or Ladefoged's set. List the examples of each type of error. Outline a treatment plan for systematically 'training' single pairs of phonemes which might lead to generalisation to other pairs of phonemes dependent on the same feature contrasts. As there are 'multiple' feature errors here do not expect to find one single, simple solution to the treatment plan.

JIM 5;11 (1979)

1. *cars* [dɑd]
2. *dive* [daɪb]
3. *girl* [dɜl]
4. *pig*, big [bɪd]
5. *zoo* [du]
6. *vase* [bɑd]
7. *bird* [bɜd]
8. *tub* [dʊb]
9. *van, pan* [ban]
10. *nose* [noʊd]
11. *give* [dɪb]
12. *ties* [daɪd]
13. *cave* [deɪb]
14. *bees, peas* [bid]

5. The procedure for distinctive feature analysis applied to clinical data cannot handle 'distortions'. Why are the following data samples therefore not amenable to distinctive feature analysis? Discuss the patterns with particular reference to the child's ability to signal, albeit incorrectly, the phonological contrasts required. Why is a detailed phonetic (i.e. impressionistic) transcription essential here?

(i) *MAXINE* 4;10 (1972)

1. *rose* [ʋoʊz̪]
2. *teeth* [t̪if]
3. *watch* [wɒt̪θ]
4. *fish* [ɸɪθ]
5. *soldier* ['s̪oʊd̪ðə]
6. *sugar* ['θʊgə]
7. *wings* [wɪŋz̪]
8. *rich* [ʋɪt̪θ]
9. *dress* [d̪ðɛs̪]
10. *thumb* [fʊm]
11. *garage* ['gaʋɪð]
12. *juice* [d̪ðus̪]
13. *scissors* ['s̪ɪz̪əz̪]
14. *chips* [t̪θɪpt̪s̪]
15. *fudge* [ɸʊd̪ð]
16. *trains* [t̪θeɪnz̪]
17. *satchel* ['s̪at̪θʊ]
18. *chairs* [t̪θɛəz̪]
19. *pencil* ['pɛn̪t̪s̪ʊ]
20. *jars* [d̪ðɑz̪]

(ii) *PAULINE* 7;6 (1972)

1. *stamps* [tamptç]
2. *shed* [çɛd]
3. *matches* ['maʧɪdʝ]
4. *thrush* [fwʌtç]
5. *rings* [wɪŋɟʝ]
6. *pencil* ['pɛntçʊ]
7. *watch* [wɒʧ]
8. *soldier* ['çoʊʤə]
9. *cherries* ['ʧɛwidʝ]
10. *thumb* [fʌm]
11. *garage* ['gawɪʤ]
12. *horse* [ɔtç]
13. *sugar* ['çʊgə]
14. *chips* [ʧɪptç]
15. *fish* [fɪtç]
16. *bridge* [bwɪʤ]
17. *jigsaw* ['ʤɪʔçɔ]
18. *wings* [wɪŋɟʝ]
19. *fridge* [fwɪʤ]
20. *toothbrush* ['tufbwʌtç]

NOTES

1. For an introduction to this theoretical debate see Fudge (1970), and for a sample of the original contributions see Fudge (1973: Sections A & B). Sommerstein (1977) provides a more detailed discussion in Chapter Two. Edwards & Shriberg (1983) provide a brief overview of the history of phonology in Chapter Three.

2. In fact the concept of 'natural class' is more complex than outlined here. The description provided is a working definition for clinical applications. For a discussion of the theoretical issues involved see Hyman (1975: esp. 138–42) and Sommerstein (1977: 92–5, 97).

3. Winitz (1969) outlined Jakobson's theory of phonological development using his distinctive feature system. Crocker (1969) and Pollack & Rees (1972) used distinctive features drawn from both Jakobson *et al.* and Halle's later systems, which evolved into the Chomsky–Halle system (1968).

4. Compton (1970, 1975, 1976) used a distinctive feature system which, it must be assumed, he devised to represent as closely as possible the articulatory characteristics of his data. The features are: Place 1–6, Voice, Nasal, Round, Consonantal, Friction, Stop.

5. See e.g. Dale (1976: 212–13); Ingram (1976: 17ff); De Villiers & DeVilliers (1978: 38ff); Cruttenden (1979: 17ff).

6. Following Chomsky & Halle and the majority of other American phoneticians, the terms 'glides' and 'liquids' are used here for approximants, both lateral and median, and rolls. 'Glides' are median approximants, such as [j, w], essentially identical to traditional 'semi-vowels'; 'liquids' are lateral approximants and all 'r-type' sounds, including apparently the post-alveolar median approximant[ɹ], which is the most frequent realisation of /r/ in many accents of English.

7. The first formant — Fl — of 'high/close' vowels is low; thus the relative heights of vowels are the inverse of their Fl frequencies.

8. Both Clive and Anthony were receiving remedial education in a language unit; neither was given specific treatment for his speech disorder, though both were in constant daily contact with a speech therapist. Anthony's *chocolate* [ˈkɒʔtət] at 4;9 is an instance of 'overgeneralisation'; he was just beginning to use [k], though somewhat indiscriminately: e.g. *tractor* [ˈkaʔtə], *stove* [koʊf], *cotton* [ˈkɒtən].

9. Carney makes many other points in criticism of, in particular, McReynolds & Engmann's procedure; all of them are valid. He begins his concluding remarks: 'the distinctive feature-counting scheme proposd by McReynolds & Engmann has so many obvious faults that one wonders why it was ever thought necessary' (1979): 131), an opinion with which this author wholeheartedly concurs.

6

Generative Phonology Applied to the Analysis of Disordered Speech

AN INTRODUCTION TO THE THEORETICAL BACKGROUND

Generative Phonology, like Distinctive Feature Analysis, is a theory of the sound structure of human language. As a theoretical framework of description it has been used to analyse the sound structure of many languages. It is the phonological component of the integrated theory of human language which was originally proposed by Noam Chomsky.[1] Although theoretically integrated into a comprehensive description of the structure of a language, most generative phonologies have been proposed in the absence of complete generative grammars of the syntactic components of the languages described. In addition, the generative phonologies themselves may not provide an exhaustive description of the sound structure of the language, since the intention of many generative analyses is to investigate further dimensions of the theory by attempting to describe phonologically interesting aspects of different languages.

It is therefore possible and usual to consider generative phonological descriptions without detailed reference to other levels of linguistic analysis,[2] and to discuss the technical formalities of generative phonological analysis with examples which constitute only partial descriptions of the languages analysed. In this chapter, both of these practices will be followed: no further reference will be made to syntactic or semantic structures and, as has been the practice in preceding chapters, the principles and procedures of generative analysis will be illustrated using aspects of normal English pronunciation patterns and small samples of disordered and/or child speech.

Generative phonology introduced a revolutionary new approach to phonological analysis. This revolution was set in train by an in-depth study of English phonology: *The Sound Pattern of English* (Chomsky & Halle 1968). This study illustrates the key principles of generative phonology which include the abandonment of phonemic analysis, as presented in the preceding chapters, the introduction of the concept of abstract underlying phonological representations that are mapped on to surface pronunciations by a set of formal rules, and the dependence of phonological descriptions upon information from other linguistic levels, specifically the syntactic component. This latter point need not concern us here.[3]

Thus, generative phonological analysis describes aspects of the sound patterns of languages that are not revealed in an analysis based on phonemic principles. In the analysis of English phonology, for example, a generative description will account for the regular vowel and consonant alternations that occur in the subsystems of the derivational morphology of the language. For example:

(1)	/aɪ/	/ɪ/
	derive	derivative
	invite	invitation
	precise	precision
(2)	/i/	/ɛ/
	supreme	supremacy
	receive	reception
	convene	convention
(3)	/k/	/s/
	critic	criticism
	medical	medicine
	plastic	plasticity
(4)	/aɪ/	/ɪg/
	resign	resignation
	paradigm	paradigmatic
	malign	malignant

These phonological relationships are described by postulating an abstract 'underlying representation' (or systematic phonological form) and a set of phonological rules which describes the different pronunciations of the same lexeme (word 'root') depending on the presence of particular suffixes. It can be observed that the relationships are revealed in the orthographic representation of the related words; the phonological specifications of the 'underlying representations' are frequently very similar to the orthographic forms of the words. It is unnecessary for present purposes to consider the complex details of the rules required to describe the derivational relationships exemplified above.[4] The essential point that these examples illustrate is that many of the rules in a generative description of the sound patterns in normal, adult languages have the function of generating the surface pronunciation from an abstract underlying representation.[5]

The formal techniques of generative phonological analysis involve descriptions of the sound patterns of language in terms of phonological rules. To illustrate these rules let us look at some statements describing the phonetic details of English pronunciation:

(1) Vowels are nasalised before nasal consonants:

$$\begin{bmatrix} +\text{voc} \\ -\text{cons} \end{bmatrix} \rightarrow [+\text{nasal}] \Big/ \text{—} \begin{bmatrix} +\text{cons} \\ +\text{nasal} \end{bmatrix}$$

In phonological rules, distinctive features are used to allow segments to be grouped into natural classes, since segments with features in common usually have similar phonological patterning (refer to Chapter Five, Table 5.1, for feature specifications used here). Distinctive features thus facilitate a description which reveals the regularities in the sound patterns. The feature specification on the left of the arrow describes the segments that conform to the rule (in the above example all vowels). The feature specification on the immediate right of the arrow is the 'output' of the rule. The arrow itself usually means 'becomes' or 'is realised as'. It is customary to specify in the 'output' of the rule only the additional or changed feature specifications, it being understood that all other feature values for the segments described remain the same. The diagonal 'slash mark' means 'in the context of' or 'when it occurs', that is it indicates the environment in which a particular pronunciation pattern occurs. The majority of phonological rules in generative phonologies are usually *context-sensitive.* The dash mark indicates the place of the segment described by the rule in the context specified.

(2) Voiceless plosives are aspirated word initial before a stressed vowel:

$$\begin{bmatrix} -\text{cont} \\ -\text{voice} \\ -\text{strid} \end{bmatrix} \rightarrow [+\text{aspiration}] \Big/ \ \# \ — \begin{bmatrix} +\text{voc} \\ -\text{cons} \\ +\text{stress} \end{bmatrix}$$

Here the class of segments that conforms to the rule is specified as non-continuant, voiceless and non-strident; only 'true consonants', that is obstruents (see Chapter Five), can be voiceless; the feature specification non-continuant excludes fricatives; the non-strident specification is necessary to exclude /tʃ/, although [− del rel] would have served just as well. In the description of the context in which the 'output' of the rule ocurs, # means 'word boundary'.

(3)

$$\begin{bmatrix} +\text{voc} \\ +\text{cons} \\ +\text{lat} \end{bmatrix} \rightarrow \begin{bmatrix} +\text{high} \\ +\text{back} \end{bmatrix} \Big/ \begin{bmatrix} +\text{voc} \\ -\text{cons} \end{bmatrix} — \ \#$$

It should be possible to work out the pattern described by this third example from the information provided and a knowledge of distinctive features. The segments described by the rule are 'lateral liquids', that is in English only /l/; the specification [+ high, + back] describes the secondary articulation of velarisation (see Chapter Five); the contextual information provided in the rule can be glossed as 'when the segment occurs after a vowel before a word boundary'. This is not, of course, the only context in which laterals might be velarised in English; it has merely been chosen to exemplify how a phonological rule is written.

In the formalisation of a rule the segment or feature specification between the arrow and the slash mark indicating the contextual condition of the rule, called the 'output' of the rule above, is often referred to as the *structural change*. The feature specification on the left of the arrow, in a sense the 'input' to the rule, and all the feature specifications and other symbols to the right of the slash mark, the context, are referred to as the *structural description*.

There is a great deal more that could be discussed with regard to the theoretical basis of generative phonology. These theoretical issues are not, however, relevant here as they have impinged little upon the applications of the framework to children's speech in a clinical context. The main thrust of these analyses has been to use the formal techniques of description to make explicit the regularities in the children's pronunciation patterns.

GENERATIVE PHONOLOGY AS A FRAMEWORK FOR THE ANALYSIS OF CHILD SPEECH

The theoretical framework described in the preceding section has proved a particularly attractive format for the description of child speech. Almost all generative phonological analyses of children's speech describe the child's pronunciation patterns as related to the adult pronunciations in terms of phonological rules.[6] The adult pronunciations are represented by the phonemic forms of the words or segments and these form the 'input' to the phonological rules; the 'output' is the child's pronunciation. As with the rules exemplified above, many of the patterns in child speech are context-sensitive; the context will therefore be specified as part of the structural description of the rule. A brief example will serve to illustrate the basic principles of the procedure.

PAMELA 7;2 (1975)

feet [p̄̆fit] *knife* [naɪp̄̆]
fence [p̄̆fɛʂ] *leaf* [lip̄̆]
fish [p̄̆fɪ̢ʃ]

The adult labiodental fricative /f/ is pronounced by Pamela as a homorganic affricate in word-initial position, before a vowel:

$$\begin{bmatrix} +\text{cont} \\ +\text{ant} \\ -\text{cor} \\ +\text{strid} \\ -\text{voice} \end{bmatrix} \rightarrow \begin{bmatrix} -\text{cont} \\ +\text{del rel} \end{bmatrix} \Big/ \# \, \text{—} \begin{bmatrix} +\text{voc} \\ -\text{cons} \end{bmatrix}$$

A different pronunciation, a plosive, occurs in word-final position, after a vowel:

$$\begin{bmatrix} +\text{cont} \\ +\text{ant} \\ -\text{cor} \\ +\text{strid} \\ -\text{voice} \end{bmatrix} \rightarrow \begin{bmatrix} -\text{cont} \\ -\text{strid} \end{bmatrix} \Big/ \begin{bmatrix} +\text{voc} \\ -\text{cons} \end{bmatrix} \text{—} \, \#$$

Both these rules derive the child's pronunciations from the adult pronunciations by changing features in the specification of the adult 'input' on the left of the arrow to provide a feature specification of the child's 'output' on the immediate right of the arrow. These two rules, and indeed all phonological rules for child speech in this analytical framework, therefore describe children's pronunciations in terms of their differences from the adult pronunciations. These formalised rule statements thus appear to be another framework for error analysis. It is superior to the traditional assessment procedure in that the use of features allows the analyst to identify regular patterns affecting natural classes of segments. In addition, the possibility of context-sensitive errors provides the opportunity for descriptions that explain some of the patterns that occur, by identifying the contextual motivation for the child's mispronunciation. Thus, this type of analysis has been advocated by several authorities as a more appropriate and adequate clinical assessment procedure.

There is, however, a specific theoretical viewpoint implied by applying this analytical procedure to child speech. One needs to be aware of these implications before attempting to apply the procedure. It appears to have been assumed, either implicitly or explicitly, by most analysts that the descriptive rules have some kind of 'reality' in the language processing and production system of the child. This position is exemplified most clearly by

Smith (1973) who states quite categorically that the child's underlying representation is the adult phonemic pronunciation; this is the input to the 'realisation rules', the output of which is the child's pronunciation (ibid.: 181–4). This hypothesis is fundamental to the psychological model of the child's phonological system which Smith proposes.

The evidence upon which the hypothesis is based essentially derives from three interlinked aspects of children's phonological behaviour. First, that all the child's pronunciations can be systematically generated from the adult pronunciations. It is this fact, that there are regular relationships between the pronunciation patterns, that makes the writing of a generative type of analysis possible. Furthermore, the differences between the two patterns are not, according to Smith, attributable to perceptual or articulatory deficiencies on the part of the child.

In regard to the articulatory abilities of children, there is certainly evidence that they might display articulatory proficiency in the production of sound types, but do not use the types appropriately in terms of the adult pronunciations. The pronunciation of /s/ as [θ], for example *seesaw* [ˈθiθɔ], but with /θ/ pronounced as [f], for example *thumb* [fʌm], is a well-known example of this phenomenon. Developmental factors in the control and mastery of pronunciation patterns, particularly for complex articulatory sequences, should not, however, be underestimated. Variability in pronunciation such as *sugar* [ˈtsʊgə, ˈsʊgə, ˈs̺ʊgə, ˈtˁʊgə] (Smith 1973: 252) and in sequencing such as *mendable* [ˈmɛndəbəl, ˈmɛlbədən] (ibid.: 235) are very suggestive of production difficulties. Smith seems to accord negligible significance to such factors in expounding his hypothesis. It is, however, noteworthy that in a very important but frequently overlooked section (ibid.: 140–3) he does recognise the contribution of articulatory mastery to phonological development. Despite this section, the main thrust of his argument remains that the child's pronunciations are accounted for or explained by the *phonological* realisation rules, which are in fact the adult analyst's description of the child's realisations of adult target pronuniations.

The second aspect of the evidence for the reality of these rules is the child's alleged perfect perception of the adult pronunciations. This is taken to imply that the child's underlying representation is a perfect replica of the adult phonemic form. Smith (1978) has subsequently amended slightly his view that the child has absolutely perfect perception, without however substantially altering his basic standpoint. It must be acknowledged that children's abilities to perceive speech sound differences they do not produce have frequently been demonstrated. Smith cites the example of his subject's discrimination of *card* and *cart* when both were pronounced [gɑt] (1973: 134). Most auditory perception tests are restricted to the same sort of minimal-pair discrimination task. The speech perception abilities required for the accurate pronunciation of more complex phonological forms will surely involve equally more complex perceptual processing skills. These have rarely been discussed and, no doubt because of the problems of devising an adequate procedure, have never been systematically tested. Furthermore, even in the instance of simple discrimination skills, the test procedure only reveals that the difference has been detected; it is not known from the child's response whether he has *analysed* the phonetic nature of the difference accurately, if at all. As Maxwell (1979) states in discussing this same issue in regard to children with deviant phonologies: 'It is an unsupported claim, however, that these children are perceiving precisely the same signals or interpreting them in precisely the same way as normal speakers' (ibid.: 189).

Related to this point is the fairly frequent observation that, whereas children are able to perceive differences in the speech of others, they apparently fail to monitor the absence of these differences in their own speech (see e.g. from Smith quoted above).[7] For a change in his pronunciation patterns to occur a child needs not only inter-personal perception, but also this intra-personal perceptual monitoring (see also Chapter Two). Thus the contribution of perceptual factors in phonological development is probably more important than has often been claimed. It is therefore unwise to assume on the evidence presently available that children have perfect perception of the adult phonemic form; and on this basis this form cannot be taken as the child's underlying representation for all the words he attempts to pronounce.

Smith's third argument in support of his hypothesis is equally controversial. Here, however, the counter-evidence is readily available. Smith's argument (1973: 3, 138–43) is that changes occur in the speech patterns of his subject 'across-the-board'. This term means that when a new, and usually more accurate, pronunciation pattern is used by the child it is simultaneously introduced into the pronunciation of all the words in which the pattern is appropriate. Furthermore, it is claimed that it is never used 'incorrectly' on words that were previously produced with a pattern similar to the words that are undergoing the change because the child 'knows' the correct form of all the target words from his underlying representations. Thus a child who has pronounced both /tʃ/ and /tr/ as [t], for example *chalk* [tɔk], *troddler* [ˈtɒglə] at an earlier stage, would *not*, on developing the correct pronunciation of /tr/, for example [ˈtɹɒglə], at the same time as introducing this new pronunciation, show variation and overgeneralisation of the pronunciation to /tʃ/ such that the following would occur: *chalk* [tɔk, tɹɔk], *chocolate* [ˈtɒklɪt, ˈtɹɒklɪt]. These examples are in fact taken from Smith (1973: 218, 219, 257). As a further illustration of this point, one would *not* expect a child when achieving the correct pronunciation of /r/ to begin to use this for /j/, which like /r/ had previously been sometimes realised as [l]; for example *red* changes from [lɛd] to [ɹɛd], *yet* changes from free variation between [jɛt, dɛt, lɛt] to free variation between [jɛt, ɹɛt] (Smith 1973: 78ff). It can be seen, therefore, that the data themselves contradict his argument. The 'across-the-board' nature of phonological development would appear to be an oversimplified view of the phenomena of phonological change.[8] It is much more realistic to characterise the progress of developmental change as a *gradual process*, in which at any one time there are both correct and incorrect realisations of similar phonological forms and the possible occurrence of inappropriate overgeneralisation.

The alleged occurrence of 'across-the-board' changes and no overgeneralisations supports Smith's hypothesis in that it is argued that such phenomena could only occur if the child 'knew' what he should be saying, that is his underlying representation is the adult pronunciation. If the 'across-the-board' evidence is questionable the fundamental hypothesis of the reality of the phonological realisation rules is thus further weakened.

This issue has been discussed in considerable detail here because it is important that the implications that some authors have claimed for generative phonological analyses are fully appreciated. It is hoped that the foregoing discussion has demonstrated that any claims that generative analyses of children's pronunciations patterns have some kind of 'psychological reality' can be seriously questioned. Perhaps the most convincing counter-argument has not yet been made; this relates to the characteristics of the learning process if one assumes that the child actually uses the generative rules. In order to develop a more accurate pronunciation these rules have to disappear; in effect, the child begins his phonological development with a complex set of pronunciation rules, which he eventually loses.

As has been cogently argued by Donegan & Stampe (1979: 131), this does not represent an appropriate or even logical characterisation of development.

In the light of this discussion, no claims are made here for any psychological status for the generative phonological procedures to be discussed below. These are to be viewed only as a framework within which to analyse the relationships between the adult pronunciations and the child's pronunciations. The phonological rules are *correspondence rules* which compare, when taken in their totality, two systems, the child's and the adult's (cf. Chapter Four). However, these correspondence rules are only written when differences are found between the two systems. In this capacity, as indicated above, they are descriptive statements of the error patterns in a child's speech.

PROCEDURES FOR A GENERATIVE PHONOLOGICAL ANALYSIS OF CHILD SPEECH

As outlined in Chapter Three, the traditional categories in error analysis are omissions, substitutions and distortions, with additions and transpositions occasionally being noted. The principles of generative analysis are that phonological rules can:

- change feature specifications, that is change segments; cf. substitutions and distortions;
- delete segments; cf. omissions;
- insert segments; cf. additions;
- interchange (reorder or permute) segments, that is metathesis; cf. transpositions;
- coalesce segments.

It can thus be easily appreciated why generative phonological rules came to be so readily applied to the analysis of child speech. This section will describe and exemplify the types and formalisation of rules for stating the correspondences between adult and child pronunciations.

Change of Feature Specifications

ANN 5;11 (1979)

car [tɑ]	*girl* [dɜl]
clown [tɹaʊn]	*finger* ['fɪndə]
queen [twin]	*tiger* ['taɪdə]
book [bʊt]	*egg* [ɛd]
milk [mɪʊt]	*singing* ['sɪnɪn]

In Ann's speech all three adult velar consonants /k, g, ŋ/ in all places in word and syllables structure are pronounced as alveolar consonants. Only the place of articulation features of the segments are changed and this pattern is not context-conditioned.

$$\begin{bmatrix} +\text{cons} \\ -\text{cont} \\ -\text{cor} \\ -\text{ant} \\ +\text{high} \\ +\text{back} \end{bmatrix} \longrightarrow \begin{bmatrix} +\text{cor} \\ +\text{ant} \\ -\text{high} \\ -\text{back} \end{bmatrix}$$

The input to this rule could be specified as:

$$\begin{bmatrix} -\text{cont} \\ +\text{back} \end{bmatrix}$$

which uniquely characterises the velar stops in English, the other feature specifications being strictly speaking redundant here. This rule and other similar segment changes rules could be stated using segmental specifications:

$$\begin{bmatrix} \text{k} \\ \text{g} \\ \text{ŋ} \end{bmatrix} \longrightarrow \begin{bmatrix} \text{t} \\ \text{d} \\ \text{n} \end{bmatrix}$$

Here the square bracket notation is the formal procedure for stating that the segments are matched along the same horizontal row.

RALPH 6;9 (1980)

bird [bɜt]	*cherryade* [ˈʧɛji ˈjeɪt]
dog [dɒk]	*kick* [kɪk]
garage [ˈgajɪʧ]	*jeep* [ʤip]
tent [tɛnt]	*pillow* [ˈpɪjə]

In this sample it can be seen that non-continuant obstruents (plosives and affricates) maintain the [± voice] feature contrast when they occur in word-initial position. In word-final position only voiceless segments of this type occur:

$$\begin{bmatrix} +\text{cons} \\ -\text{son} \\ -\text{cont} \end{bmatrix} \rightarrow [-\text{voice}] \, / \, \text{—}\ \#$$

This rule changes the feature of adult [+ voice] plosives and affricates, but by not specifying this feature in the input it also states the generalisation that all segments of these types are voiceless in the word-final position. For these two examples it should be apparent that rules framed in terms of features enable more general statements of 'error' patterns; the next two examples demonstrate how it is possible to extend this aspect of the framework further.

BOB 4;10 (1980)

side [taɪd]	*zoo* [du]
seven [ˈtɛbən]	*zebra* [ˈdɛbə]
scissors [ˈtɪdəd]	*eyes* [aɪd]
mouse [maʊt]	*horse* [hɔt]

This sample has been selected to illustrate Bob's pronunciation of adult /s, z/, which in all contexts are realised as [t, d] respectively:

$$\begin{bmatrix} \text{s} \\ \text{z} \end{bmatrix} \rightarrow \begin{bmatrix} \text{t} \\ \text{d} \end{bmatrix}$$

or

$$\begin{bmatrix} +\text{cons} \\ +\text{cor} \\ +\text{ant} \\ +\text{cont} \\ +\text{strid} \end{bmatrix} \rightarrow \begin{bmatrix} -\text{cont} \\ -\text{strid} \end{bmatrix}$$

Bob's pronunciation of adult /ʃ/ is also [t]. For example:

shoes [tud]	*fish* [fɪt]
sheet [tit]	*washer* ['wɒtə]
shed [tɛd]	*sugar* ['tʊdə]

$$\begin{bmatrix} +\text{cons} \\ +\text{cor} \\ -\text{ant} \\ +\text{cont} \\ +\text{strid} \end{bmatrix} \rightarrow \begin{bmatrix} -\text{cont} \\ +\text{ant} \\ -\text{strid} \end{bmatrix}$$

As can be seen when expressed in feature terms the two rules are very similar; the only difference in the feature specification affects the Anterior feature which has to be changed to describe the difference between target /ʃ/ and Bob's [t]. These two rules can be expressed as one rule by employing another device of formal notation, *angled brackets*, viz. [‹feature›]. Thus:

$$\begin{bmatrix} +\text{cons} \\ +\text{cor} \\ +\text{cont} \\ +\text{strid} \\ \langle -\text{ant} \rangle \end{bmatrix} \quad \begin{bmatrix} -\text{cont} \\ -\text{strid} \\ \langle +\text{ant} \rangle \end{bmatrix}$$

The angled brackets allow segments that have all the features as specified, including [− ant], to be inputs to the rules, but indicate that just those segments that are [− ant] show a feature change to [+ ant] in the output. Thus the feature specifications and the angled bracket notation allow the analysis to reveal the obvious phonetic relationship between the adult and child pronunciations.

On the other hand the natural class /s z ʃ/ can be more simply specified by its common features and the output would thus only specify the feature changes, as follows:

$$\begin{bmatrix} +\text{cont} \\ +\text{cor} \\ +\text{strid} \end{bmatrix} \longrightarrow \begin{bmatrix} -\text{cont} \\ +\text{ant} \\ -\text{strid} \end{bmatrix}$$

Similarly in Julia's sample the feature specification allows us to capture the natural class of velar plosives that are all involved in the same pattern of place of articulation change.

JULIA 8;0 (1980)
go [toʊ]   *cake* [teɪt]
game [teɪm]   *cap* [tap]
sugar ['lʊtə]   *cow* [tɑʊ]
egg [ɛt]   *leaking* ['litɪn]
pig [pɪt]   *pick* [pɪt]

From this example it is evident that Julia, like Ann, pronounces adult velar plosives /k g/ as alveolars, but unlike Ann both are realised as [t]. This can be indicated by specifying the value of the voicing feature shared by the output of the rule, thus:

$$\begin{bmatrix} +\text{cons} \\ -\text{son} \\ -\text{cont} \\ +\text{back} \end{bmatrix} \longrightarrow \begin{bmatrix} +\text{cor} \\ +\text{ant} \\ -\text{high} \\ -\text{back} \\ -\text{voice} \end{bmatrix}$$

A different type of notational device makes it possible to express in one rule an identical segment correspondence that occurs in two different contexts. This device is *braces notation.*

ANN 5;11 (1979)
fish [fɪʔ]   *saucer* ['sɔʔə]
coffee ['tɒʔɪ]   *shoe* [ʃu]
knife [naɪʔ]   *cushion* ['tʊʔən]
pussy ['pʊʔɪ]   *house* [ɑʊʔ]
stamps [sants]   *socks* [sɒts]

In this sample it can be seen that the realisations of adult fricatives in word-initial position are correct pronunciations. Within words in intervocalic position and in word-final position when immediately following a vowel the fricatives are pronounced as [ʔ].

$$\begin{bmatrix} -\text{son} \\ +\text{cons} \\ +\text{cont} \end{bmatrix} \rightarrow [\text{ʔ}] \bigg/ \text{V} — \begin{Bmatrix} \text{V} \\ \# \end{Bmatrix}$$

In this rule, the braces notation indicates that the contexts in which the rule applies are either before a vowel or at a word boundary, in both contexts immediately following a vowel. Two further points should be noted about this rule. First, that 'V' can be used as a 'cover symbol' for vowels and 'C' can be used as a 'cover symbol' for consonants. Secondly the phonetic symbol [ʔ] is used as a simpler notation for this segment which if specified in features would require all the features to be listed for place of articulation as all are changed in this glottal realisation of target labial and lingual fricatives.

Another example of the application of braces notation will be demonstrated in the next section.

Deletion of Segments

DAVID 5;9 (1979)

spoon [bun]	*smoke* [moʊk]
star [dɑ]	*snow* [noʊ]
spade [peɪd]	*stove* [toʊf]

In this sample of David's speech the realisations of the word-initial clusters involve the omission of the /s/ before a 'stop' consonant, either plosive or nasal. This pattern can be described in a context-sensitive rule:

$$\begin{bmatrix} +\text{cons} \\ +\text{cor} \\ +\text{ant} \\ +\text{cont} \\ +\text{strid} \\ -\text{voice} \end{bmatrix} \rightarrow \theta \bigg/ \# — \begin{bmatrix} +\text{cons} \\ -\text{voc} \\ -\text{cont} \end{bmatrix}$$

This rule would also describe omission of /s/ before /k/, which did occur at this time in David's speech; but in this context he realised /k/ as [t] or [d], for example *skipping* ['dɪpɪn], *school* [tul] (cf. Ann above).

A different type of segment deletion pattern is exemplified in the following sample.

JONATHAN 4;7 (1978)
plate [peɪ] *brush* [bʌ]
glove [də] *tree* [ti]
clock [tɒ] *grass* [da]

In Jonathan's pronunciation patterns, the word-initial clusters of the adult system in which a plosive is followed by the approximants ('liquids') /l, r/ are realised by a single consonant, a plosive. The following rule describes this segment deletion pattern.

$$\begin{bmatrix} +\text{cons} \\ +\text{voc} \end{bmatrix} \rightarrow \theta \Big/ \# \begin{bmatrix} +\text{cons} \\ -\text{voc} \\ -\text{cont} \end{bmatrix} —$$

This rule describes the patterns in the six words cited above and would also account for the following, all of which occurred in Jonathan's speech:

pram [pa] *dress* [dɛ]
blue [bu] *crisps* [tɪ]

As in the data of Ann and David, a feature-change rule would be required to describe the realisations of target velar consonants as [t, d].

As in the analysis of feature-change correspondences, the braces notation can be used to describe two similar omission patterns in one rule.

RICHARD 4;2 (1972)
horse [hɔ] *seesaw* [ˈʧiʧɔ]
pencil [ˈpɛnʧʊ] *Christmas* [ˈʧɪmə]
desk [dɛk] *nest* [nɛt]
custard [ˈkʊtə] *icecream* [ˈaɪkim]
saucepan [ˈʧɔpən] *jigsaw* [ˈʧɪʔʧɔ]

Analysis of Richard's realisations of adult /s/ in the above sample reveals that this segment is omitted in word-final position (*horse, Christmas*) and before a consonant both in word-final clusters (*desk, nest*) and within words before consonants (*Christmas, custard, icecream, saucepan*). The following rule states the deletion pattern for the two types of contexts.

$$\begin{bmatrix} +\text{cons} \\ +\text{cor} \\ +\text{ant} \\ +\text{cont} \\ +\text{strid} \\ -\text{voice} \end{bmatrix} \rightarrow \theta \Bigg/ \left\{ \begin{array}{l} \text{—} \ \# \\ \\ \text{—} \begin{bmatrix} +\text{cons} \\ -\text{voc} \end{bmatrix} \end{array} \right\}$$

Further rules would, of course, be required to describe the other patterns in Richard's speech.

Insertion of Segments

In clinical data, and in normal developmental patterns in child speech, there is one well-attested and frequently occurring correspondence pattern which involves the insertion of a segment. Anthony's sample exemplifies this pattern (see further Chapter Seven).

ANTHONY 5;8 (1980)
blue [bə'lu] *drum* [də'wʌm]
brush [bə'ɹʌs] *cleaner* [kə'linə]

Here a neutral vowel is inserted between the two consonants in a word initial cluster.

$$\theta \rightarrow \begin{array}{c} \text{V} \\ \begin{bmatrix} -\text{high} \\ -\text{back} \\ -\text{low} \end{bmatrix} \end{array} \Big/ \ \# \ \text{C–CV}$$

Interchange of Segments

Metathesis or permutation of ordering of segments in children's speech does not appear to occur very regularly or very often, despite the well-known mispronunciations of 'efelant' and 'agillator'. Smith (1973: 98–101) provides a sample which shows some regularity of patterning, and in view of the number of examples quoted the phenomena presumably occurred with noticeable frequency. Examples include:[9]

milk [mlɪk] *film* [flɪm]
self [slɛf] *shelf* [slɛf]

The pattern here appears to involve the metathesis of the vowel to separate a sequence of two consonants involving a lateral followed by a non-apical consonant. A rule involving the interchange of segments can be formulated as follows:

$$\underset{1}{\text{V}}\ \underset{2}{[+\text{lat}]}\ \underset{3}{\begin{bmatrix}+\text{cons}\\-\text{cor}\end{bmatrix}} \rightarrow \underset{2}{[+\text{lat}]}\ \underset{1}{\text{V}}\ \underset{3}{\begin{bmatrix}+\text{cons}\\-\text{cor}\end{bmatrix}}$$

In fact, in the sample these consonants are sometimes interchanged without metathesis of the vowel:

bulb [bʌbl] *helping* ['ɛplɪn]
wolf [wʊfl] *silver* ['sɪvlə]

The rule describing this pattern is:

$$\underset{1}{\text{V}}\ \underset{2}{[+\text{lat}]}\ \underset{3}{\begin{bmatrix}+\text{cons}\\-\text{cor}\end{bmatrix}} \rightarrow \underset{1}{\text{V}}\ \underset{3}{\begin{bmatrix}+\text{cons}\\-\text{cor}\end{bmatrix}}\ \underset{2}{[+\text{lat}]}$$

The formulation of metathesis rules is simple and obvious; indeed the numbering of the segments makes it unnecessary to rewrite the feature specifications of the segments on the right of the arrow (Schane 1973: 66–8).

Coalescence of Segments

In the early stages of phonological development children usually realise word-initial clusters as single segments (see further Chapter Seven). Sometimes their realisations involve a phonetic combination of the two segments composing the adult pronunciation of the cluster. For example:

/sl/ → [ɬ] e.g. *slide* [ɬaɪd]

in which the voiceless friction of /s/ and the lateral airstream of /l/ are both present in [ɬ];

/sw/ → [ʍ] e.g. *swim* [ʍɪm]

in which the voiceless friction of /s/ and the labial-velar articulation of /w/ are both present in [ʍ]. These realisations can be described as involving coalescence, which is formulated in the following type of rule:

$$\begin{matrix} /\text{sl}/ & & & [\text{ɬ}] & \\ \begin{bmatrix} +\text{cons} \\ +\text{cor} \\ +\text{ant} \\ +\text{cont} \\ +\text{strid} \\ -\text{voice} \end{bmatrix} & \begin{bmatrix} +\text{cons} \\ +\text{voc} \\ +\text{ant} \\ +\text{cor} \\ +\text{lat} \\ +\text{voice} \end{bmatrix} & \rightarrow & \begin{bmatrix} +\text{cons} \\ -\text{voc} \\ +\text{cont} \\ +\text{strid} \\ +\text{lat} \\ -\text{voice} \end{bmatrix} & \Big/ \;\; \# \text{—} V \\ (1) & (2) & & (3) & \end{matrix}$$

$$\begin{matrix} /\text{sw}/ & & & [\text{ʍ}] & \\ \begin{bmatrix} +\text{cons} \\ +\text{cor} \\ +\text{ant} \\ +\text{cont} \\ +\text{strid} \\ -\text{voice} \end{bmatrix} & \begin{bmatrix} -\text{cons} \\ -\text{voc} \\ +\text{high} \\ +\text{back} \\ -\text{cor} \\ -\text{ant} \\ +\text{voice} \\ -\text{strid} \\ +\text{round} \end{bmatrix} & \rightarrow & \begin{bmatrix} +\text{cons} \\ -\text{voc} \\ +\text{high} \\ +\text{back} \\ -\text{cor} \\ -\text{ant} \\ -\text{voice} \\ -\text{strid} \\ +\text{round} \end{bmatrix} & \Big/ \;\; \# \text{—} V \\ (1) & (2) & & (3) & \end{matrix}$$

From the feature specifications of the three different segments described in each rule it can be seen that the child's pronunciation is a combination of the phonetic components of the adult's. In this way these rules make explicit the phonetic motivation for the child's realisations.

Rule Ordering

It is often claimed that the phonological rules in generative analyses must be ordered to apply in a particular sequence.[10] Both Compton (1970: 335) and Oller (1973: 45) show that rule ordering may be applied in the description of the correspondences between child and adult pronunciations. Rule ordering is required when one rule removes, by feature change or deletion, the input to another rule. For example, as has been seen above in David's sample, /s/ is frequently deleted before consonants in the child's realisations of adult word-initial clusters. Sometimes, however, the child's realisations of the retained segment involve a feature change which is most easily described by specifying the context of /s/, for example:

smoke [m̥^{F}oʊk] *snow* [n̥^{F}oʊ]
cf. *mat* [mat] *no* [noʊ]

These realisations of /s/ + nasal clusters can be formulated by two rules:[11]

Rule (1)

$$\begin{bmatrix} +\text{cons} \\ -\text{voc} \\ +\text{nasal} \\ +\text{voice} \end{bmatrix} \rightarrow [-\text{voice}] \Big/ \ \# \begin{bmatrix} +\text{cons} \\ +\text{ant} \\ +\text{cor} \\ +\text{cont} \\ +\text{strid} \\ -\text{voice} \end{bmatrix} \_\_$$

Rule (2)

$$\begin{bmatrix} +\text{cons} \\ +\text{ant} \\ +\text{cor} \\ +\text{cont} \\ +\text{strid} \\ -\text{voice} \end{bmatrix} \rightarrow \emptyset \Big/ \ \# \_\_ \begin{bmatrix} +\text{cons} \\ +\text{nasal} \end{bmatrix}$$

Rule (2) could NOT apply before Rule (1), since Rule (2) deletes the segment which is the context required for the application of Rule (1) here.

Another instance where rule ordering appears to be necessary is where one rule has as its output a segment which could form the input to another rule, but which apparently does not. For example, Robbie (5;5 1980) had the following pattern:

Rule (1)

$$\begin{bmatrix} \text{t} \\ \text{d} \end{bmatrix} \rightarrow \begin{bmatrix} \text{ʧ} \\ \text{ʤ} \end{bmatrix} \Big/ \ \# \text{—} \text{V}$$

e.g. *two* [ʧu] *daddy* ['ʤadi]
tie [ʧaɪ] *dont* [ʤoʊnt]

Rule (2)

$$\begin{bmatrix} \text{k} \\ \text{g} \end{bmatrix} \rightarrow \begin{bmatrix} \text{t} \\ \text{d} \end{bmatrix} \Big/ \ \# \text{—} \text{V}$$

e.g. *cat* [tat] *girl* [dɜl]
cup [tʌp] *gun* [dʌn]

Here Rule (2) must be ordered AFTER Rule (1), otherwise the [t, d] output from Rule (2) would form an input to Rule (1), and adult /k, g/ through the sequential application of the two rules would be realised as [tʃ, dz], which is not the case in Robbie's speech.

These are two examples where the formulation of the rules seems to require that their application be ordered. In many instances, however, although more than one rule is required to describe the child's pronunciation of a particular adult target, no particular order of application is apparently needed. For example, to describe David's pronunciation of *skipping* [ˈdɪpɪn] (see above), three rules would be required:

Rule (1) Deletion of /s/ before a consonant in word-initial position (see above);
Rule (2) Feature change of velar consonants to alveolar consonants (see above);
Rule (3) Feature change of voiceless consonants to voiced before vowels; this is not an absolutely regular pattern, so that the rule here would be 'optional', that is it does not always apply (see below).

There are apparently no reasons for imposing an order upon the application of these rules. Indeed they could all three be said to apply simultaneously rather than sequentially, although it is probably easier to appreciate the patterning in children's pronunciations by describing the phonological rules in some logical sequence. Any order could be possible here; one would have to refer to the whole data sample to establish a logical order.

Assimilative Feature Changes

There are instances where different feature changes occur in a segment dependent upon the features of the other segments in the conditioning context. This type of feature change usually involves assimilation and it is useful to be able to indicate this assimilative aspect of the pattern in the rule. For example, in their first realisations of /s/ + consonant clusters as clusters, children sometimes use a fricative realisation that is influenced by the place of articulation of the following consonant, for example:

(1) /sp/ → [fp], /sm/ → [fm]
(2) /st/ → [θt] /sn/ → [θn]
(3) /sk/ → [çk]

Here the fricative is assimilated to the following stop (cf. Anthony *et al.* 1971: 37, 42).

The places of articulation of these fricatives can be succinctly described in a rule using variables for the feature specifications:

$$\begin{bmatrix} +\text{cons} \\ -\text{voc} \\ +\text{cont} \end{bmatrix} \rightarrow \begin{bmatrix} \alpha\text{ant} \\ \beta\text{cor} \\ \gamma\text{high} \end{bmatrix} \Big/ \# \text{---} \begin{bmatrix} \alpha\text{ant} \\ \beta\text{cor} \\ \gamma\text{high} \end{bmatrix}$$

It will be recalled that the features Anterior, Coronal and High are required to specify the place of articulation of labial, dental/alveolar and palatal/velar consonants. Thus /s/, when assimilated, is realised as:

(1) labial $\begin{bmatrix} +\text{ant} \\ -\text{cor} \\ -\text{high} \end{bmatrix}$

(2) dental/alveolar $\begin{bmatrix} +\text{ant} \\ +\text{cor} \\ -\text{high} \end{bmatrix}$

(3) palatal/velar $\begin{bmatrix} -\text{ant} \\ -\text{cor} \\ +\text{high} \end{bmatrix}$

In the rule the Greek-letter feature specifications indicate that for each of these three features the value is variable (i.e. it may be 'plus' or 'minus'), but that the value of each of the features is always the same for the output of the rule, the fricative, and the following consonant (plosive or nasal), which is part of the structural description of the rule. The use of variables thus indicates the assimilative nature of the feature change.[12] It also enables one to express similar feature changes by a single rule which makes explicit the phonetic motivation of the feature changes.

Optional Rules

As has been indicated in Chapter Four and in the first section of this chapter, developmental change in children's phonological patterns tends to be gradual. Children's speech is usually characterised by some degree of variability. This factor is usually handled in generative analyses by stating that some of the rules are *optional.* This implies that the rule does not describe all of the data specified in the structural description of the rule; that is it does not always apply. Some analysts calculate the percentage application of the optional rules (e.g. Compton 1975, 1976). Rules that always apply, that is that describe the realisations of all the data that fit the structural description, are *obligatory.*

Bearing in mind that all generative rules describe correspondences between adult and child pronunciations, rules may be optional in two different ways. First, a rule may be optionally in alternation with another rule, in which instance the child has two variable realisations, both being different from the adult pronunciation. For example, Robbie (see above) realised initial /s/ variably as [ʃ] or [tʃ], for example:

summer [ˈʃʌmə]	*singing* [ˈʃɪnɪn]
see [ʧi]	*some* [ʧʌm]

This pattern of variability requires two optional rules; *opt.* is used to indicate optional rules.

$$(1)\quad \begin{bmatrix} +\text{cons} \\ +\text{cor} \\ +\text{ant} \\ +\text{cont} \\ +\text{strid} \\ -\text{voice} \end{bmatrix} \rightarrow [-\text{ant}] \;/\; \# \text{—} V \qquad \textit{opt.}$$

$$(2)\quad \begin{bmatrix} +\text{cons} \\ +\text{cor} \\ +\text{ant} \\ +\text{cont} \\ +\text{strid} \\ -\text{voice} \end{bmatrix} \rightarrow \begin{bmatrix} -\text{cont} \\ -\text{ant} \\ +\text{del rel} \end{bmatrix} \;/\; \# \text{—} V \qquad \textit{opt.}$$

Secondly, where a child's variable pronunciations involve alternation between a correct and incorrect pronunciation there is only one optional rule for the incorrect realisation, the correct pronunciation being represented by the absence of any rule, of course (see above). For example, David's variable realisations of the voicing features of /p, t, k/ in target /s/ clusters require an optional feature-change rule which alternates with no rule. Thus, to describe David's pronunciation of word-initial /s/ clusters as:

/sp/ → [p ~ b]
/st, sk/ → [t ~ d],

one optional and two obligatory rules are required:

Rule (1) Deletion of /s/ *oblig.*
Rule (2) Feature change of velars *oblig.*
Rule (3) Voicing feature change *opt.*
(see above).

In an analysis of child speech for clinical purposes these two different types of rule optionality (or variable realisations) must be clearly distinguished. Variability between two 'error' pronunciations has very different clinical implications from variability between correct and incorrect realisations. The latter often indicates a positive prognosis since change is apparently already in progress. The implications of the former must be assessed with reference to the nature of both the optional rules and the other speech patterns used by the child.

GENERATIVE PHONOLOGICAL ANALYSIS OF CHILD SPEECH: AN EXAMPLE

In the preceding section the procedures and types of rules used in generative analysis have been illustrated on small speech samples from a variety of children. These samples were selected to illustrate as simply and as clearly as possible the different types and formulations of generative rules. A full generative phonological analysis of a child's speech will involve a series of inter-related rules with, for example, the output of one rule feeding into the input of a second rule, in which instance rule ordering is crucial, as we have seen above. As mentioned in the second section of this chapter, Smith (1973) provides a complete generative phonology of the pronunciation patterns of a child developing speech along normal lines. Oller *et al.* (1972; see Oller 1973 for a summary of the results of these studies), and Compton (1975, 1976) provide what appear to be complete generative analyses of the pronunciation patterns of children with disordered phonologies. In this section generative phonological procedures are applied to a selected representative sample of the speech of a child who had a severe developmental phonological disorder, (see Grunwell & Pletts 1974). The aim of this analysis is to show how an (almost) complete description of a child's speech patterns can be made using generative principles.

ROSEY 6;8 (1974)

(1) *monkey* ['mʊʎi]
(2) *bottle* ['bɒbɒ]
(3) *garage* ['daʎi]
(4) *feathers* ['fɛfɛ]
(5) *telly* ['dɛʎi]
(6) *christmas* ['dɪdɪ]
(7) *indian* ['ʎiʎi]
(8) *scissors* ['tɪtɪ]
(9) *chimney* ['dɪʎi]
(10) *letter* ['lɛlɛ]
(11) *pinny* ['bɪʎi]
(12) *flowers* ['fafa]
(13) *budgie* ['bʊʎi]
(14) *elephant* ['ʎɛʎi]
(15) *little* ['lɪlɪ]
(16) *dressing* ['dɛʎi]
(17) *fire* ['fafa]
(18) *pencil* ['bɛbɛ, 'pɛpɛ]
(19) *matches* ['maʎi]
(20) *finger* ['fɪfɪ]

(21) *paper* ['bɛbɛ]
(22) *settee* ['dɛʎi]
(23) *dolly* ['dɒʎi]
(24) *sugar* ['tʊtʊ, 'dʊdʊ]
(25) *aeroplane* [bɛ 'bɛ]
(26) *Cheryl* ['dɛʎi]
(27) *middle* ['mɪmɪ]
(28) *kitchen* ['dɪdɪ, 'tɪtɪ]
(29) *sleeping* ['tiʎi]
(30) *chocolate* ['dɒdɒ]

Rule (1)

$$[+\text{cons}] \rightarrow \theta / \text{—} \ \#$$

i.e. all word-final consonants are deleted. This rule actually needs to be extended to describe (14) *elephant*, where the final syllable is deleted; this is the only trisyllabic word included in this sample;[13] it is included because it exemplifies the insertion rule (9.1) below.

e.g. (2), (3), (4), (6), (7), (8), (12), (14), (15), (16), (18), (19), (25), (26), (27), (28), (29), (30).

Rule (2)

$$\begin{bmatrix}+\text{cons}\\+\text{voc}\end{bmatrix} \rightarrow \theta \Big/ \begin{bmatrix}+\text{cons}\\-\text{voc}\end{bmatrix} \text{—} \underset{[+\text{stress}]}{\text{V}}$$

i.e. /r,l/ are deleted after consonants in clusters, initial in a stressed syllable. This context description is required to include (25) *aeroplane*; all other examples are of word-initial (stressed) syllables. The feature specification of the preceding consonant covers /k/ in (6) which is subject to Rule (3) and Rule (5), /p/ in (25) which is subject to Rule (5), and /s/ in (29) which is subject to Rule (4).

e.g. (6), (12), (16), (25), (29).

Rule (3)

(3.1)
$$\begin{bmatrix}+\text{cons}\\-\text{ant}\\-\text{cor}\\+\text{high}\\+\text{back}\\-\text{cont}\end{bmatrix} \rightarrow \begin{bmatrix}+\text{ant}\\+\text{cor}\\-\text{high}\\-\text{back}\end{bmatrix} \Big/ \ \# \text{—}$$

i.e. velar plosives /k,g/ are realised as alveolar plosives [t,d] word-initially.

(3.2)
$$\begin{bmatrix} +\text{cons} \\ -\text{ant} \\ +\text{cor} \\ +\text{high} \\ -\text{cont} \\ +\text{del rel} \end{bmatrix} \rightarrow \begin{bmatrix} +\text{ant} \\ -\text{high} \\ -\text{del rel} \end{bmatrix} \Big/ \# \_\_$$

i.e. postalveolar affricates /tʃ, dz/ are realized as alveolar plosives [t, d] word-initially.

Because velar plosives and the postalveolar affricates uniquely share a set of common features, they can be specified as a natural class and these two rules can be collapsed into one.

$$\begin{bmatrix} +\text{cons} \\ -\text{cont} \\ -\text{ant} \\ +\text{high} \end{bmatrix} \rightarrow \begin{bmatrix} +\text{ant} \\ -\text{high} \\ +\text{cor} \\ -\text{back} \\ -\text{del rel} \end{bmatrix} \Big/ \# \_\_$$

e.g. (3), (6), (9), (26), (28), (30).

Rule (4)

(4.1)
$$\begin{bmatrix} +\text{cons} \\ +\text{ant} \\ +\text{cor} \\ +\text{cont} \\ +\text{strid} \\ -\text{voice} \end{bmatrix} \rightarrow \begin{bmatrix} -\text{cont} \\ -\text{strid} \end{bmatrix} \Big/ \# \_\_$$

i.e. /s/ is realised as an alveolar plosive in word-initial position.

(4.2)
$$\begin{bmatrix} +\text{cons} \\ -\text{ant} \\ +\text{cor} \\ +\text{cont} \\ +\text{strid} \\ -\text{voice} \end{bmatrix} \rightarrow \begin{bmatrix} +\text{ant} \\ -\text{cont} \\ -\text{strid} \end{bmatrix} \Big/ \# \_\_$$

i.e. /ʃ/ is realised as an alveolar plosive in word-initial position. Once again /s/ and /ʃ/ are a natural class and so these two rules can also be collapsed into one, by specifying them using the features they share in common:

$$\begin{bmatrix} +\text{cons} \\ +\text{cor} \\ +\text{cont} \\ +\text{strid} \\ -\text{voice} \\ -\text{ant} \end{bmatrix} \rightarrow \begin{bmatrix} -\text{cont} \\ -\text{strid} \\ +\text{ant} \end{bmatrix} \Big/ \# \_\_$$

e.g. (8), (22), (24), (29).

Rule (5)

$$\begin{bmatrix} +\text{cons} \\ -\text{cont} \end{bmatrix} \rightarrow [+\text{voice}] \Big/ \_\_ \underset{[+\text{stress}]}{\text{V}} \qquad \textit{opt.}$$

i.e. plosives are realised as voiced, initial in stressed syllables. As with Rule (2), this context is required to describe (25). This rule must be ordered to follow both Rules (3) and (4), so that it will account for the voiced realisations of the plosives that are the outputs of these rules in (9), (22), (24), (26), (30).
This is an optional rule; it applies in the realisations of (5), (6), (9), (11), (18), (21), (22), (24), (25), (26), (28), (30). It does not apply in the realisations of (8), (18), (24), (28), (29), where the correct value of the voicing feature is used; in (18), (24) and (28), the rule is optionally applied to the same word.

Rule (6)

$$\underset{(1)}{[+\text{cons}]}\ \underset{(2)}{[+\text{cons}]} \rightarrow \underset{(3)}{[+\text{cons}]} \Big/ \underset{[+\text{stress}]}{\text{V}} \_\_ \underset{[-\text{stress}]}{\text{V}}$$

i.e. a sequence of two consonants in intervocalic position, between a stressed vowel and an unstressed vowel, is realised as a single intervocalic consonant. The formulation of this rule is extremely crude; the features of the output consonant are left unspecified as the characteristics of the single intervocalic consonant described by this structural change rule are specified by Rules (7) and (8). The format of the rule is similar to that of coalescence rules; a rule specifying deletion of one of the two consonants in the intervocalic sequences might have been more satisfactory, but there is no indication in the data as to which consonant should be regarded as undergoing deletion.

e.g. (1), (6), (7), (9), (20), (30).

Rule (7)

$$[+\text{cons}] \rightarrow \begin{bmatrix} +\text{voc} \\ -\text{ant} \\ -\text{cor} \\ +\text{lat} \\ +\text{voice} \\ +\text{high} \\ -\text{back} \end{bmatrix} \Bigg/ \begin{matrix} \text{V} \\ [+\text{stress}] \end{matrix} \_\_ \begin{matrix} \text{V} \\ \begin{bmatrix} -\text{stress} \\ +\text{high} \\ -\text{back} \end{bmatrix} \end{matrix}$$

i.e. an intervocalic consonant is realised as a voiced palatal lateral [ʎ], when followed by an unstressed close front vowel, i.e. [i] or [ɪ]. This rule must obviously follow Rule (6); it must also precede Rule (8), since the following rule has as its output unstressed close front vowels preceded by consonants which do not undergo palatalisation and lateralisation.

e.g. (1), (3), (5), (7), (9), (11), (13), (14), (16), (19), (22), (23), (26), (29).

Rule (8)

$$\begin{bmatrix} +\text{cons} \\ -\text{voc} \end{bmatrix} \begin{bmatrix} +\text{voc} \\ -\text{stress} \end{bmatrix} \rightarrow \begin{bmatrix} +\text{cons} \\ \alpha\text{fea's} \end{bmatrix} \begin{bmatrix} +\text{voc} \\ \beta\text{fea's} \end{bmatrix} \Big/ \begin{bmatrix} +\text{cons} \\ \alpha\text{fea's} \end{bmatrix} \begin{bmatrix} +\text{voc} \\ \beta\text{fea's} \\ +\text{stress} \end{bmatrix} \_\_$$

i.e. this rule ‘copies’ all the features of the consonant and vowel in the first stressed syllable of a disyllabic word on to the consonant and vowel of the second syllable; i.e. the constituent segments of the syllables are reduplicated, (see Chapter Seven). This rule is a perfect example of the use of variables in feature specifications, since they provide the formal notation for showing that the segments are identical. As mentioned above, rule ordering is crucial here, since the output of this rule in the instances of (6), (8), (15), (20), (27) and (28) would meet the structural description of Rule (7); equally, if Rule (8) applied first, (1), (3), (5), (13), (16), (19), (22), (23) and (26) would no longer meet the structural description of Rule (7), as they would be reduplicated forms, for example (1) *[ˈmʊmʊ], (16) *[ˈdɛdɛ].[14] Therefore, to provide an appropriate description of these data, Rule (7) must precede Rule (8).

e.g. (2), (4), (8), (10), (15), (18), (20), (21), (24), (27), (28), (30).

Rule (9)

(9.1) $$\theta \rightarrow \begin{bmatrix} +\text{cons} \\ \alpha\text{fea's} \end{bmatrix} / \ \# - \text{V} \begin{bmatrix} +\text{cons} \\ \alpha\text{fea's} \end{bmatrix} \text{V}$$

i.e. a consonant is inserted before a word-initial vowel; the consonant is identical to the consonant in intervocalic position within the word; once again the use of variables allows one to show that all the features are 'copied' on to the inserted consonant.

e.g. (7), (14), (25).

(9.2) $$\theta \rightarrow \begin{bmatrix} +\text{cons} \\ \alpha\text{fea's} \end{bmatrix} / \ \# \begin{bmatrix} +\text{cons} \\ \alpha\text{fea's} \end{bmatrix} \text{V} - \text{V}$$

i.e. a consonant is inserted between a sequence of two vowels within a word; the consonant is identical to the word-initial consonant.[15]

e.g. (12), (17).

Since these two rules describe the same type of insertion in different contexts, they can be collapsed using braces notation:

$$\theta \rightarrow \begin{bmatrix} +\text{cons} \\ \alpha\text{fea's} \end{bmatrix} \Bigg/ \left\{ \begin{matrix} \# - \text{V} \begin{bmatrix} +\text{cons} \\ \alpha\text{fea's} \end{bmatrix} \text{V} \\ \\ \# \begin{bmatrix} +\text{cons} \\ \alpha\text{fea's} \end{bmatrix} \text{V} - \text{V} \end{matrix} \right\}$$

It should be noted that the patterns in Rosey's speech are

somewhat unusual, though in every instance a similar pattern has been reported by another researcher.[16] Indeed many of her pronunciation patterns are found in the early stages of normal phonological development, especially syllable reduplication (Rule 8), cluster simplification (Rule 2), and final consonant deletion (Rule 1), (see further Chapter Seven). It is the idiosyncratic combination of these patterns with the less common patterns that gives the impression that Rosey's speech is unusual, and indeed as a result of the formalism of the generative rules rather complex. As demonstrated by Spencer (1984), Rosey's speech patterns are essentially very simple indeed; yet they do conform to the universal principles of phonological organisation. They fail, however, to take account of the specific patterns of phonology required to realise the target English pronunciations.[17] In fact the combined output of these nine phonological rules is an extremely rudimentary pronunciation system. As we shall see in the following chapter there is an alternative framework of phonological description which performs essentially the same analytical function as generative rules, but presents the child's pronunciations by comparison with the adult pronunciations in a much more explicit format so that their simplified nature is clearly evident.

REVIEW OF THE CLINICAL APPLICATIONS OF GENERATIVE PHONOLOGY

Several research investigations of children's phonological disorders have adopted the theoretical framework of generative phonology (e.g. Compton 1970, 1975, 1976; Lorentz 1976; Oller 1973; Grunwell (1975) also based a 'phonology of substitutions' on a generative approach; Maxwell (1979) presents a generative analysis only to reject it).

Compton's papers best exemplify the clinical applications of generative phonology. He presents the child's generative phonology as 'an analysis of the underlying principles characterising all of [the child's] misarticulations'. These phonological principles or rules are in fact, as we have seen above, formalised statements of the sound substitution and omission patterns in a child's speech. Furthermore most of the rules in his published studies are independent of each other. For example in Compton (1976) he presents fifteen rules of which only one relates to another rule by optionally providing an input to it. One is therefore left with the impression that these phonological rules are very little different from formalised error analysis statements of substitutions and omissions.

As with all phonological analyses, however, the chief clinical advantage of generative phonology is that the phonological rules describe *patterns* of 'errors'. It is hypothesised that if one manifestation of an 'error pattern' is corrected, the new pronunciation will be correctly generalised to the other segments in the pattern that are included in the structural description of the rule (Compton 1975: 74ff, 1976: 74ff). It must be appreciated that in principle this is a much stronger claim than the generalisation hypothesis proposed in relation to the clinical implications of distinctive feature analysis. In that, where the phonological rules in a generative analysis are seen to be interdependent, which is sometimes found to be so, as we have seen in Rosey's data, then the generalisation, it is claimed, should spread to the segments related to the targeted error through the dependent rules. It is suggested, therefore, that by judicious selection of a pivotal pattern in the set of rules, the clinician can set in train a series of changes in the child's pronunciation system. Grunwell (1975), for example, illustrated a 'chain' of three substitution rules:

$$\left.\begin{array}{l}\text{/f/}\\ \text{/θ/}\end{array}\right\} \rightarrow \left.\begin{array}{l}\text{[ʃ]}\\ \text{/ʃ/}\end{array}\right\} \rightarrow \left.\begin{array}{l}\text{[tʃ]}\\ \text{/tʃ/}\end{array}\right\} \rightarrow \text{[j]}$$

In order to 'break this chain' it was suggested that the first target for remediation should be the anterior fricative /f/ (and hopefully /θ/ would follow in train, most probably as [f]). In spite of the limited amount of rule interdependence in his analyses Compton appears to place considerable emphasis on this implication of generative analysis. He summarises his ideas behind this type of approach as follows:

> The basic assumption underlying the clinical use of phonological analysis is that the elimination of any specific articulatory error effects a change in the principle giving rise to that error. Hence all the other articulatory errors arising from that principle will also be eliminated without having to work directly with them. (1976: 74)

> . . . the analysis itself is not a recipe for therapy. Rather it is more like a map to aid us in choosing the best route to reach a destination. In the process of selecting the specific key sounds to include in therapy we are formulating our working hypotheses of the most effective routes to follow in correcting a child's speech; the effects of therapy upon the child's speech constitute a test of these hypotheses. (ibid.: 87)

Compton's case studies illustrate some examples of generalisation which appear to be the result of therapy based on this type of hypothesis. There are, however, changes in the speech of the children that are not accounted for by the rule-based therapy. In addition he does not provide any control studies to corroborate the claim that the changes were specifically facilitated by the intervention. In any event should rule-based therapy prove to be an effective approach to organising intervention, which is at face value not an unreasonable contention, then the formal complexities of generative phonology are not essential in order to describe the systematic correspondence patterns between the child and adult pronunciations, as we shall see in the following chapter.

Compton–Hutton Phonological Assessment (1978)

The Compton–Hutton Phonological Assessment (Compton & Hutton 1978; henceforward CHPA), is the only formal clinical assessment procedure known to the author which is claimed to be based on generative phonological principles. It consists of an elicitation procedure whereby 50 phonetically balanced words are obtained using a set of pen-and-ink drawings. The words sampled provide a representative set of target English consonants and clusters in word-initial and word-final position. The authors state that they have restricted their sample to mostly monosyllabic words (there are only five disyllabic words), in order to minimise interference from complex phonetic sequences and multisyllabic words. This reveals a very limited view of the phonological organisation of the pronunciation system of the language; at its most basic it excludes the examination of the consonant system within words; but it also excludes investigation of the child's ability to pronounce more complex phonotactic patterns. Another unusual and limiting facet of the elicitation procedure in CHPA is that the child is required to say each word twice in succession; this, according to the authors, is designed to assess the consistency of the child's articulation. Again this reveals a limited view of the potential range and characteristics of consistency and variability in children's pronunciation patterns. For developmental and clinical purposes it is equally if not more relevant to investigate the child's consistency/variability in the realisations of the same target phoneme in different words and positions in words and syllables.

It is not, however, the elicitation procedures that are our main concern here, but the analytical procedures. The first procedure is called a 'pattern analysis' and simply requires the child's realisations to be classified according to the traditional manner of articulation categories. That is, the target consonants are all grouped together into the appropriate manner categories to which they belong: plosives, nasals, 'frictions', affricates, liquids, glides and cluster types; the child's realisations are then entered for each target consonant phoneme included in these categories. This analysis enables the clinician to discern any pattern in the child's realisation of target phonemes belonging to the same target type.

The second type of analysis makes explicit the generative base of the procedure by stating such patterns in terms of 'phonological rules'. It is this aspect of the CHPA that is derived from Compton's studies. The record form details 40 phonological rules: 24 for initial consonants and clusters and 16 for final consonants. All except one describe either the omission of a group of consonants, e.g. $\begin{bmatrix} \mathrm{l} \\ \mathrm{r} \end{bmatrix} \rightarrow \emptyset$ in initial clusters; or a phonemic replacement pattern (a substitution), e.g. $\begin{bmatrix} \mathrm{f} \\ \mathrm{v} \end{bmatrix} \rightarrow \begin{bmatrix} \mathrm{p} \\ \mathrm{b} \end{bmatrix}$ word initially. The exception is the occurrence of unreleased plosives in word-final position; this is an allophonic realisation rule and it is a curious 'error', since it is acceptable in many accents of English.

There is thus a predetermined set of rules describing what Compton & Hutton describe as 'Common Deviant Phonological Rules'. In fact they are all common *normal* phonological patterns in children's speech which occur during the period of normal phonological development; such as cluster reduction, fronting of velars, stopping of fricatives, etc. It is unfortunate that these patterns have been labelled 'deviant' in themselves. It is their persistent use by children over a certain age that is 'deviant'. This is regrettably not explained by the devisers of CHPA.

While the phonological rule framework in CHPA is derived from the generative approach, it is radically different from the type of generative phonological analysis attempted above for Rosey's sample. These predetermined rules are simply statements of common error patterns which the user of the assessment procedure is alerted to look for in the data. None of these rules are interdependent; they are all 'free-standing', though many of them are of course context-sensitive. The fact that the generative approach can be reduced to this type of simplicity in its analytical statements does, however, highlight the basic nature of its application to the analysis of clinical data: it simply provides a systematic and formal description of the relationships between the target pronunciations and the child's mispronunciations. In sum, this is a statement of the error patterns in the child's speech.

EXERCISES

1.1 Write the phonological rules which will describe the following aspects of the pronunciation of English:
   (a) /l, r/ are devoiced after a voiceless plosive in a word-initial cluster before a stressed vowel.
   (b) Alveolar plosives /t, d/ and alveolar nasal /n/ are realised as postalveolar before /ʃ, tʃ, dʒ, (ʒ)/; e.g. *hatshop, red cheese, inch, engine, mention.*
   (c) Alveolar plosives /t, d/ are palatalised before /j/.

1.2 Explain and give examples in transcription of the aspects of English pronunciation described by the following rules:

(a) $[+\text{cons}] \rightarrow [+\text{round}] \;/\; \underline{\quad} \begin{bmatrix} +\text{voc} \\ -\text{cons} \\ +\text{back} \\ +\text{round} \end{bmatrix}$

(b) $$\begin{bmatrix}-\text{cont}\\-\text{voice}\\-\text{strid}\end{bmatrix} \rightarrow [-\text{aspiration}] \Big/ \begin{bmatrix}+\text{cons}\\+\text{cor}\\+\text{ant}\\+\text{cont}\\+\text{strid}\\-\text{voice}\end{bmatrix} \underline{\quad} \underset{[+\text{stress}]}{\text{V}}$$

(c) $$\begin{bmatrix}-\text{cont}\\+\text{ant}\\+\text{cor}\end{bmatrix} \rightarrow [-\text{ant}] \Big/ \underline{\quad} \begin{bmatrix}+\text{voc}\\+\text{cons}\\-\text{ant}\\-\text{lat}\end{bmatrix}$$

2.1 Write the phonological rules which will describe the correspondence between the adult and child pronunciations of /ʃ/ in the following data.

DAVIE 5;8 (1975)

ship [tɪp] *teeshirt* [ˈditɜ]
shoes [tu] *cushion* [ˈtʊtə]
shop [tɒp] *fish* [fɪ]
sugar [ˈtʊtə] *wash* [wɒ]

2.2 Write the phonological rules which will describe the correspondence between the adult and child pronunciations of /tʃ/ and /dʒ/ in the following data (also from Davie).

chip [tɪp] *satchel* [ˈtatʊ]
chocolate [ˈtɒtə] *sergeant* [ˈtɑdən]
jelly [ˈdɛli] *cabbage* [ˈkabɪ]
jar [dɑ] *match* [ma]

2.3 How can these two patterns be described in one rule?

3. Write one rule to describe the two patterns of context-sensitive ‘omissions’ of /l/ in the following data.

ALISON 5;3 (1977)

1. *blue* [bu]
2. *like* [laɪ]
3. *bottle* [ˈbɒtə]
4. *balloon* [bəˈlun]
5. *clock* [kɒk]
6. *apple* [ˈapə]

7. *playing* [ˈpeɪjɪn]
8. *tickle* [ˈtɪkə]
9. *glasses* [ˈgaʔɪ]
10. *lorry* [ˈlɒwi]
11. *castle* [ˈkaʔə]
12. *smiling* [ˈmaɪlɪn]
13. *bubble* [ˈbəbə]
14. *colour* [ˈkələ]

(Note: For this child's accent, the target adult pronunciation of syllable final /l/, especially in potentially syllabic contexts, was a very noticeably velarised (even perhaps pharyngealised) lateral, e.g. *little* [ˈlɪtəɫ].)

4. Write the phonological rules which will describe the correspondences between the adult and child pronunciations of the *word-initial consonants* in the following data. Do you think that any of the rules should apply in a particular sequence? If so, what is the order and why?

PAUL 6;11 (1975)

1. *spoon* [pu]
2. *see* [s̺i, θi]
3. *tent* [tʰɛ]
4. *smell* [fɛ]
5. *school* [tu]
6. *more* [mɔ]
7. *snow* [s̺oʊ]
8. *stove* [toʊ]
9. *car* [tʰɑ]
10. *small* [fɔ]
11. *saw* [s̺ɔ]
12. *paint* [pʰeɪʔ]
13. *snake* [s̺eɪʔ]
14. *spade* [peɪ]
15. *take* [tʰeɪ]
16. *smoke* [foʊ]
17. *pen* [pʰɛ]
18. *sky* [taɪ]
19. *mat* [maʔ]
20. *stir* [tɜ]

5. Write the phonological rule which will describe the correspondence between the child and adult pronunciations in the following data. You will need to use braces notation and variables in the feature specifications and the structural description in order to state the child's pronunciation pattern in one rule.

DEREK 5;1 (1976)

1. *cup* [pʌp]
2. *bed* [bɛd]
3. *gun* [dʌn]
4. *cake* [keɪk]
5. *peg* [pɛb]
6. *tap* [tap]
7. *egg* [ɛg]
8. *neck* [nɛt]
9. *come* [pʌm]
10. *dog* [dɒd]
11. *bat* [bat]
12. *car* [kɑ]

13. *back* [bap]	17. *game* [beɪm]
14. *mug* [mʌb]	18. *cart* [tɑt]
15. *gate* [deɪt]	19. *go* [goʊ]
16. *king* [kɪŋ]	20. *take* [teɪt]

NOTES

1. Lyons (1970) provides a general introduction to the ideas and work of Chomsky. Smith & Wilson (1979) have written the most recent review that goes beyond the introductory level, without engaging in a great deal of detailed theoretical debate.

2. There is almost always some reference to syntactic/semantic categories, since a crucial theoretical claim of generative grammarians and phonologists is that syntactic information is essential in providing an adequate, economical description of phonological structure; e.g. classification into word classes provides the basis for stress-placement patterns in English; see Hyman (1975: 198–203) for a brief summary of the original analysis by Chomsky & Halle (1968).

3. There is one area of clinical linguistics where the relationship between a generative phonological analysis and syntactic structures has been explored. This is in the explanation of agrammatism in Broca's aphasia (Kean 1977, 1979). Kean argues that Broca's aphasia can be accounted for as resulting from a purely phonological deficit arising from the morphophonological characteristics, including stress assignment, of different types of words and affixes in English. This is arguably a much too limited view of the linguistic nature of agrammatic aphasia, as Garman (1982) cogently demonstrates.

4. For further brief details, see Fudge (1970: 93) and Schane (1973: 80). Once again the source text is Chomsky & Halle (1968).

5. This is, of course, exactly analogous to the syntactic component of a 'standard' generative grammar, which contains 'deep structure', 'transformational rules' and 'surface structure'.

6. There have been a few studies in which the child's speech is analysed as an independent system in a generative framework: e.g. Braine (1974); Smith (1973). This is very much a minority approach and is in fact rejected, although not altogether convincingly, by Smith in favour of the popular approach described here (1973: 178–80). For a more detailed discussion of the issues involved see Grunwell (1981b).

7. For a more detailed discussion of this point see Grunwell (1981b).

8. For a clear acknowledgement of this see Smith (1973: 139–43).

9. The sample used here to illustrate metathesis rules has been selected to present a regular, easily analysed pattern. The data are in fact much more complex; see Smith (1973). The vowel transcription has been adjusted to follow the conventions used throughout this book; see Appendix.

10. This principle of analysis is subject to considerable controversy; see Hyman (1975: 125–31); Sommerstein (1977: Chapter Seven).

11. These realisations could also be described by a single rule, analysing the [m̥^{F}] as involving coalescence of the voiceless feature of /s/ and the place and nasality features of /m/; likewise the /n̥^{F}]. This analysis would, however, overlook the generalisation of the rule deleting /s/ before all 'stop' consonants.

12. The same type of rule can be used to describe juxtapositional assimilation in adult speech, such as *that pen* /ðæp pɛn/, *that man* /ðæp mæn/, *that cup* /ðæk kʌp/, *that girl* /ðæk gɜl/.

13. The adult pronunciation of *indian* is taken as /'ɪndʒən/, /'ɪndjən/ or /'ɪndʒɪn/; this last form would best account for Rosey's realisation, as this word is subject to Rule (7). Although words with syllabic laterals are included in the list of examples to which this rule applies (viz. (2), (15), (18), (27) and perhaps also (26), the majority of adult pronunciations which Rosey would hear would involve vocalic laterals, e.g. *bottle* ['bɒtʊ]. This does not affect this analysis, except insofar as these four/five words should be deleted from the list of examples of Rule (1).

14. Following the usual linguistic convention, the asterisk * here, outside the phonetic brackets, indicates an impossible form for Rosey's phonology.

15. The adult pronunciation is taken as *flower* /'fɑʊə/, *fire* /'faɪə/.

16. For further details about this case, see Grunwell & Pletts (1974). The most unusual patterns here are Intervocalic Palatalisation, Rule (7) (cf. Priestly 1977; in fact Rosey's realisations varied phonetically between [l̡, j, ʎ]; the data have been regularised here to enable a simpler rule formulation for pedagogic purposes) and Initial Consonant Insertion, Rule (9) (for further discussion of which see Grunwell 1981b). For discussion of the other patterns here, see Chapter Seven.

17. Spencer (1984) presents a reanalysis of Rosey's data as a set of more succinct generalised generative phonological rules. The account presented above has been designed for pedagogic purposes and makes transparent the phonological changes in Rosey's pronunciation patterns, by comparison with the adult pronunciations, which are described by the rules. The purpose of Spencer's paper is to demonstrate the applications of a different phonological theory to Rosey's data: the theory of autosegmental phonology. Gandour (1981) has also reanalysed a clinical data sample using this theory; the sample here is that of Lorentz (1976). No other researchers to date have adopted this approach, and no routine clinical analysis or assessment procedures have been proposed based on this theory. A discussion of autosegmental phonology as applied to clinical data has not therefore been included in this textbook. Readers interested in the potential clinical applications of this type of phonological analysis are referred to the papers of Gandour (1981) and Spencer (1984).

7

Natural Phonology Applied to the Analysis of Disordered Speech

BASIC CONCEPTS OF NATURAL PHONOLOGY

The concept of 'naturalness' in phonological patterning has already been mentioned in Chapters Five and Six. In Chapter Five the theory of markedness in distinctive feature analysis was introduced as having been specifically developed to explain phonological tendencies in languages. It was also seen to have been invoked in the analysis of disordered speech to account for the most typical substitution patterns. These, it will be recalled, most commonly involve a shift to a less marked feature specification; i.e. a more 'natural' (or 'easier') segment to pronounce. In examining generative phonological rules in the immediately preceding chapter reference was also occasionally made to the fact that the techniques of formal rule statements made explicit the phonetic motivation of the rule (see especially coalescence and assimilative feature changes). The implication of these observations is that the rules reveal the phonetic naturalness of the substitution patterns in these instances.

This theme of naturalness in phonological patterning has come to play an increasingly important role in phonological analysis. The concept of naturalness is used to explain the motivation for the occurrence of phonological patterns. Naturalness is related to phonetic factors, which may be the physiological/articulatory and/or psychological/perceptual characteristics of sounds. As in the theory of markedness, certain sounds are more natural, easier to pronounce/perceive than others. Use of more natural sounds entails use of simpler pronunciation patterns.

The theory of Natural Phonology was originally proposed by

David Stampe (1969, 1979). It has since been taken up by several researchers, most notably David Ingram (1976: *passim*), as a framework for describing child phonologies, both normal and disordered, and disordered adult speech (e.g. Crary & Fokes 1980). It should be noted, however, that from the earliest stages in the elaboration of the theory, Stampe has emphasised its significance as an explanation of the development of phonology.

The theory states that the patterns of speech, that is its phonological organisation, are governed by certain universal phonological processes. It is claimed that there is a universal set of natural phonological processes which are innate. The concept of 'phonological process' is fundamental to the theory and its applications. The original definition of this concept must therefore be the first consideration of this chapter.

> A phonological process merges a potential opposition into that member of the opposition which least tries the restrictions of the human speech capacity. (Stampe 1969: 443, 1979: vii)

> A phonological process is a mental operation that applies in speech to substitute for a class of sounds or sound sequences presenting a common difficulty to the speech capacity of the individual, an alternative class identical but lacking the difficult property. (Stampe 1979: 1)

These definitions are best understood by examining examples of phonological processes. If two different types of sound may occur, they may function contrastively; they are a 'potential phonological opposition': for example, fricatives may contrast with plosives, [s] with [t]. One of the two types of sound may appear to be easier to articulate than the other; this type 'tries the restrictions of the human speech capacity' less than the other: for example, plosives are generally taken to be less difficult to produce than fricatives. It is therefore regarded as a 'natural phonological process' to use plosives instead of fricatives; that is the contrast/opposition is lost/merged by the use of the easier member. Thus, *Stopping* of fricatives to plosives is a well-attested phonological process in child speech (see below).

It will be noted that in the second definition, phonological processes are described as operating on sound sequences as well as classes of sounds. For example, a single sound may contrast with a sequence of two sounds, as in syllable onset [p] *v.* [sp], [t] *v.* [st], [k] *v.* [sk]. A single sound is evidently easier to articulate than a sequence; thus it is a natural phonological process to omit one sound in a sequence of two: this is known as *Cluster Reduction* (see below). Furthermore, given that, in terms of the difficulty of individual sounds, plosives are easier than fricatives, the plosives in the exemplified sequences will be retained and the fricatives deleted, thus merging [p] *v.* [sp] to [p], [t] *v.* [st] to [t], [k] *v.* [sk] to [k].

In these target clusters the fricative is frequently referred to as the 'marked', i.e. less natural, member of the cluster. This highlights the explanation as to why it is the /s/ that is deleted.

Phonological processes do not just operate on the paradigmatic dimension of sound contrasts and the syntagmatic dimension of sound sequences, they may also reflect the interaction between the two, taking into account the effects of context. For example, a sequence of sounds involving two different places of articulation is arguably more difficult to produce than a sequence in which only one place is used; that is a sequence alveolar-V-velar (e.g. [dək]) would be harder to say than a sequence such as velar-V-velar (e.g. [gək]). Thus *Consonant Harmony* (see below) is another phonological process. It would also appear to be easier to produce certain types of sound in one context, and other types in another. For example, voiced (lenis) consonants are apparently more 'natural' in prevocalic position, where they might be interpreted as 'anticipating' the voicing of the vowel, while the postvocalic (and word-final) position is easier for voiceless (fortis) consonants, in anticipation, presumably, of the voicelessness of the potential silence of a pause. Thus, [bɪp] is apparently easier than [bɪb] or [pɪb] or [pɪp]. There is, therefore, a natural phonological process of *Context-Sensitive Voicing* (see below).

Stampe, in formulating the theory, demonstrated its applications to both the historical and developmental aspects of phonology. In their historical evolution, the spoken forms of the languages of the world often appear to have operated with these processes and then to have changed to a more complex pattern in order to sustain efficient communication. Furthermore, sociolinguistic differences, most interestingly differences between more or less 'casual' styles of speaking, can be accounted for in terms of phonological processes.[1]

With regard to clinical phonology, phonological processes have been applied to the analysis of both child and adult disordered speech. These clinical applications have also drawn almost exclusively on the developmental studies of natural phonology. The latter obviously have special relevance for clinical practice, because a large proportion of the clinical population is children with 'delayed speech development' or 'developmental speech disorders'. In this chapter we shall therefore examine in some detail the natural phonological description of children's speech development. In addition to the developmental dimension, it must be remembered that phonological processes *per se* describe the ultimate in phonological simplicity. As a set of phonological hypotheses they provide a simplicity metric with which to measure and evaluate pronunciation patterns. Clinically relevant findings could result therefore from investigating disordered speech for the occurrence of phonological processes.

PHONOLOGICAL DEVELOPMENT FROM THE PERSPECTIVE OF NATURAL PHONOLOGY

Stampe proposes that speech development begins with the child using his 'innate phonological system' to organise his speech output. Being innate, this natural system is universal; that is, all children embark on the development of their pronunciation systems from the same beginnings. Here all the natural phonological processes are operating and speech production has its simplest organisation. In this 'language-innocent state' speech is composed of simple sequences of consonants and vowels: CVCVCV ..., where C is a nasal or lenis plosive, and V is an open vowel; i.e. [mama, baba, nana, dada]. These are of course the utterances that tend to become the child's first words. However, they have usually emerged earlier as frequently recurring vocalisations in a child's babbling. Indeed, there is a considerable amount of research demonstrating the phonetic continuity between babbling and early speech patterns (Oller *et al.* 1976; Locke 1983a).[2] Thus the tendencies predicted by natural phonological processes are found to characterise the phonetic patterns of babbling.

The development of phonology itself is described as a progression from these innate speech patterns to the learned language-specific pronunciation system of the child's language(s). In order to learn the phonological structures and contrasts of his language the child has to revise the universal system in ways particular to his language and thus increase the complexity of his own pronunciation system. These revisions involve suppression of the phonological processes or limitations on their application. 'Suppression' is a relatively straightforward concept, implying that the process disappears and the previously merged oppositions are used contrastively; e.g. fricatives become contrastive with plosives. As an example of a revision which involves a limitation of a process, there are many languages (e.g. German, Russian) which have a contrast between voiced and voiceless consonants in prevocalic position, whereas in postvocalic word-final position only completely voiceless obstruents occur. There is therefore no contrast in word-final position between voiced and voiceless obstruents; in phonemic terms the opposition is neutralised (see Chapter Four). In natural phonological terms there is systematic partial occurrence of the Context-Sensitive Voicing process; thus implying that in children's development of the pronunciation patterns of these languages this process was not completely suppressed, but limited to this context in its application. Eventually the child will have unlearned almost all the natural processes and will have achieved the relatively more complex patterns that constitute the language-specific pronunciation system of his community.

This appears to be a plausible and attractive account of phonological development until one looks more closely at Stampe's views on the 'reality' of the natural processes. As can be seen from his definition given above, Stampe endows the processes with 'psychological reality' since he refers to them as 'mental operations'. He apparently regards them as reflexes of the natural production constraints which restrict the speech mechanism. In his view they are specifically *articulatory* restrictions, which inhibit the child *producing* sound differences he is well able to perceive auditorily. Stampe (like Smith 1973, see Chapter Six), believes that the child's underlying representations of words are the same as the adult phonemic form; i.e. that the child has a perfect, fully developed perceptual phonological system at the very beginning of the development of meaningful speech. This notion has already been seriously questioned in respect of Smith's theory (see Chapter Six). Stoel-Gammon & Dunn (1985: 67) raise similar doubts about the viability of this hypothesis with reference to Stampe's views. They also (following Kiparsky & Menn 1977), point to another inadequacy of Stampe's account of phonological development. He presents a very deterministic picture of developmental phonological change in describing the child's learning as the somewhat passive suppression of the innate processes, rather than the active acquisition of language-specific phonological patterns.

Thus Stampe's view of phonological development is somewhat less than satisfactory. Other researchers, however, have taken the basic concept of Stampe's approach — the phonological process — and proposed less deterministic accounts of phonological development. Ingram, for example as early as 1976 (48–50) describes the processes as operating variously on the child's perceptual abilities, his phonological organisation and his production of speech sounds. This is a very interesting and potentially valuable hypothesis. Unfortunately Ingram does not definitively describe at which level in speech processing each of the phonological processes operates. Furthermore, evidence for the perceptual operation of processes is tenuous.[3]

More recent accounts of phonological development (see Ferguson 1978; Macken & Ferguson 1983; Menyuk, Menn & Silber 1986) accord children an active role in the development of their phonological systems through the formulation of hypotheses, the selection and avoidance of lexical items and phonological forms and the creation of segments and phonological patterns/rules (e.g. see Fey & Gandour 1982). This approach has been called the cognitive theory of phonological development, and as such we shall return to a discussion of this theory in the final chapter. In the present chapter it is important to highlight both the comparison and the compatibility between the natural phonology and the cognitive theory approaches. Natural phonology emphasises, almost to the exclusion of any other factors, the universality of the natural processes. As a consequence natural phonology concentrates upon discovering the common patterns that children learning the same pronunciation system share, and indeed the patterns that occur in child speech cross-linguistically. Cognitive theory, on the other hand, highlights the individual differences in children's phonological learning strategies. However this is not to the exclusion of the possibility of a baseline of common strategies. Indeed the fact that there are apparently universal tendencies is readily acknowledged (Macken & Ferguson op. cit.; see also Stoel-Gammon & Dunn op. cit.: 68–70). Therefore the concept of natural processes continues to be important in the description and explanation of children's phonological development.

PHONOLOGICAL PROCESSES IN CHILD SPEECH

It is evident from the definitions of 'phonological process' that the effect of a process is a simplification of the pronunciation of a phonological unit, either a segment or a combination of segments. Following the descriptive framework adopted throughout this book, the phonological processes operating in children's speech patterns can be classified as effecting simplifications in the structure of phonological units, words or syllables, or simplifications in the system of contrasts.[4] Each process will be illustrated with typical examples; these are not, however, attributed to specific sources (cf. Ingram 1976). Only those processes which are attested in a majority of the studies of pronunciation development in normal children are discussed in detail.

Processes Effecting Structural Simplications

Weak Syllable Deletion. Children often simplify the structure of multisyllabic words by omitting one or more unstressed (weak) syllables. The most 'vulnerable' weak syllables are those before the stressed syllables; these are sometimes called the pretonic syllables.

e.g. *banana* [ˈnɑnə]
pyjamas [ˈdɑməd]
forgot [dɒ]

Unstressed syllables after the stressed syllable may also be deleted.

e.g. *wheelbarrow* [ˈwiba]
telephone [ˈdɛdoʊ]

This process may continue to affect some words, especially pretonic weak syllable deletion, up to the age of 3;6–4;0. Indeed, the adult pronunciations of certain words in informal speech are often subject to weak syllable deletion, for example *banana, pyjamas, potato, television.* It is, therefore, not just a developmental phonological process.

Final Consonant Deletion. Consonants in word-final position are frequently omitted in the earliest stages of speech development, thus resulting in open syllables, the dominant structure in child speech.

e.g. *juice* [du] *cheese* [di]
milk [mɪ] *bed* [bɛ]
spoon [bu] *ball* [bɔ]

The order in which consonants begin to be used in final position has not been definitively described (for a discussion of this issue see Ingram 1976: 30). Most types of consonants are beginning to occur in word-final position by 3;0. Normally the process has completely disappeared by 3;3–3;6.

Vocalisation. This process has an essentially similar effect to Final Consonant Deletion. It is, however, distinguishable from the latter as it affects consonants that may be syllabic in adult pronunciations. In British English this process is only unequivocally attested for syllabic laterals, and even here many adult accents use a vocalic pronunciation for /l/, that is [ʊ], in similar contexts; therefore the simplification is not just developmental.

e.g. *bottle* [ˈbɒtʊ]
apple [ˈapʊ]

The alleged Vocalisation of syllabic nasals, for example *garden* pronounced [ˈdɑdə], is a dubious interpretation of this pattern; it is probably just simply Final Consonant Deletion. Vocalisation of syllabic /r/, for example *flower* [ˈfawa], is alleged for children learning American English; there is no evidence available for children learning rhotic British English accents. The chronology of this process is also not well documented, probably because it is noticed as part of the overall massive simplification of speech patterns in the earliest stages but, although still present, subsequently goes unnoticed as the child's speech becomes more complex in later stages. As is evident from the examples quoted, it does not result in a very different pronunciation from the target.

Reduplication. This involves the well-known child pattern seen in the conventional 'first words' (see above). Reduplication is the repetition of the first syllable, which is usually also the stressed syllable, to constitute the second, and occasionally subsequent, syllable(s) in a multisyllabic word. This repetition may involve the whole syllable, Complete Reduplication, or just one of its constituents, the consonant or vowel, Partial Reduplication.

e.g. *Complete Reduplication*

bottle ['bɒbɒ] *pudding* ['pʊpʊ]
mirror ['mɪmɪ] *umbrella* ['bɛbɛ]
(Note Weak Syllable Deletio

Partial Reduplication

blanket ['babə] *donkey* ['dɒdi]
cabbage ['daba]

Reduplication usually only occurs in children's 'first words'. Indeed, some children do not give evidence of an active reduplication process ('non-reduplicators', see further Schwartz *et al.* 1980). In any event, it is a process which disappears between 2;0 and 2;6 at the latest.

Some children give evidence of reduplicated forms for target monosyllabic words:

cat ['kaka] *ball* ['bɔbɔ]

As these examples indicate, the tendency is for the initial consonant to be repeated as the second consonant in the word which is then followed by the reduplicated vowel. Effectively the final consonant appears to have been deleted and replaced by the reduplicated syllable. It has been found that children who are 'frequent reduplicators' show a stronger tendency to use final consonant deletion (Fee & Ingram 1982; Schwartz & Leonard 1983; Schwartz *et al.* 1980). It has been proposed that the occurrence of reduplicated target monosyllables represents a strategy to facilitate the maintenance of target second consonants (see especially Fee & Ingram op. cit.). This hypothesis, however, was not supported by the data analysed in their study. Nevertheless it is still worthy of consideration as a possible strategy when examining the pronunciation patterns of individual children (e.g. see Lahey, Flax & Schlisselberg 1985).

While the outcomes of both types of the reduplication process are reduplicated forms in the child's pronunciations, it is desirable to have a terminological means of distinguishing the two types. Following Stoel-Gammon & Dunn (1985: 37–8, 41) reduplicated forms of target multisyllabic words can be viewed as evidence of a reduplication process; reduplicated forms of target monosyllabic words can be viewed as evidence of a *doubling* process. Both processes effect a simplification in the structure of the targets in that reduplication reduces the complexity of the consonant and vowel sequences required for the pronunciation of the multisyllabic words, while doubling overwrites the final consonant with a second open syllable which does not add greatly to the sequential complexity of the word as it is a repeat of the first syllable, without its final consonant.

Consonant Harmony. In some children's pronunciations all the consonants in a word may be 'harmonised' so that they all share one or more phonetic characteristics. This process is often called assimilation (e.g. Ingram 1976; Stoel-Gammon & Dunn 1985). Consonant Harmony most commonly involves 'assimilation at a distance' (cf. Chapter Three) and usually affects the place of articulation features. The most frequent pattern is anticipatory (or regressive) harmony to velar consonants. This is called variously 'Velar Harmony' (Smith 1973), 'Back Assimilation' (Ingram 1976), 'Deapicalisation' (Cruttenden 1979), 'Velar Assimilation' (Stoel-Gammon & Dunn 1985). Alveolar consonants are most susceptible to harmony.

e.g.	*dog* [gɒg]	*donkey* ['gɒŋki]
	tiger ['kaɪgə]	*neck* [ŋɛk]

The process effects a structural simplification because, first, it results in a phonetically simpler sequence of consonants, and secondly, the harmonised target consonants are usually found to occur in other contexts. Thus, a child with Velar Harmony of the type exemplified above will probably use alveolar consonants 'correctly' when they do not precede velars: for example *door* [dɔ], *teddy* ['tɛdi], *nut* [nət], *dummy* ['dəmi], *table* [teɪbʊ]. It is therefore evident that the consonants are not actually lacking in the child's system; it is the patterns of structural organisation that govern their occurrence.

Different patterns of Consonant Harmony may also occur in children's speech. For example, alveolar consonants may harmonise to labials; i.e. labial harmony:

e.g. *dummy* ['bəmi] *table* ['peɪbʊ]

Or, velars may harmonise to alveolars and/or labials; i.e. alveolar and/or labial harmony:

e.g.	*cart* [tɑt]	*goat* [doʊt]
	cup [pəp]	*game* [beɪm]
BUT	*car* [kɑ]	*go* [goʊ]

It should also be noted that Consonant Harmony is not always anticipatory; it may be perserverative (or progressive).

e.g. *coat* [koʊk] *again* [gɛŋ]
(Note Weak Syllable Deletion)

Consonant Harmony may also be evidenced as affecting the manner of articulation of consonants. The most frequently attested (though still rather rare), process here is nasal assimilation:

drum	[nʌm]	*pencil*	['mentʊ]
bunny	['mʌni]		

Like Reduplication, Consonant Harmony does not occur in the speech of all young children. Also, it is only evidenced at the beginning of speech development. The speech patterns of a child at 2;0 may contain many examples of Consonant Harmony; by 2;6 harmonisation processes have begun to disappear. Consonant Harmony does not persist in normal children's speech beyond about 3;0.

Cluster Reduction. The structural simplification that is evidenced in almost all children's speech is Cluster Reduction. This involves the deletion of one or more consonants from a target cluster so that only a single consonant occurs at syllable margins. There are different patterns of reduction for the different types of adult clusters in both onsets and terminations. Each type of cluster also shows a different pattern of development. Substantial evidence is currently available for onset (initial) clusters only. The discussion will therefore be confined to the types that occur here (see also examples in Chapter Six).

Obstruent + Approximant Clusters

i.e. Plosive + Approximant: /pr, pl, br, bl,/
/tr, dr,/
/kr, kl, kw, gr, gl/.
Fricative + Approximant: /fr, fl, θr/.

Reduction Process

These are realised by children in the first stages of speech development as the plosive or fricative. The pattern can be stated as:

$$C_1 + C_2 \rightarrow C_1$$

e.g.	*plate* [peɪt]	*frog* [fɒg]
	brick [bɪk]	*flower* [faʊə]
	drum [dəm]	*three* [fi]
	cream [kim]	

Patterns of Development

Clusters of this type begin to be evidenced (i.e. realisations of this type of target as a cluster) in the speech of some children by 2;6–3;0. Clusters are being used by most children by 3;6 and at the latest 4;0. The structural simplification process is therefore suppressed at this point. The clusters will, however, continue to evidence other simplification processes, since when clusters first appear for this target type the approximants are not usually pronounced correctly.

e.g.	*plate* [pjeɪt]	*frog* [fʊɒg]
	brick [bwɪk]	*flower* [fjaʊə]
	drum [dwəm]	*three* [fwi]
	cream [kɰim]	

Occasionally the approximant may influence the pronunciation of the obstruent, so that in the first pronunciations in which clusters are used there is an assimilation process. This may involve changes in the place and/or manner of articulation of the obstruent; plosives are most frequently affected.

e.g. *twins* [ɸwɪnz]
drum [bwəm]
green [bwin]

This type of cluster is usually pronounced correctly by 4;6.

/s/ + Plosive/Nasal Clusters
i.e. /sp, st, sk, sm, sn/.

Reduction Process
These are realised as the plosive/nasal, thus:

$C_1 + C_2 \rightarrow C_2$

e.g.	*spade* [peɪd]	*star* [tɑ]	*sky* [kaɪ]
	smoke [moʊk]	or [m̥ᶠoʊk]	
	snow [noʊ]	or [n̥ᶠoʊ]	

The alternative realisations of /s/ + Nasal clusters shown here exemplify *feature synthesis*, where phonetic characteristics of both constituents of the adult pronunciations are combined in the single segment of the child's realisation, that is the voiceless friction of /s/ and the place of articulation of /m/ in [m̥ᶠ] (see also Chapter Six).

Patterns of Development
Cluster realisations are used by about 3;6, though the child's pronunciation is usually not correct with regard to the fricative. Once again the structural simplification disappears, but systemic simplifications may then emerge.

e.g. *spade* [fpeɪd] *star* [θtɑ]
smoke [m̥ᶠmoʊk]

Here, as before, there may be interaction between the phonetic constituents involving assimilation, usually to the place of articulation of C_2 as shown in the examples above (see also

Chapter Six). This cluster type tends to show slow development of phonetic accuracy, so that between 4;0 and 4;6, although the fricative is an 's' type, it is still not correct by comparison with the adult pronunciation.

e.g. *spade* [s̪peɪd] or [ʂpeɪd]

The correct pronunciation of these clusters will usually have been mastered by most children by 5;0.

/s/ + Approximant Clusters
i.e. /sl, sw/.

Reduction Process
These clusters may be realised according to the *Obstruent + Approximant* reduction pattern:

$C_1 + C_2 \rightarrow C_1$
e.g. *slide* [saɪd]

Or, they may be reduced following the */s/ + Plosive* pattern:

$C_1 + C_2 \rightarrow C_2$
e.g. *slide* [laɪd] *swing* [wɪŋ]

They are also often reduced to a single consonant which shows *feature synthesis*:

e.g. *slide* [l̥aɪd] or [ɬaɪd]
swing [ʍɪŋ] or [fɪŋ]

Here the realisations incorporate the voicelessness, and the friction, of /s/ and the place of /w/ and the laterality of /l/.

Patterns of Development
Development follows that of other /s/ clusters, with a strong tendency for assimilation processes to be evidenced (see also Chapter Six).

e.g. *slide* [l̥laɪd] or [ɬlaɪd]
swing [ɸwɪŋ] or [fwɪŋ]

The chronology is also the same as for other /s/ clusters.

/s/ + Plosive + Approximant Clusters
i.e. /spl, spr, str, skr, skw/.

Reduction Process
These are reduced to a single consonant, usually the plosive, in the child's first realisations:

$$C_1 + C_2 + C_3 \rightarrow C_2$$

e.g. *splash* [pat] *string* [tɪn] *squash* [kɒt]

Patterns of Development
The development of a cluster realisation may involve the appearance of the initial fricative:

e.g. *string* [θtɪŋ]

Or, the approximant may be realised first:

e.g. *string* [twɪŋ]

As with other cluster types the phonetic mastery of the pronunciation of these complex articulatory sequences is gradual, and shows the same types of systemic simplifications of both /s/ and the approximants.

For all types of clusters the emergence of a sequence of consonants or the development of a different pronunciation of one element in a cluster may be preceded by a transition phase in which the sequence is lengthened. This can be regarded as another type of structural simplification process, since it affects the sequencing of the segments. It may involve either lengthening of a segment:

e.g. *plate* [plleɪt] *smoke* [smmoʊk]

or the insertion of a vowel between the two segments:

e.g. *drum* [də'wəm] or later [də'ɹəm]
snow [θə'noʊ] or later [s̪ə'noʊ]

This vowel-insertion pattern is called *epenthesis*; the vowel is called an *Epenthetic vowel* (see also Chapter Six). From the above description of children's developing mastery of the pronunciations of clusters, there is very clear evidence that:

(1) children's speech development is patterned, that is systematic;
(2) children's speech development is gradual.

Processes Effecting Systemic Simplifications

Fronting. One of the most well-attested patterns in early child speech is the realisation of target velar consonants as alveolar;

i.e. /k, g, ŋ/ → [t, d, n].

This is known as a process of Fronting. Occasionally, children use palatal pronunciations for velars:

i.e. /k, g, ŋ/ → [c, ɟ, ɲ].

This can also be termed Fronting. In this pattern, although phonetically velars are 'incorrect' and 'fronted', the use of palatal consonants for velar targets maintains the contrast between target alveolar and velar plosives and nasals. Strictly speaking, this is therefore not a systemic simplification.

Fronting of velars is usually suppressed by 2;6–3;0; velar consonants are established in most children's speech by 3;3 at the latest.

The realisations of palato-alveolar fricatives and affricates /ʃ, ʒ, tʃ, dʒ/ as alveolar consonants, which may be at various times [t, d, ts, dz, s, z] (see further below) is also frequently referred to as involving a Fronting process (Grunwell 1985a) or a Depalatalisation process (e.g. Stoel-Gammon & Dunn 1985).

Stopping. Fricatives and affricates may not be used in the beginning stages of speech development; where target fricatives and affricates occur the most common child pronunciation is to use a *plosive at the same place (or nearest place) of articulation.* This process is called *Stopping*

e.g. *face* [peɪt] *van* [ban]
shoes [dud] *juice* [dut]

i.e. /f/ → [p] /v/ → [b]
/s/, /ʃ/, /ʧ/ → [t] /z/, /ʒ/, /ʤ/ → [d]

The dental fricatives /θ, ð/ may follow either the /f/ or /s/ patterns:

i.e. /θ/ → [p] or → [t]
e.g. *thumb* [pəm] or [təm]
/ð/ → [b] or → [d]
e.g. *feather* [ˈpɛbə] or [ˈpɛdə]

Patterns of Development

Stopping begins to disappear for most fricatives and affricates by 2;6–3;0, but the emergence of correct pronunciations is gradual (see esp. Ingram *et al.* 1980).

Usually [f] is the first fricative used in child speech; indeed it may be present in the 'first words' and some children never 'stop' target /f/. An 's' type fricative may also occur early in the development of speech. This fricative often appears in syllable termination, word-final position first (Ferguson 1978). With the appearance of fricative pronunciations the systemic simplification processes tend to change. Stopping is suppressed and fricative simplifications occur. The most common patterns are:

/θ/ → [f] /ð/ → [v]
/ʃ/ → [s]
/ʧ/ → [ts] /ʤ/ → [dz]
(/ʒ/ is excluded because of its low frequency of occurrence.)

The 'stopped' pronunciations of /v/ → [b] and /ð → [d] may, however, continue for some time. Also labiodental realisations of /θ, ð/ may continue until 6;0 or even later. With these two consonants the locally, or familiarly, acceptable pronunciation must be ascertained as both [f, v] and [t, d] are often acceptable adult pronunciations.

The development of the palato-alveolar fricative /ʃ/ is

usually gradual, involving, after Stopping, systemic simplification of the contrast with /s/, until eventually the full contrastive system emerges:

e.g. /s/ → [t] → [s̪] → [s̪] → [s] → [s]
/ʃ/ → [t] → [s̪] → [ʂ] → [ʃ] → [ʃ]

The pronunciations [ʂ, ʃ], exemplified here, can be designated as a phonetic process of *Palatalisation.* This is quite common in children's speech in 'Almost Mature' realisations of /s, z, ʃ, ʒ, tʃ, dʒ/ (Anthony *et al.* 1971: 43). The development of the palato-alveolar affricates is also gradual; although here, with the suppression of Stopping, the systemic simplification of the contrast with the plosives /t, d/ disappears and the subsequent development of the affricates involves primarily phonetic mastery.

e.g. /ʧ/ → [t] → [ts] → [tʂ] → [tʃ] → [ʧ]

With the emergence of the palato-alveolar pronunciation, however, there is occasionally evidence of confusion between these affricates and the clusters /tr, dr/ which are, in many adult pronunciations, phonetically the affricates [t̠ɹ̥, d̠ɹ].[5] Thus, some children may be heard to say around 4;6–5;0:

e.g. *satchel* ['sat̠ɹ̥əɫ] *petrol* ['pɛʧəɫ]

The palato-alveolar affricates, and the fricative /ʃ/, are usually pronounced correctly by 4;0–5;0.

One final noteworthy pattern that is often evidenced in normal development is that lenis fricatives tend to lag behind homorganic fortis fricatives in the order of emergence of contrasts in children's speech. This is always the case with /ʒ/, undoubtedly the result of the low frequency of occurrence of this fricative. It is also often found, however, that /v/ and even /z/ appear later than the fortis members of the pairs.

Gliding of the Fricatives

The above are the most common patterns in the development of fricatives. A less usual pattern is for target fricatives to be realised as approximants at the beginning of speech development:

e.g. /f/ → [w]
/s/ → [l] or [j]

Or, the Stopping process may disappear and fricatives be realised as approximants before fricative realisations emerge (e.g. Smith 1973).

Gliding of Approximants. The first approximants used in child speech are [w, j]; these are also known as 'glides'. Usually target /l, r/, also known as 'liquids', are realised by [w, j]. This process is called *Gliding.*

Patterns of Development of Approximants
There is much individual variation in the development of the approximant subsystem. Two 'routes' are traced below.

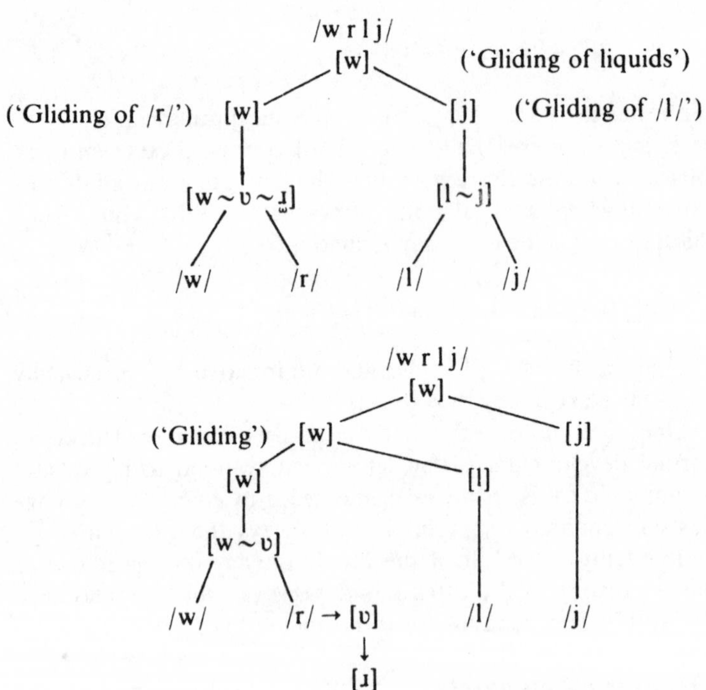

It is difficult to provide age norms for the various 'cross-roads' in these developmental progressions. [w] as the first approximant will be used 'correctly' at 2;0–2;6, but will also be used as the realisation of other approximants. [l] is used 'correctly' by 3;0–3;6, but again may also be the realisation of other approximants, for example /r/ and most notably /j/ in *yellow*. In other words however, [j] is probably 'correctly' used by 3;0, though again this may also be used to realise /r/. The pronunciation of /r/ as [w] is, however, the most common and most well-known child pattern in the development of the approximants; it may be used until 4;0–5;0, and even later in some immature speakers, without being regarded as a major 'speech defect'. /r/ mispronunciations may, of course, continue into adulthood.

Stopping of /l, r/ to [d]. This is a much less common process and pattern of development for the two liquids. The development here tends to follow the route as shown below.

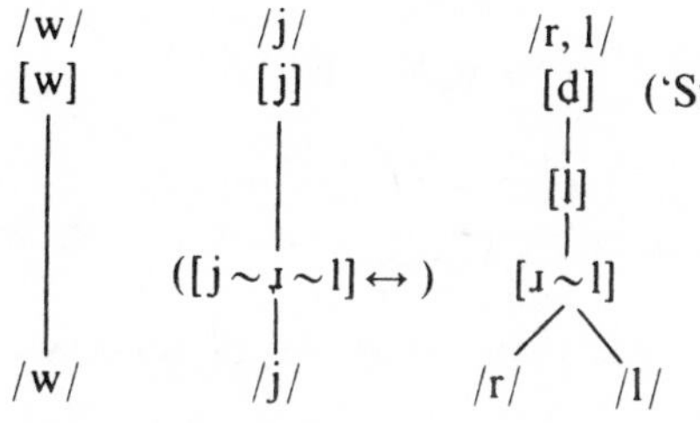

```
/w/          /j/              /r, l/
[w]          [j]              [d]   ('Stopping of liquids')
 |            |                |
 |            |               [l]
 |            |                |
 |     ([j ~ ɹ ~ l] ↔ )      [ɹ ~ l]
 |            |               /  \
/w/          /j/            /r/  /l/
```

Context-Sensitive Voicing. This last systemic simplification process involves a different type of pattern in child speech from those discussed so far. Here both types of target consonants, specifically obstruents, are used in the child's pronunciations, but they cannot function contrastively because they are in complementary distribution (see Chapter Two). The most common pattern is for lenis ('voiced') obstruents to occur only in prevocalic positions (as syllable onsets word-initial and within words), and fortis ('voiceless') obstruents to occur only in postvocalic positions (as terminations word-final). Thus the 'voicing' of obstruents is Context-Sensitive.

e.g.	*party* ['bɑdi]	*cub* [gəp]
	card [gɑt]	*peg* [bɛk]
	ticket ['dɪgɪt]	*pussy* ['bədi]

This type of pattern only occurs at the beginning of speech development. If Final Consonant Deletion is also present at this stage then the evidence for Context-Sensitive Voicing will not be available until final consonants are used. Context-Sensitive Voicing may occur up to about 3;0, although it usually begins to disappear by 2;6. Some children continue to use voiceless, and often fortis, obstruents in word-final position for some time after 3;0 for all types of obstruents; but by this time both fortis and lenis obstruents are used word-initial and within words. Thus, 'voicing;' is no longer wholly context-sensitive. Not all children exhibit context-sensitive voicing patterns. Some use only fortis or only lenis obstruents at the beginning of speech development; others may have both types evidenced even in their 'first words' and apparently use them contrastively from the very beginning. Any simplification of the fortis–lenis contrast can be designated as a *Voicing* process, whether the process is voiceless → voiced, or vice-versa.

CO-OCCURRENCE OF PHONOLOGICAL PROCESSES

As several of the examples quoted above have indicated, the phonological simplifications effected by the processes frequently co-occur in children's realisations of target words. In this section we shall examine some examples of process co-occurrence in more detail.

Two or more processes may co-occur at different places in syllable structure in the child's pronunciation of a word.

black	[bat]	SIWI Cluster Reduction: /bl/
		SFWF Fronting: /k/
cough	[top]	SIWI Fronting: /k/
		SFWF Stopping: /f/
peg	[bɛk]	SIWI Voicing: /p/
		SFWF Devoicing: /g/.

As can be seen from these examples this type of co-occurrence of processes compounds the losses of contrasts entailed by the processes. As a result there are many more potential child homophones (homonyms), i.e. words with the same pronunciation and different meanings.

Two or more processes often co-occur at the same place in structure; i.e. operate on the child's pronunciation of one target segment or cluster, thus simplifying different phonetic properties of the same target.

car	[da]	SIWI Fronting SIWI Voicing	: /k/
chair	[dɛə]	SIWI Stopping SIWI Voicing	: /t/
glue	[du]	SIWI Cluster Reduction SIWI Fronting	: /gl/
sky	[daɪ]	SIWI Cluster Reduction SIWI Fronting SIWI Voicing	: /sk/ : /k/

Of course more often than not both types of co-occurring processes are present in a child's pronunciation patterns.

space	[beɪt]	SIWI Cluster Reduction SIWI Voicing	: /sp/ : /p/
		SFWF Stopping: /s/	
thread	[dɛt]	SIWI Cluster Reduction SIWI Stopping SIWI Voicing	: /r/ : /θ/
		SFWF Devoicing: /d/	
scratch	[dat]	SIWI Cluster Reduction SIWI Fronting SIWI Voicing	: /skr/ : /k/
		SFWF Stopping: /t/	
shreddies	[ˈdwɛdit]	SIWI Stopping SIWI Voicing	: /ʃ/
		SIWI Gliding: /r/	
		SFWF Stopping SFWF Devoicing	: /z/

Very occasionally it appears that processes have to be described as operating in a particular order so as to account for the pronunciation patterns used by a child. For example, if a child pronounces *dark* as [gɑ], then the Velar Consonant Harmony (Assimilation) process has to precede the Final Consonant Deletion process; in the opposite order the /k/, source of the velar harmony, would be removed by the Final Consonant Deletion process before the Consonant Harmony process has operated, and there would be no contextual justification for the occurrence of the [g] pronunciation of /d/. Processes can potentially enter into a number of rather complex ordering relationships which have differential effects on children's abilities to signal phonological contrasts, and thus on the occurrence of homophones. In this overview of phonological process analysis the detailed technical analysis of process co-occurrence and the complexities of the possible ordering relationships need not concern us further here (for a comprehensive examination of these issues see Leinonen-Davies 1987). In the majority of instances of co-occurring processes ordering appears to be neither necessary nor relevant.

CHRONOLOGY OF PHONOLOGICAL PROCESSES

From the preceding description of the common phonological processes and the patterns of development of the target segments and sequences to which they apply, it is evident that there is a chronology of phonological process occurrence and disappearance. Table 7.1 summarises the chronology of the most commonly evidenced phonological processes in children's speech development. Where a process is entered on this chart as a continuous black line across an age band this indicates that almost all children at this age will evidence use of the process. Where a broken line of dashes marks the occurrence of a process this indicates that in the child population as whole at that age an appreciable number of children will not be using the process or will be using it variably. Thus any one individual child is likely to evidence inconsistent use of the process. Where the occurrence of a process is annotated this indicates the likely phonetic form of children's realisations of the target. Thus for target /θ/, Stopping *per se* disappears approximately between 2;6 and 3;0, being replaced not by the correct pronunciation but by [f], a different though extremely common child pronunciation. Thus also with regard to Stopping, this disappears for /ʃ/ between 2;6 and 3;0 as well, being replaced by [s].

Table 7.1 is based on information drawn from a large number of sources providing normative data on children's speech development (see Grunwell 1981a for a detailed discussion of how this table was devised). The validity of the age norms suggested by this table has been supported by an empirical study carried out by Vihman (1984). She studied the phonological patterns of 10 children at age 3;0–3;1 and found that 11 of the 16 processes predicted to occur at that age were present in her subjects at the expected level, i.e. always present or variably

Table 7.1: Chronology of Phonological Processes

	2;0–2;6	2;6–3;0	3;0–3;6	3;6–4;0	4;0–4;6	4;6–5;0	5;0→
Weak Syllable Deletion							
Final Consonant Deletion							
Reduplication							
Consonant Harmony							
Cluster Reduction (Initial) obstruent + approximant							
/s/ + consonant							
Stopping							
/f/							
/v/							
/θ/		/θ/	→[f]				
/ð/				/ð/→	[d] or [v]		
/s/							
/z/							
/ʃ/		Fronting '[s] type'					
/ʧ, ʤ/			Fronting [ts, dz]				
Fronting /k, g, ŋ/							
Gliding /r/→[w]							
Context-Sensitive Voicing							

present. The main discrepancies were as follows: only 2 (out of 10) subjects displayed syllable deletion and only 3 displayed /s/ +consonant cluster reduction. Also Stopping of /z/ did not occur regularly in the data; this might be expected given the dashed line which starts before 3;0 and peters out just after 3;6. Similarly the opposite finding that Gliding of /r/ occurred in more than half the subjects also complies with the interpretation of the dashed line. The finding that one subject was still using

Consonant Harmony at 3;0 would not be predicted by this table. On the whole, however, Vihman's findings provide confirmation of the general picture suggested by this table. Like Vihman we must emphasise that there is much individual variation in the processes and progress of phonological development, and therefore any normative profile of this type must be interpreted flexibly.

The information in Table 7.1 can be combined with Table 4.6, which displays the development of the child's pronunciation system of consonants (see Chapter Four). This results in a Profile of Phonological Development as shown in Table 7.2 (see also Grunwell 1985c: Chapter Five). The right-hand column of this table displays the Chronology of Phonological Processes in a different format. Processes that are almost always present at a particular stage are shown in upper case letters. The gradual disappearance of processes is shown by a change to lower case. Thus when a process is entered in lower case the implication is that either in the child population as a whole an appreciable number of children would not display the process, or in an individual child's speech variable use of the process is likely to be evidenced (i.e. lower case is exactly analogous to the dashed lines on Table 7.1). Optional processes are in parentheses. By combining information from both the left and right sides of this profile one can deduce how a child uses his own pronunciation system, as shown in the left-hand column, to realise the adult pronunciation patterns. That is, by relating the contrasts missing in the child's system to the processes operating one can identify how the child will pronounce any of the target phonemes. Thus, for example, at Stage IV there is neither [tʃ] nor [dʒ] in the child's system; from the phonological process analysis, specifically the entry indicating the use of Stopping, it is evident that the child is likely to use his [t d] to realise target /tʃ dʒ/. This profile can also be used as a Developmental Assessment (see Grunwell op. cit.; and below).

CLINICAL APPLICATION OF PHONOLOGICAL PROCESS ANALYSIS

Since the publication of Ingram's monograph *Phonological Disability in Children* (1976), phonological process analysis has come to occupy a pre-eminent position in the description and

Table 7.2: Profile of Phonological Development

Stage	Consonants		
Stage I (0;9–1;6)	NASAL PLOSIVE FRICATIVE APPROXIMANT LABIAL LINGUAL	*First Words* tend to show: — individual variation in consonants used; — phonetic variability in pronunciations; — all simplifying processes applicable.	
Stage II (1;6–2;0)	m n p b t d w	Reduplication Consonant Harmony FINAL CONSONANT DELETION CLUSTER REDUCTION	FRONTING of velars STOPPING GLIDING /r/ → [w] CONTEXT SENSITIVE VOICING
Stage III (2;0–2;6)	m n (ŋ) p b t d (k g) w h	Final Consonant Deletion CLUSTER REDUCTION	(FRONTING of velars) STOPPING GLIDING /r/ → [w] CONTEXT SENSITIVE VOICING
Stage IV (2;6–3;0)	m n ŋ p b t d k g f s j h w (l)	Final Consonant Deletion CLUSTER REDUCTION	STOPPING /v ð z ʧ ʤ/ /θ/ → [f] FRONTING /ʃ/ → [s] GLIDING /r/ → [w] Context Sensitive Voicing
Stage V (3;0–3;6)		Clusters appear: obs.+ approx. used; /s/ clusters may occur	STOPPING /v ð/ (/z/) /θ/ → [f] FRONTING of /ʧ ʤ ʃ/ GLIDING /r/ → [w]
Stage VI (3;6–4;0) (4;0–4;6)	m ŋ p b t d ʧ ʤ k g f v s z ʃ h w l (r) j	Clusters established: obs.+approx.: approx. 'immature' /s/ clusters: /s/ → FRICATIVE obs. + approx. acceptable /s/ clusters: /s/ → type FRICATIVE	/θ/ → [ŋ] /ð/ → [d] or [v] (PALATALISATION of /ʧ ʤ ʃ/) GLIDING /r/ → [w]
Stage VII (4; 6 <)	m n ŋ p b t d ʧ ʤ k g f v θ ð s z ʃ ʒ h w l r j	(/θ/ → [ŋ]) (/ð/ → [d] or [v]) (/r/ → [w] or [ʋ])	

assessment of disordered child speech. As is evident from the foregoing section, investigating children's disordered pronunciation patterns from the perspective of Natural Phonology provides information which is clinically relevant on two counts. First, a developmental assessment can be made: this will indicate whether a child's 'disordered' speech is extremely delayed or even arrested developmentally, or whether it is developmentally deviant. Secondly given that phonological processes effect simplifications, the identification of the occurrence of processes pinpoints the targets for remediation; that is the analysis identifies the more complex pronunciation patterns that the child has to achieve in order to acquire a more adequate pronunciation system.

This latter interpretation is also applicable when phonological process analysis is employed in the description of adult speech disorders. Relatively few studies have been carried out to date in this area. Those that have been published will be summarised briefly at the end of this section.

PHONOLOGICAL PROCESSES IN CHILDREN'S PHONOLOGICAL DISORDERS

Phonological process analysis of disordered child speech (like generative phonological analysis before it) has firmly established that the children's pronunciation patterns have a systematic relationship to the target adult pronunciation patterns. All studies have found that processes can be easily identified and that there is much that is normal in the processes that are discovered (for detailed reviews see Edwards & Shriberg 1983: 215–51; Grunwell 1981b: Chapters 2 and 4; Ingram 1976: 98–121; Stoel-Gammon & Dunn 1985: Chapter 5). However, differences have been found between normal child speech and disordered child speech. These differences largely relate to the *use* of the processes and can be classified as follows:

Persisting Normal Processes
Chronological Mismatch
Systematic Sound Preference
Unusual/Idiosyncratic Processes
Variable Use of Processes.

In the following sections these characteristics will be illustrated and discussed using examples of pronunciation patterns found in the speech of children with developmental phonological learning disorders.[6]

Persisting Normal Processes

The early simplifying processes are usually evidenced in children's phonological disorders. At least some of the pronunciation patterns are similar to those found in normal development; more often than not there are several normal processes. Because of the children's age, the continuing use of the early processes is indicative of a developmental disorder; hence the occurrence of Persisting Normal Processes is a characteristic of developmental phonological disorders.

In some instances only the earliest simplifying processes are evidenced. This suggests that there has been a precocious stabilisation of the first pronunciation patterns and a virtually complete failure to progress phonologically in language development; that is development is 'arrested'. The following data illustrate this type of disorder.

SARAH 4;3 (1974)

shop, top, pop, chop [bɒp]	*face, case* [deɪt]
cat, grass [dat]	*brush* [dət]
pig [gɪk]	*dress* [dɛt]
cot [dɒt]	*slide* [daɪt]
picture ['dɪdə]	*dougall* ['gugʊ]
stable ['beɪbʊ]	*pussy* ['dʊdi]

Here, there is: Cluster Reduction, e.g. *stable, brush*;
Stopping of Fricatives, e.g. *grass, face*;
Stopping of Affricates, e.g. *chop, picture*;
Anticipatory Consonant Harmony, e.g. all words;
Context-Sensitive Voicing, e.g. all words.

All of these processes are found simultaneously only in the very earliest stages of phonological development (see Tables 7.1 and 7.2).

Chronological Mismatch

It is often found that some of the earliest simplifying processes persist, but co-occur with pronunciation patterns characteristic of later stages in phonological development. Such a situation involves a developmental Chronological Mismatch. The following data samples illustrate this type of disorder.

JOANNE 5;0 (1974)

bridge [bə'wɪʤ̥]	*clouds* [klaʊdz̥]
dresses ['ʤɛs̬ɪz̥]	*flowers* ['flaʊwəz̥]
glove [gə'lʊb̥]	*plunge* [pə'lʊŋʤ̥]
thread [fwɛd]	*trumpet* ['ʧʊmpət]

The pronunciations of these words indicate that the development of clusters and fricatives is almost complete. However, as the following words illustrate, Velar Harmony persists in Joanne's speech.

cat [kak]	*dog* [gɒg]
card [kɑg]	*digging* ['gɪgɪn]
cart [kɑk]	*donkey* ['gɒŋki]
string [kɪŋg]	*swing* [kwɪŋg]
middle ['mɪgʊɫ]	*needle* ['nigʊ]

In the last two words the target /d/ is apparently harmonised to the velarised lateral (cf. Smith 1973: 14). The process of Velar Harmony normally only occurs in the earliest stages of speech development, simultaneous with Cluster Reduction and Stopping of Fricatives and Affricates. There is, therefore, a clear instance of Chronological Mismatch here, with regard to the developmental status of the different pronunciation patterns used by the child.

DAVID 5;7 (1975)

flower ['baʊwə]	*shop* [dɒp]
fence [dɛnt]	*sun* [dʊn]
chip [tɪp]	*jelly* ['dɛli]

These words give evidence of a process of Stopping of Fricatives and Affricates, which occurred throughout David's speech; there was no systematic or contrastive use of any fricative phones. At the same time, however, there were an appreciable number of pronunciations which showed that initial consonant clusters were developing; most involved an epenthetic vowel, as the following examples illustrate.

blue [bə'lu]	*clean* [kwin]
crown [kwaʊ̃]	*dress* [tə'wɛ]
grapes [də'weɪp]	*trousers* [tə'waʊwə]

This is not the normal order of emergence of these pronunciation patterns; some fricatives are established and used contrastively before clusters appear in most children's speech. Thus, here again there is a clear example of Chronological Mismatch.

Systematic Sound Preference

From the discussion of the characteristics of normal phonological processes in preceding sections of this chapter it is evident that the results of the operation of several processes are in fact the same type of segment. For example:

Stopping	/s/ /ʃ/ /tʃ/	[t]
Fronting	/k/	[t]
Cluster Reduction	/st/ /tr/	[t]

If all these processes are evident in a child's pronunciation patterns they can be said to operate in a 'conspiracy', i.e. conspiring toward the same resultant sound. This type of patterning is normal in the speech of very young children at the earliest stages of phonological development when the child's pronunciation patterns are phonetically and phonologically very simple in nature.

With older children who are adjudged to have developmental phonological disorders a different type of process 'conspiracy' has been quite frequently observed in their pronunciation patterns. This involves the combination of common normal processes with less common or unusual/idiosyncratic processes which conspire to simplify a wide range of different sound types to a single phonetic realisation. For example, from the data sample of Martin's speech (see Chapter Four) it is evident that all fortis initial fricatives that is /f θ s ʃ/ and the affricates /tʃ dʒ tr dr/ are realised as [f]. This pattern is of course normal for targets /f θ/ but unusual/idiosyncratic for the other targets. Another example of a similar type of process is seen in Clive's speech (see Chapter Two) where a very wide range of different targets in word-initial position are realised by [h]; these include /s ʃ tʃ br fr θr sw/. This process is even more remarkable given the occurrence of almost acceptable realisations of word-final consonants. Cruttenden's subject (1972: 32) exhibited a pattern similar to Martin's and Clive's, realising word-initial /s f fl h t d k dʒ/ as [s]. These combinations of processes could be interpreted as conspiring towards the use of the child's *favourite articulation*; i.e. that the child shows a *systematic sound preference.*

Weiner (1981) discussed this type of patterning in detail, illustrating patterns of systematic sound preference in eight children. These subjects exhibited patterns of an essentially similar type to those illustrated above. For example one child's preference was to use [h] for all initial fricatives and plosives (cf. Clive); another child used [θ] for all initial voiceless fricatives and affricates and some liquids and glides (cf. Martin). Weiner observes that systematic sound preference tends to operate primarily on fricatives and is frequently limited to word-initial position. He suggests that it might be viewed differently from other simplifying processes which operate on homogeneous classes of sounds changing one feature, e.g. stopping of fricatives. In contrast to these, systematic sound preference appears to be a 'collapsing process' whereby a large group of target sound types are realised in a child's speech by a single sound segment type. This interpretation points up the difference between the normal developmental phonological processes which conform to Stampe's original definitions of natural simplifying processes and the massive reduction in contrasts resulting from the use of sound preferences. However, it does not take account of the fact that conspiracies also occur in the early stages of normal development, and that within a systematic sound preference process there are patterns that are developmentally normal.

A different interpretation of systematic sound preference can be put forward which takes account of these observations. Systematic sound preference is the patterning that results from a conspiracy of normal persisting processes and unusual/ idiosyncratic processes, and has as its consequence a massive reduction in the child's ability to signal phonological contrasts; i.e. it entails a major simplification in the child's pronunciation patterns by comparison with the target. This interpretation has the attraction of aligning systematic sound preference with the other characteristic patterns of developmental phonological disorders; viz.: persisting normal processes and unusual/ idiosyncratic processes (to be described below; it should be noted that Stoel-Gammon & Dunn (1985) classify Sound Preference as an Idiosyncratic Process (op. cit.: 117)).

The following data illustrate another unusual process which is also similar to those involving systematic sound preferences:

PAMELA 7;2 (1975)
bus [bəs̡]   *soup* [d̡up]
dish [dɪʃ]   *ship* [d̡ɪp]
match [maʔʃ]   *chip* [d̡ɪp]

Here it is evident that Pamela 'stops' fricatives and affricates in word-initial onsets, but not in word-final terminations. In the following two words there is evidence that fricatives have 'preferred occurrence' in terminations:

shed [dɛʔʃ]   *slide* [daɪʃ]

These exemplify Ingram's process of 'fricative preference' (1976: 116-17) whereby fricatives are retained, but often metathesised (or 'transposed'). However, the use of fricatives in terminations is not necessarily determined by the characteristics of the target in Pamela's speech patterns, as the following words illustrate:

bike [baɪʔs̡]   *gate* [deɪs̡]   *kite* [daɪs̡]

The occurrence of fricatives in terminations is thus probably a context-conditioned sound preference (or favourite articulation).

Karen shows a similar pattern to Pamela in regard to fricative preference in word-final position while at the same time giving evidence of a systematic sound preference process conspiracy in word-initial position.

KAREN 4;4 (1985)

bed	[dɛs]	*jug*	[dʌs]
catch	[dats]	*pig*	[dɪs]
dress	[dɛs]	*roof*	[dus]
fish	[dɪs]	*shoe*	[du]
glass	[das]	*teeth*	[dis]
chair	[dɛə]	*vest*	[dɛs]

Thus in word-initial position /p b t d tʃ dʒ k g f v s ʃ/ and clusters including these targets are realised as [d]; while in word-final position /d g f θ s ʃ/ (and /b v/ as well; not illustrated in this sample), are realised as [s]. As can be readily appreciated both these patterns entail a massive destruction of phonological contrasts. Both also involve the combination in a conspiracy of both normal and unusual processes (cf. Leonard & Brown 1984 whose subject, like Pamela and Karen, showed a preference for [s] in word-final position).

Unusual/Idiosyncratic Processes

As has been indicated in the discussion of systematic sound preference, processes have been observed in the pronunciation patterns of children with developmental phonological disorders which have been described as 'unusual' or 'idiosyncratic'. It is, however, advisable to adopt a rather cautious interpretation of what is alleged to be 'normal' and even more what is designated to be 'abnormal' in phonological development. Since the end of the 1960s there has been a sustained programme of research into phonological development in children supposed to be developing normal pronunciation patterns along normal lines. While many studies have highlighted the common patterns in children's speech, and indeed in the speech of children learning different languages (e.g. Ingram 1976; Locke 1983); almost as many others have emphasised the individual variation that is observed in children's production patterns and apparent learning strategies (e.g. Menyuk, Menn & Silber 1986; Stoel-Gammon & Cooper 1984). Accepting that both common (or universal) and individualistic trends can be observed in children's phonologies, several researchers have attempted to account for both in proposing explanations which describe the learning mechanisms which might underlie such patterning (e.g. Macken 1986).

In describing children's phonological disorders similar trends have also occurred. The processes described in the earlier section on phonological development are those which can be designated as 'normal' with a fair degree of certainty, as these are the most common processes reported in 'normal' child phonologies. It is suggested at certain points in that section that some processes, for example Gliding of fricatives or Stopping of liquids, are less common in normal child speech. There are other processes which occur less commonly in normal child speech; for example the reduction of Obstruent+Approximant clusters to the approximant rather than the obstruent (e.g. *green* [win]; *tree* [wi]); the Frication of approximants (e.g. *lock* [ðɒk]; *walk* [vɔk]). These can be called Unusual Processes. They have been frequently noted in disordered child phonologies; for example Simon (at 4;7 see Chapter Four) gives evidence of both Gliding of fricatives and an unusual cluster reduction pattern; Darren (see Chapter Two) shows, amongst other very unusual patterns (see further below), Frication of approximants.

It is sometimes found that processes are described as occurring in disordered child phonologies which have not as yet been reported as occurring in normal speech development. These are therefore not just uncommon or unusual patterns; they could be called Idiosyncratic Processes.

However, in the author's experience, more often than not an analogous process can be found in apparently normal speech development which throws into question this designation; compare, for example, Priestly (1977) with the pattern in Paul's data quoted below for within-word consonants (see also Rosey's sample in Chapter Six). The distinction between Unusual and Idiosyncratic Processes is therefore necessarily tentative.

The following data samples exemplify the type of pronunciation patterns that can be regarded as unusual and are perhaps idiosyncratic. It must be emphasised that in the speech of all the children quoted here there were also many processes that were normal (for further details see Grunwell 1981b). Several of the data samples in preceding chapters have been taken from the same children; indeed in many instances these pronunciation patterns have already been used to illustrate the applications of other analytical concepts.

DARREN 6;3 (1975)

Consonant–Vowel Harmony

In this process the place of articulation of the preceding consonant, labial/labiodental *v.* dental, is determined by the quality of the following vowel: dental consonants only occur before /i, ɪ, ɛ, eɪ, ɛə/.

e.g. *seat*, *feet* [θit] *four*, *saw* [fɔ, ɸɔ]
shake [θeɪk] *shop* [fɒp]
(for further examples, see Chapter Two; Grunwell 1981b; cf. Camarata & Gandour 1984)

PAUL 6;11 (1975)

/s/ + Nasal Cluster Reduction

In this Cluster Reduction process, contrary to the usual pattern, the nasal is omitted and the fricative retained in Paul's pronunciations. There is, furthermore, *feature synthesis* in the [f] realisations of /sm/ clusters.

e.g. *smack* [faʔ] *snail* [s̬ɛʊ]
smaller [ˈfɔɹə] *snake* [s̬eɪʔ]
smelly [ˈfɛji] *snow* [s̬oʊ]

Glottal Stop Realisations of Within-word Consonants

In many instances the pronunciation patterns of children with speech disorders involve Glottal Stop Realisations of many, often the majority of, different consonant types within words. This constitutes an extreme simplification of both the structural patterns and systemic contrasts at this place in structure.

Darren's speech illustrates this pattern; though here both [h] and [ʔh] occur as well as [ʔ], for all consonant targets.

DARREN 6;3 (1975)

rabbit ['waʔɪʔ]	*scissors* ['θɪʔəɬ]
pirate ['paʔəʔ]	*blowing* ['boʊʔɪ, boʊhɪ]
finger ['θɪhə]	*shopping* ['fɒhɪŋ]
painting ['deɪʔhɪ]	*bottle* ['bɒʔhə]

A similar type of pattern involving the simplification of all within-word consonants is evidenced in Paul's data. Here, the glottal stop is usually followed by an apical fricative, most often dental. This fricative could be called a *favourite articulation*, in Paul's speech; he appeared to use this pattern to avoid less practised, more complex articulatory sequences (cf. Ingram 1976: 117).

PAUL 6;11 (1975)

candle ['taʔs̪ʊ]	*chocolate* ['tɒʔs̪ə]
donkey ['tɒʔθi]	*window* ['wɪʔθə]
water ['wɔʔsə]	*pussy* ['pʊʔsi]

These within-word glottal stop realisations are also similar to systematic sound preference in that they entail a massive destruction of the child's potential to signal phonological contrasts.

It should be noted that Paul's pattern for within-word consonants involves in many instances an addition. Other types of patterns have also been observed that involve additions. For example, Darren inserted a consonant before a vowel in word-initial position:

eye [βaə] *owl* ['wahə]

This is called *initial consonant adjunction.*

Tanya (see Chapter Two) also evidenced a pattern that appeared to involve an addition. In her speech the approximants in Plosive+Approximant clusters are realised as laterals, which may suggest a favourite articulation. This interpretation is supported by the observation that Tanya 'creates' clusters in word-initial position by metathesis of a word-final lateral (though it often remains in the word-final position in its vocalic form):

bell [plɛʊ] *bottle* [ˈplɒʔtʊ]
girl [tlɜ].

Leonard (1985) provides an interesting overview of the characteristics of unusual processes in disordered child phonologies, by classifying them into three types with several subcategories in each type. His three types are:

salient but unusual sound changes with readily detectable systematicity;

salient but unusual sound changes with less readily detectable systematicity;

subtle behaviours.

This last type is somewhat beyond the scope of our discussion here as it is mainly concerned with imperceptible differences in children's pronunciations which are detectable using acoustic analysis such as sound spectrography. The systematic occurrence of such behaviours indicates that the child is signalling a contrast and thus has the phonological knowledge of that contrast, but has not yet mastered the mature phonetic encoding of the contrast. As well as this type of subtle behaviour, Leonard also includes in this category *avoidance*, which he suggests is a subtle behaviour since it is only detectable by considering what the child does not say. It has been observed that young normal and older phonologically disordered children may not attempt to say certain types of words, probably because they present the child with certain pronunciation difficulties. As will be appreciated, while these subtle behaviours do not strictly speaking fall within the purview of the clinical applications of natural phonological analysis as presented in this chapter, they are nevertheless closely related to the basic premises of natural phonological theory.

The other two types of unusual sound changes that Leonard proposes are directly relevant to the foregoing outline of unusual/idiosyncratic processes. In his first type — unusual changes with readily detectable systematicity — Leonard includes:

early sounds replaced by late sounds; as an example he gives fricative preference. It should be noted that this is different from chronological mismatch which involves precocious development of one aspect of the target system. In the instance of early sound replaced by late sound there is an unusual error pattern;

e.g. /t/ → [ʃ]; /f/ → [θ];

additions to adult target forms, such as initial consonant adjunction (see above);

the use of sounds not in the model language, such as ingressive fricatives; Darren frequently used an ingressive voiceless alveolar lateral fricative in word-final position (see Grunwell 1981b):

e.g. *dish* [dɪɬ] *bus* [bʊɬ]

the use of sounds absent from natural languages; for example Edwards & Bernhardt (1973) describe a child who used an ingressive nasal snort.

In his second type of unusual sound changes — those with less readily detectable systematicity — Leonard includes the context-based sound changes such as consonant–vowel harmony, which has been illustrated in Darren's samples. One could also include *metathesis*, such as some of the examples of Pamela's fricative preference, and Tanya's cluster creation, and *dissimilation*, such as the pronunciation of *pipe* as [paɪk] (see further examples in Grunwell 1981b: 124). Leonard's discussion of the implications of these unusual phonological behaviours focuses mainly on how such patterns can contribute to our understanding of phonological learning and phonological disorders. This issue is taken up in some detail in the following and final chapter, and therefore we shall postpone our examination of Leonard's points until then. However Leonard also emphasises the implications of such behaviours for clinical analysis and assessment, indicating the importance of a large speech sample and the need to carry out detailed analysis of that sample looking for consistency of sound changes (i.e. systematic relationships to the adult target), across different contexts, and the importance of searching for contextual factors that may account for certain types of sound changes. These are crucial points that must be borne in mind when undertaking any phonological analysis and assessment.

Without entering into any detail at this stage (see Chapter Seven) it is evident that the occurrence of unusual/idiosyncratic processes in disordered child speech provides further support for the theory of phonological development which credits the child with an active and creative role in the learning of his pronunciation patterns. Thus once again children with developmental phonological disorders can be seen to be very similar to children exhibiting normal developmental behaviours, except that in the disordered population their phonological patterns apparently are in certain dimensions somewhat different, or in some instances deviant from the norm.

Variable Use of Processes

Variable use of phonological processes has often been proposed as a characteristic of disordered children's pronunciation patterns (see especially Grunwell 1981b; Stoel-Gammon & Dunn 1985: 119-20). The variability has been observed to take different forms:

— variability between the presence *v.* absence of a process i.e. variably correct and incorrect pronunciations:

/k/	*car*	[ta] i.e. Fronting
	cow	[kaʊ]

— variability between two different processes, i.e. variably incorrect pronunciations:

/k/	*mack*	[mat] i.e. Fronting
	back	[ba] i.e. Final Consonant Deletion.

It is also important to consider whether the variability occurs in pronunciations of the same word or in different words, and the amount of variability that is present. Very often in the speech of children with phonological disorders there is extreme variability with several different sounds being used for the same target type and occasionally in pronunciations of the same word; for example Joanne pronounced *some* as [sʊm; s̺ʊm; tʃʊm; tʊm] (see Grunwell 1981b: 153–5).

As we have already seen in Chapter Four, the occurrence of

variability may be a prognostically positive indicator of incipient developments in the child's pronunciation patterns.

OTHER EVALUATIVE FACTORS

Phonological process analysis has also been used as a basis for other approaches to the evaluation of the speech of children with developmental phonological disorders. For example Norris & Harden (1981) compared the phonological processes occurring in the pronunciation patterns of children rated as having a high error rate with those with a lower error rate. Their findings indicated that there were no processes unique to children with high error rates, but that these children either used more processes in *unusual* ways or overused a few processes, especially deletion processes. These findings conform to the characteristic patterns outlined above; the first observation being predicted from the occurrence of unusual/idiosyncratic processes, the second from the characteristics of persisting normal processes and systematic sound preference.

Hodson & Paden (1981) address a similar question from a slightly different standpoint. They analysed the phonological processes in the speech of unintelligible children (i.e. children with developmental phonological disorders) by comparison with those used in the speech of normal intelligible children at age 4;0. They found that the unintelligible children's speech evidenced one or more of the following processes: final consonant deletion; fronting; backing; weak syllable deletion; prevocalic voicing; glottal replacement. The intelligible children rarely gave evidence of these patterns, but used postvocalic voicing, fricative simplifications of /θ; ð/ (i.e. realisations as either [f;v] or [s;z] and vocalisation. Once again these findings are predictable from the characteristics already described; their intelligible children evidenced the patterns of maturing phonologies, while their unintelligible children evidenced persisting normal early processes and some unusual processes.

PHONOLOGICAL PROCESSES IN OTHER SPEECH DISORDERS

As was indicated earlier, phonological process analysis has

achieved a pre-eminent position as the most common analytical procedure employed in the investigation of children's developmental phonological disorders. Given this position it is rather surprising to find that there are relatively few studies employing phonological processes in the analysis of other types of speech disorders. The most prolific area is the study of the pronunciation patterns of mentally retarded children and Down's syndrome children (Prater 1982; Stoel-Gammon 1980; Mackay & Hodson 1982; Smith & Stoel-Gammon 1983; Bleile 1982; Bleile & Schwartz 1984). All of these studies consistently point to the normality of the phonological processes observed. Indeed unlike the studies of developmental phonological disorders no salient qualitatively different characteristics appear to emerge from these studies.

There have been two published reports applying phonological processes in the analysis of acquired speech disorders (Klich *et al.* 1979; Crary & Fokes 1980) and one important unpublished report (see Edwards & Shriberg. 1983: 263–7). These studies were primarily directed towards demonstrating the feasibility of applying this analytical approach to this type of disordered speech. In this regard they are successful. Using the process analysis the systematicity of many of the pronunciation errors in the disordered speech is revealed, as is also the tendency of these patterns to lead to a systematic reduction in the complexity of speech produced. It must be noted, however, that in analysing acquired apraxia of speech both Crary & Fokes and Klich *et al.* only examine phonemic substitutions, and that therefore the less regular and indeed more complex error productions may have been overlooked (see further Chapter Eight below). Edwards (as reported in Edwards & Shriberg) specifically highlights the occurrence of 'unnatural processes', such as the production of affricates for fricatives, of clusters for singleton targets and of metatheses. However she found that over half the processes were indeed natural processes essentially similar to those found in phonological development.

CLINICAL IMPLICATIONS OF PHONOLOGICAL PROCESSES IN DISORDERED SPEECH

As has already been indicated in several comments in the preceding discussion, very clear implications have been drawn from the applications of phonological process analysis to disordered speech. The occurrence of phonological processes has been taken as indicative of simplified speech production patterns. Very often this interpretation strictly adheres to Stampe's original conception of phonological processes. For example: Weiner (1984) defines phonological processes as 'mental substitutions which unconsciously adapt phonologic intentions to phonetic capabilities', and observes that 'Because of the orderliness of sound errors in these children, researchers have inferred mentalistic rules must govern surface level sound production' (op. cit.: 75). Similarly Shriberg & Kwiatkowski (1980) describe natural processes as 'sound changes' that involve 'phoneme deletions and phonemic substitutions (replacements)' and which are in effect simplifications of underlying forms. Such descriptive explanations emphasise two aspects of process analysis: firstly that processes describe error patterns; secondly that processes explain these error patterns as simplifications in productions. Thus the treatment implications can also be very simply and clearly stated as requiring suppression of the processes in order to increase the complexity of the person's pronunciation patterns. One might be forgiven for wondering how much progress has been made beyond traditional error classifications. We are now able to highlight the systematicity and simplicity of the disordered pronunciation patterns, and thus in therapy to target these patterns systematically rather than targeting individual phonemes, but these limited and limiting explanations of phonological processes do not take us much further (Hodson & Paden 1983).

This is an underestimate of the impact of natural phonology on clinical phonology. As we have seen in the preceding discussion, the detailed analyses and investigations that have been carried out, and are in progress, to discover the nature of disordered phonologies, were largely initiated by the concepts of natural phonology. As we shall see in the next chapter, clinical phonology is already beginning to address the critical question posed by Locke in 1983(b).

> At times we have said or been told that children do such-and-such because this 'simplifies' the adult system. But is this the child's reason for doing something, or is it — in the opinion of the observer — the effect of the child's behaviour?' (op. cit.: 341)

REVIEW OF CLINICAL ASSESSMENT PROCEDURES

There are currently five major clinical assessment procedures which are based on phonological process analysis. These are:

Phonological Process Analysis (PPA; Weiner 1979)
Natural Process Analysis (NPA; Shriberg & Kwiatkowski 1980)
Assessment of Phonological Processes (APP; Hodson 1980)
Procedures for the Phonological Analysis of Children's Language (PPACL; Ingram 1981)
Phonological Assessment of Child Speech (PACS; Grunwell 1985c).

All five procedures employ different sets of phonological processes (see Table 7.3). However, as is evident from this table, although the names and the level of detailed classification vary in each procedure, all five provide a framework of analysis based on the processes outlined in the preceding section of this chapter discussing children's phonological development. In addition four of the five (the exception being NPA) include some unusual processes which have typically been reported as frequently occurring in the speech of children with developmental phonological disorders; for example glottal replacement (PPA, APP, PACS), denasalisation (PPA, PPACL). As has been indicated above the classification of the processes in PPA, APP and PPACL differs from that put forward in this chapter (and in PACS). Both PPA and PPACL operate with three basic types of processes, following Ingram (1976):

Syllable Structure Processes
Substitution Processes
Assimilation Processes

APP does not identify processes according to their structural or systemic implications; both the categories of Basic Processes and Miscellaneous Processes include both structural and systemic simplifications. APP, unlike the other four procedures, also includes 'Articulatory Shifts' which except for substitutions involving [f v s z] for /θ ð/ do not have phonological implications.

Given that phonological process analysis of child speech in a clinical context is derived from and an extension of the applications of this approach to normal child speech (see Ingram 1976) one would reasonably expect that these clinical procedures would provide a developmental assessment of the child speech data analysed using the procedure. There is, however, only one procedure, PACS, in which the phonological analysis leads directly to a developmental assessment profile. Shriberg & Kwiatkowski and Ingram include descriptions and discussion of normal developmental patterns in their manuals, but do not put forward a formal assessment procedure. Only Ingram and Grunwell discuss the characteristics of disordered use of phonological processes, though Shriberg & Kwiatkowski and Hodson, provide detailed case studies which are illustrative of disordered phonology.

With regard to the type of sample analysed: NPA, PPACL and PACS are intended for use with spontaneous speech samples. PPA is based on the presentation of line drawings which elicit 136 words testing for the occurrence of the processes examined. APP also uses a prescribed set of words: 20 in a screening version and 55 in the full version. In spite of these various differences in detail these five clinical procedures are essentially very similar, and would be expected to provide convergent results when employed to assess a child's speech. This point has in fact been demonstrated in respect of NPA, APP and PPACL (Paden & Moss 1985) and for selected processes only on APP and PPACL (Benjamin & Greenwood 1983).

PHONOLOGICAL PROCESS ANALYSIS (1979)

Weiner's approach to PPA involves a carefully designed elicitation procedure which tests for the occurrence of each process in a set of four to eight words illustrated by line drawings. The child's response to each picture is also carefully controlled: the examiner elicits a delayed imitation of the intended word and attempts also to elicit a sentence recall response by asking the child to repeat the examiner's description of the picture. There are 136 pictures so this is therefore an extremely lengthy procedure. Weiner optimistically estimates that a skilled examiner with a co-operative child would be able to complete the elicitation task in 45 minutes. This elicitation technique, and the demands it puts upon the child's memory and attention skills,

Table 7.3: Clinical Assessment Procedures Using Phonological Process Analysis

Weiner (1979)	Shriberg & Kwiatkowski (1980)	Hodson (1980)
Syllable Structure Process		Basic Phonological Processes
Deletion of final consonant	1. Final Consonant Deletion	Syllable reduction
Cluster Reductions:		Cluster reduction
Initial stop + liquid	2. Velar Fronting:	Prevocalic obstruent singleton omissions
Initial fricative + liquid	Initial	Postvocalic obstruent singleton omissions
Initial /s/ clusters	Final	Strident deletion
Final /s/ + Stop	3. Stopping:	Velar deviations
Final liquid + stop	Initial	
Final nasal + stop	Final	Miscellaneous Phonological Processes
Weak Syllable Deletion	4. Palatal Fronting:	
Glottal Replacement	Initial	Prevocalic voicing
	Final	Postvocalic devoicing
Harmony Processes		Glottal replacement
	5. Liquid Simplification:	Backing
Labial assimilation	Initial	Stopping
Alveolar assimilation	Final	Affrication
Velar assimilation		Deaffrication
Prevocalic voicing	6. Assimilation:	Palatalisation
Final consonant devoicing	Progressive	Depalatalisation
	Regressive	Coalescence
Feature Contrast Processes	7. Cluster Reduction:	Epenthesis
	Initial	Metathesis
	Final	
Stopping	8. Unstressed Syllable Deletion	Sonorant Deviations
Gliding of fricatives		Liquid /l/
Affrication		Liquid /r ɚ/
Fronting		Nasals
Denasalisation		Glides
Gliding of liquids		Vowels
Vocalisation		
		Assimilations
		Nasal
		Velar
		Labial
		Alveolar
		Articulatory Shifts
		Substitutions of /fvsz/ for /θð/
		Frontal lisp
		Dentalisation of /tdnl/
		Lateralisation

Ingram (1981)

Deletion of Final Consonants

1. Nasals
2. Voiced stops
3. Voiceless stops
4. Voiced fricatives
5. Voiceless fricatives

Reduction of Consonant Clusters

6. Liquids
7. Nasals
8. /s/ clusters

Syllable deletion and Reduplication

9. Reduction of disyllables
10. Unstressed syllable deletion
11. Reduplication

Fronting

12. of palatals
13. of velars

Stopping

14. of initial voiceless fricatives
15. of initial voiced fricatives
16. of initial affricates

Simplification of Liquids and Nasals

17. Liquid Gliding
18. Vocalisation
19. Denasalization

Other Substitution Processes

20. Deaffrication
21. Deletion of initial consonant
22. Apicalisation
23. Labialisation

Assimilation Processes

24. Velar assimilation
25. Labial assimilation
26. Prevocalic voicing
27. Devoicing of final consonant

Grunwell (1985c)

Structural Simplifications

Weak Syllable Deletion:
pretonic
posttonic
Final Consonant Deletion:
nasals
plosives
fricatives
affricates
clusters — 1
— 2 +
Vocalisation:
/l/
other C
Reduplication:
complete
partial
Consonant Harmony:
velar
alveolar
labial
manner
other
S.I. Cluster Reduction:
plosive + approx.
fricative + approx.
/s/ + plosive
/s/ + nasal
/s/ + approx.
/s/ + plosive + approx.

Systemic Simplifications

Fronting:
velars
palato-alveolars
Stopping:
/f/
/v/
/θ/
/ð/
/s/
/z/
/ʃ/
/ʧ/
/ʤ
/l/
/r/
Gliding:
/r/
/l/
fricatives
Context-Sensitive Voicing:
WI and WF
Voicing WI
Voicing WW
Devoicing WF
Glottal Replacement:
WI
WW
WF
Glottal Insertion

provoke serious questions about this aspect of the methodology, in particular with regard to the representativeness of the sample obtained.

The child's responses are recorded on record sheets for each process; each process is tested in a set of words in sequence. On these record sheets there are examples in transcription of pronunciations that exemplify the process. While being useful these could prejudice the examiner's perception and recording of the child's pronunciations. There is space on each record form to include other words the child says. In addition Weiner provides 'control items' to confirm whether a child's pronunciations involve assimilative processes or substitution processes. For example *duck* is one of the words which tests for Velar Assimilation; if the child says [gʌk] the examiner elicits the nonsense syllable [dʌ] by imitation to check that the [g] realisations of target /d/ is in fact a context-conditioned pronunciation. Ingenious though this technique is, it has to be questioned, in that an imitation of a nonsense syllable is not the same type of response as that obtained by the delayed recall of a real word.

Some of Weiner's process definitions are somewhat heterogeneous. For example labial assimilation includes /θ/ → [f] in *thumb*; /t/ → [p] in *table*; /s/ → [f] in *sweater* and others. As these patterns are both phonologically and developmentally different, it is misleading to view them as manifestations of the same process. There is also an unfortunate omission from Weiner's list: the stopping of affricates /tʃ, dʒ/ → [t,d]. This is a serious oversight as it is often found to be a persistent problem in the speech of children with developmental phonological disorders (Grunwell 1981b). Weiner advises examiners that with experience they will be able to notice other processes in children's speech. This is of course very important in the assessment of disordered child phonologies. In spite of this device the methodology and format of PPA are not conducive to open-ended identification of phonological processes.

The analysis of the PPA responses involves completion of a Process Profile Form. On this is recorded the frequency of occurrence of the processes tested, and there is space to record other processes. There is also a 'Phonetic Inventory' on which the presence or absence of *target* English consonant phonemes is noted. As has been mentioned, the developmental status of the processes is not indicated. Furthermore, Weiner includes both normal and unusual processes in his illustrations of the processes; for instance in his examples of Cluster Reduction he gives /sk/ reduced both to [k] and to [s]. In the final section of the manual, however, Weiner provides useful guidelines with regard to the interpretation of PPA in planning treatment programmes and strategies.

NATURAL PROCESS ANALYSIS (1980)

NPA is intended for use in the analysis of spontaneous speech samples. It is, however, extremely limited in its applications because of the procedures Shriberg & Kwiatkowski advocate for its use. With regard to the sampling procedure, although the intention is to obtain a natural spontaneous sample, the examiner is instructed to repeat word for word what the child has said immediately after the child's utterance is finished. This will hardly make for natural continuous interaction. With regard to NPA *per se*, only monosyllabic words are analysed in detail for the occurrence of processes; this entails discarding very important data. Furthermore, only the first occurrence of a word is analysed; repeated occurrences (i.e. any repetitions of the word in subsequent utterances) are ignored. Therefore the occurrence of variable pronunciations is not examined. These two limitations on the data analysed mean that NPA does not assess aspects of a child's pronunciation patterns which are of considerable clinical significance.

As is evident from Table 7.3, only eight processes are included in NPA. Furthermore these processes only handle omissions and phonemic substitutions. Because the authors doubt the ability of examiners to achieve reliable transcriptions of certain aspects of speech, voicing errors are excluded and coded as correct, as are glottal stop realisations. This is an extremely unfortunate and misguided decision which seriously distorts any assessment of children's pronunciation patterns based on NPA. In addition to coding voicing errors as correct the authors advise that distortions such as /s/ → [ɬ] and additions such as /s/ → [ts] should also be scored as correct. A further shortcoming of the NPA approach to process analysis is the procedure whereby any substitution is only attributed to one process, instead of identifying the co-occurrence of processes as in, for example, /kl/ → [t], which involves both Cluster Reduction and Fronting of Velars, but which would be analysed as a single process in NPA; though which of the two possible processes can be justifiably selected is not clear.

On completion of the process analysis the occurrence of processes is recorded on a Summary Sheet in four categories of frequency: 'always occurs'; 'sometimes occurs'; 'never occurs'; 'no data available'. The summary also includes a 'Phonetic Inventory' which, as with Weiner's PPA, is once again the target English consonant phoneme system. The occurrence of these targets is similarly recorded as: 'correct anywhere'; 'appears anywhere'; glossed but never correct or never appears; never glossed, i.e. 'never appears'. As with the other procedures in NPA this is a very limited assessment of a child's pronunciation patterns and their relationship to the adult target system. This summary assessment furthermore fails to take account of the number of potential occurrences of any process or target phoneme in measuring frequency of occurrence; a crucial factor in evaluating the status of a process or indeed a consonant in a child's pronunciation. The authors justify NPA on the grounds that clinicians need a simplified assessment procedure. They achieve this end at great expense: by discarding or misclassifying a large proportion of the relevant data.

ASSESSMENT OF PHONOLOGICAL PROCESSES (1980)

APP combines the articulation test elicitation procedure with phonological process analysis. Hodson provides a list of 55 words which are selected to illustrate the potential occurrence of phonological processes. There is also a screening list of 20 words which can be used to indicate if any of the most common processes are present. The word list is provided but no stimulus pictures. Hodson suggests that objects can be easily collected to elicit the words and indeed indicates that the words were selected with, amongst other factors, the availability of appropriate objects in mind.

The analysis itself involves transferring the transcription of the child's pronunciation of a word from a Record Form on which the target pronunciation is already recorded, to an Analysis Sheet. The 55 words are listed on this sheet, and against each word are shown the phonological processes that could possibly occur in a child's pronunciation of the word. The examiner enters a check/tick in the appropriate box when a process does occur. Finally the frequency of occurrence of each process is entered on a Summary Sheet. Because the sample is predetermined, for most processes the number of possible occurrences can also be predetermined. Calculating the percentage frequency of occurrence is thus quite straightforward. Frequency of occurrence is not calculated for Assimilation Processes or Articulatory Shifts. At the bottom of the Summary Sheet two lines are provided to enter other patterns/preferences.

As is evident from Table 7.3, APP provides a very comprehensive list of processes. These are all described and illustrated in the manual. In the examples provided it is evident that APP analyses the co-occurrence of two processes as two separate processes, unlike NPA. The classification of processes as Basic and Miscellaneous is somewhat unsatisfactory, especially the inclusion of the Voicing Processes and Stopping in the Miscellaneous category. There are also some unusual and inconsistent definitions of some of the processes. For example, examples of *Palatalisation* include /s/ realised as [ʂ] or [ʃ], and /gr/ realised as [dʒ]; *Coalescence* is exemplified by /sm/ → [f] and /st/ → [tʃ]. In discussing other patterns and preferences Hodson specifically mentions reduplications and nasalisation/denasalisation, which are in themselves unfortunate omissions from her otherwise adequate list of normal and more frequently occurring unusual processes.

While there is no developmental assessment *per se* in APP, the definitions and descriptions of the individual processes frequently include reference to the normality and chronology of the processes. An overview, however, is difficult to achieve from these references, and such a synthesis is especially necessary in the instance of APP as both normal and unusual processes are included and many of the normal processes are taken from different stages in development. Hodson mainly concentrates upon the occurrence of processes in children with phonological disorders and makes frequent reference to the effects of these processes upon intelligibility. These are supported by a study of process occurrence in 60 intelligible children and 60 unintelligible children (reported above; Hodson & Paden 1981). Hodson outlines five illustrative cases and provides a list of fundamental principles in the remediation of phonological disorders.

Although many of the processes examined on APP can

potentially occur many times in the 55 selected words that form the data base for APP, it has to be acknowledged that the reliability of the approach is limited by the size of this data base. Although there may be several occurrences of each process there is in effect in the sample only one or at most two occurrences of each cluster or phoneme type at each position in structure. The potential for detecting variability in a child's pronunciation patterns is thus highly constrained. In other respects, however, APP has much to recommend it.

PROCEDURES FOR THE PHONOLOGICAL ANALYSIS OF CHILDREN'S LANGUAGE (1981)

As has already been mentioned, Ingram's PPACL are intended for the analysis of spontaneous speech samples. One of the four types of analysis included in his procedures — Substitution Analysis — has already been outlined at the end of Chapter Three. Ingram suggests that the Phonological Process Analysis in PPACL can best be compiled from the Substitution Analysis. Alternatively, if a Substitution Analysis has not been carried out, the processes can be identified from a direct examination of the data sample. As well as indicating the occurrence of a process Ingram's procedure includes the calculation of the frequency of occurrence of each process by calculating how many items underwent the process that were susceptible to the application of the process. On the basis of this calculation a summary of the most frequently occurring processes is made. It would appear that Ingram's criterion of frequency is 50 per cent occurrence of a process; though there appears to be no explicit statement of this.

It is evident from Ingram's procedure that this approach to process analysis entails in effect a systematisation of the error patterns already detected in a child's pronunciations. As we have already seen, Ingram's list of processes includes both normal and unusual processes; for example fronting of velars alongside apicalisation of labial plosives. It is thus a comprehensive list of patterns, though there are some anomalies. For example Stopping of fricatives is defined as only ocurring in syllable-initial position in word-initial position. The cluster reduction patterns do not distinguish between the different types of /s/+consonant clusters; most importantly here there should be a distinction between the /s/+plosive or nasal clusters and the /s/+approximant clusters (see preceding section of this chapter).

With regard to the assessment of the occurrence of processes Ingram provides some guidelines in the final chapter of his manual with regard to which processes are normal, which might be encountered in disordered phonological development and what might be a typical normal profile of phonological development. He is, however, cautious, and advises that although much progress has been made in investigating children's phonological patterns, both normal and disordered, there is much fundamental research still to be done in both areas.

PHONOLOGICAL ASSESSMENT OF CHILD SPEECH (1985c)

PACS is intended for use in the analysis of spontaneous speech samples, and as with Ingram's PPACL the phonological process analysis is part of a set of procedures. Unlike PPACL the process analysis in PACS is totally free-standing and does not depend upon any prior procedure.

The processes analysed include all those illustrated in the preceding section of this chapter describing normal phonological development, with the addition of Glottal Replacement and Insertion. In the PACS manual it is emphasised that this is not a normal process but has been included on the preprinted analysis sheets because it is a process that has been found to occur very frequently in the speech of children with phonological disorders, which is the clinical population for whom PACS is primarily, but not exclusively, designed. As well as these listed processes, space is provided for entering other systemic and structural processes. The manual provides some examples of these, such as Backing, Weakening (Spirantisation) of plosives, Denasalisation, Initial Consonant Adjunction, Perseveration. This list is illustrative, not definitive nor exhaustive.

The procedure for process analysis in PACS involves entering the occurrence of a process on a table in terms of its frequency of occurrence (number of tokens *v.* number of possible tokens), together with a description and/or examples of its occurrence. Note is also made of any other realisations of the target types that could be susceptible to the process but do not give evidence of the process having operated, and note is also made of any other aspects of the child's pronunciation relevant to the assessment of the process, such as for example its developmental status. Co-occurring processes are analysed as separate occurrences of two processes. As well as analysing process occurrence, the disappearance or suppression of the processes is noted as Evidence of Systemic or Structural Development. Thus emergence of more adult-like pronunciation patterns and the occurrence of progressive variability are identified and recorded for subsequent evaluation.

On completion of the process analysis the child's pronunciation patterns in terms of the combinations of processes that are used can be assessed on a Developmental Profile (see Table 7.2, which is in fact the PACS Developmental Assessment chart). Caution is of course advised in the use of the age norms stated on this chart; and users are reminded that there is much individual variation in the use of processes and the occurrence of developmental patterns in normal children, as well as in the population of children who exhibit difficulties in learning the pronunciation system of their language. In the PACS Manual the developmental characteristics of children's phonological disorders are also discussed in outline, specifically those characteristics already examined above:

Persisting Normal Processes
Chronological Mismatch
Unusual/Idiosyncratic Processes
Variable Use of Processes
Systematic Sound Preference.

The PACS Phonological Process Analysis is thus an explicitly open-ended and freely structured procedure which is intended to facilitate a developmental assessment of a child's pronunciation patterns, as well as simply to identify the phonological processes that occur in those patterns.

EXERCISES

Analyse the pronunciation patterns in the following six data samples in terms of phonological processes. Classify each process you identify as effecting Structural or Systemic Simplifications. You should describe the process in detail, identifying as appropriate the context or contextual factors involved in its operation. Every word in which the process occurs should be listed as an example. When you have accounted for all the patterns you can discover in the data, illustrate the co-occurrence of processes in words whose pronunciation is accounted for by the operation two or more processes.

After analysing the processes, make a developmental assessment of the processes you have identified. Indicate occurrences of Persisting Normal Processes, Chronological Mismatch, Unusual and Idiosyncratic Processes and Systematic Sound Preference.

As well as analysing these data samples you could also analyse the data presented in exercises in preceding chapters in terms of phonological processes, especially Chapter Two: Exercises 2, 4, 5, 6, 7, 8, 9; and Chapter Four: Martin 6;3, Simon 4;7 and 5;2.

1. *PETER* 6;0 (1978)

1. *dog* [dɒd]
2. *pushing* ['pʊʔɪn]
3. *feather* ['bɛdə]
4. *black* [bat]
5. *scissors* ['dɪdəd]
6. *jacket* ['daʔɪt]
7. *keys* [tid]
8. *big* [bɪd]
9. *dress* [dɛt]
10. *sugar* ['dʊdə]
11. *crossing* ['tɒʔɪn]
12. *bridge* [bɪd]
13. *glasses* ['daʔɪd]
14. *soldier* ['doʊdə]
15. *catch* [tat]
16. *teeth* [tit]
17. *shopping* ['dɒʔɪn]
18. *trousers* ['taʊdəd]
19. *fish* [bɪt]
20. *cheating* ['tiʔɪn]

2. *IAN* 5;2 (1975)

1. *monkey* ['ŋʌŋki]
2. *soldier* ['doʊdə]
3. *jug* [gʌg]
4. *stamps* [dam]
5. *ball* [bɔ]
6. *gate* [geɪt]
7. *pig* [gɪg]
8. *saucepan* ['dɔpən]
9. *duck* [gʌk]
10. *picture* ['bɪʔdə]
11. *sugar* ['gʊgə]
12. *tap* [dap]
13. *cat* [gat]
14. *smoke* [ŋoʊk]
15. *door* [dɔ]
16. *mat* [mat]
17. *bag* [gag]
18. *sock* [gɒk]
19. *cap* [gap]
20. *string* [gɪŋg]

3. *MARK* 6;0 (1976)

1. *fish* [hɪt]
2. *grass* [dat]
3. *rock* [jɒt]
4. *truck* [tʌt]
5. *peach* [pit]
6. *salad* [ˈhajəd]
7. *place* [peɪt]
8. *garage* [ˈdajɪd]
9. *sock* [hɒt]
10. *crash* [tat]
11. *carrot* [ˈtajət]
12. *black* [bat]
13. *cherry* [ˈtɛji]
14. *sugar* [ˈhʊdə]
15. *golly* [ˈdɒji]
16. *brush* [bʌt]
17. *log* [jɒd]
18. *shed* [hɛd]
19. *fairy* [ˈhɛəji]
20. *jelly* [ˈdɛji]

4. *JOHN* 4;4 (1979)

1. *baby* [ˈdeɪdi]
2. *cake* [teɪç, teɪx]
3. *mice* [naɪç]
4. *sauce* [tɔç]
5. *window* [ˈlɪndoʊ]
6. *table* [ˈteɪdʊ]
7. *blocks* [dlʒɒx]
8. *cooker* [ˈtʊtə]
9. *postman* [ˈtoʊxnən]
10. *ships* [tɪç]
11. *gate* [deɪx]
12. *ring* [lʒɪn]
13. *dish* [dɪç, dɪx]
14. *pusy* [ˈtʊti]
15. *grass* [dlʒaç]
16. *biscuits* [ˈdɪtɪx]
17. *meat* [niç]
18. *letter* [ˈlɛtə]
19. *skates* [teɪç]
20. *lorry* [ˈlɒli]
21. *brown* [dlʒaʊn]
22. *sweets* [tix]
23. *rabbit* [ˈladɪx]
24. *book* [bʊx]
25. *washing* [ˈlɒtɪn]
26. *spots* [tɒç]

5. *JULIA* 8;0 (1980)

1. *baking* [ˈpeɪtɪn]
2. *clock* [lɒt]
3. *raspberry* [ˈɹatpəɹi]
4. *stick* [tɪt]
5. *supper* [ˈlʊpə]
6. *yes* [lɛt]
7. *cabbage* [ˈtapɪt]
8. *digging* [ˈtɪtɪn]
9. *prize* [ɹaɪt]
10. *bed* [pɛt]
11. *slipper* [ˈlɪpə]
12. *drink* [ɹɪnt]
13. *leaking* [ˈlitɪn]
14. *table* [ˈteɪpʊ]
15. *tree* [ɹi]
16. *sugar* [ˈlʊtə]
17. *cup* [tʊp]
18. *bread* [ɹɛt]
19. *ladder* [ˈlatə]
20. *speak* [pit]
21. *rich* [ɹɪt]
22. *big* [pɪt]
23. *seaside* [ˈlitaɪt]
24. *go* [toʊ]
25. *black* [lat]
26. *rubbish* [ˈɹəpɪt]

27. *skate* [teɪt]
28. *grass* [ɹat]
29. *said* [lɛt]
30. *press* [ɹɛt]

6. *ANTHONY* 4;7 (1979)

1. *satchel* [ˈsaʔs̬ʊ]
2. *peach* [bis]
3. *strawberries* [ˈdɔjiz]
4. *break* [beɪt]
5. *christmas* [ˈdɪʔs̬əs]
6. *shoes* [suz]
7. *chicken* [ˈdɪʔs̬ɪn]
8. *polish* [ˈbɒjɪs]
9. *trees* [diz]
10. *saddle* [ˈs̬ajʊ]
11. *bottle* [ˈbɒʔs̬ʊ]
12. *flag* [s̬ad]
13. *donkey* [ˈdɒʔs̬i]
14. *cabbage* [ˈdajɪz]
15. *sugar* [ˈsʊjə]
16. *grass* [das̬]
17. *tanker* [ˈdaʔs̬ə]
18. *feather* [ˈsɛjə]
19. *castle* [ˈdaʔsʊ]
20. *prize* [baɪz̬]
21. *scissors* [ˈsɪjəz]
22. *brush* [bəs̬]
23. *glasses* [ˈdaʔs̬ɪz̬]
24. *bandage* [ˈbajɪz]
25. *tractor* [ˈdaʔs̬ə]
26. *crate* [deɪt]
27. *garage* [ˈdajɪz̬]
28. *cooker* [ˈdʊʔs̬ə]
29. *soldier* [ˈsoʊjə]
30. *chopper* [ˈdɒʔsə]

7. Analyse the pronunciation patterns in these twenty words in terms of phonological processes. State the processes that occur at each stage/age and trace the changes in the processes from one age to another.
Make a developmental assessment of the processes operating at each age; indicate occurrences of Persisting Normal Processes, Chronological Mismatch and Unusual and Idiosyncratic Processes.
(During this period Christine was receiving special education in a language unit, cf. Simon, Chapter Four.)

CHRISTINE (1979–1980)

	4;9	4;11	5;2	5;6
1. finger	[ˈwɪwɪ]	[ˈfɪndə]	[ˈfɪŋgə]	[ˈfɪŋgə]
2. garage	[ˈdada]	[ˈdawɪ]	[ˈgawɪd]	[ˈgawɪd]
3. soldier	[ˈdoʊdʊ]	[ˈjoʊdə]	[ˈtsoʊdə]	[ˈs̬oʊdə]
4. feather	[ˈdɛdɛ]	[ˈfɛdə]	[ˈfɛvə]	[ˈfɛvə]
5. sugar	[ˈdʊdə]	[ˈjʊdə]	[ˈt̪s̬ʊgə]	[ˈs̬ʊgə]
6. sleeping	[wi]	[ˈwibɪ]	[ˈwipɪn]	[ˈslipɪn]
7. rabbit	[ˈbaba]	[ˈwabɪ]	[ˈwabɪt]	[ˈwabɪt]
8. scissors	[ˈdɪdə]	[ˈjɪdə]	[ˈʧɪdə]	[ˈt̪s̬ɪdəd]

9. chocolate	['dɒdɒ]	['tɒʔtə]	['tsɒʔkə]	['ʧɒʔkət]
10. bridge	[wɪ]	[wɪd]	[bwɪd]	[bwɪd]
11. train	[deɪ]	[deɪn]	[weɪn]	[tʊ'weɪn]
12. glasses	['dada]	['latɪ]	['latsɪ]	['glatsɪd]
13. flag	[da]	[fa]	[fag]	[flag]
14. tractor	['dada]	['waʔtə]	['waʔkə]	[tə'waʔtə]
15. pram	[bam]	[bam]	[wam]	[pwam]
16. red	[dɛd]	[wɛ]	[wɛd]	[wɛd]
17. claws	[dɔ]	[dɔd]	[wɔd]	[kə'wɔd]
18. elephant	['ɛdɪ]	['ɛ-ɪvɪ]	['ɛwəfənt]	['lɛlifənt]
19. butterfly	['bʊda]	['bʊʔədaɪ]	['bʊtəfaɪ]	['bʊtəfaɪ]
20. aeroplane	['ɛdə]	['ɛəbeɪ]	['ɛwəbeɪn]	['ɛəwəpleɪn]

NOTES

1. For a brief review of some of the theoretical issues involved see Sommerstein (1977: 233–7). The references given there will provide the interested reader with a thorough introduction to the theory.

2. Oller *et al.* found that there were few consonant clusters in babbling and that open syllables predominated. With regard to phonetic content, plosives far outnumbered fricatives, amongst other more detailed findings. It would appear, therefore, that babbling is also constrained by the natural restrictions of the speech production mechanism and furthermore that there is a natural *phonetic* link between babbling and beginning to talk.

3. This is not to say that the child has 'perfect perception'; that is that all children can perceive all the differences in sounds and sequences when they begin to talk (cf. Stampe 1969 and Smith 1973, who claim that this is so. See also Chapter Six). While perception normally always precedes production, it is not known by how much. The main problem is the lack of a suitable experimental design whereby linguistic perceptual abilities can be investigated, that is not just the ability to discriminate minimal pairs, but also to retain and analyse complex sound sequences and to identify phonetically-different sounds as having phonological identity. For a preliminary investigation of the last mentioned see Tallal *et al.* (1980).

4. Ingram (1976: 29–44) uses a different classification:
   - (i) *syllable structure processes*: e.g. Final Consonant Deletion, Weak Syllable Deletion, Reduplication, Cluster Reduction;
   - (ii) *assimilation processes*: e.g. Consonant Harmony, Context-Sensitive Voicing;
   - (iii) *substitution processes*: e.g. Stopping, Fronting, Gliding, Vocalisation.

5. Indeed /tr, dr/ may pattern with the affricates in the earlier stages of development; see Martin's data sample in Chapter Four.

6. It is to this type of child speech disorder that this framework of

analysis is most applicable. It is potentially misleading to describe the types of patterns in disordered speech which clearly result from identifiable organic impairments (e.g. hearing loss, cleft palate) as involving these *phonological* processes (cf. Ingram 1976: 122–9). Simplifications in these disorders are determined, or at least influenced, by the physical disabilities of the impaired speech mechanisms; these are speech disorders at the phonetic (articulatory) level. (See Chapter Eight.)

8

Issues in Clinical Phonology

This final chapter addresses general issues in the clinical applications of phonology, issues that were touched on briefly in Chapter One. In the intervening chapters attention has mainly been focused on examining the principles and procedures of the analytical frameworks presented. The clinical relevance of each of the frameworks has been discussed, and through these discussions certain ideas about what might constitute the principles of clinical phonology have begun to emerge. An exploration of these ideas can be most usefully organised in a clinically applicable framework under the headings of assessment, diagnosis and treatment. In addition to these issues which address the practice-oriented applications of clinical phonology, the theoretical implications of clinical phonological investigations must also be examined. The increasing interest in the cognitive domain of phonetic and phonological descriptions requires consideration of the nature of such theoretical explanations in clinical phonology.

In this chapter we shall therefore be identifying the impact of phonological concepts and analyses on clinical assessment procedures by elaborating the prerequisites and principles for clinical phonological assessment. The diagnostic contributions of clinical phonology are in large part based on the descriptive frameworks provided by the analytical assessment procedures. The discussion in the second section of this chapter examines some of the descriptive classifications and definitions of speech disorders that have been proposed on the basis of phonological analyses. This discussion leads us to two further issues: (1) what principles and procedures of treatment can be derived from the phonological definitions and descriptions of speech disorders, and (2) what implications are entailed for the explanation of the nature of such speech disorders. These two issues will be addressed in this order since aspects of the treatment process also relate to the more fundamental issue of attempting to achieve an understanding of the nature of speech disorders.

ASSESSMENT

Stoel-Gammon & Dunn (1985) state:

> It is necessary to identify the unique characteristics of each child's system in order to design the most appropriate treatment plan for each child. (op. cit.: 127)

Likewise Elbert & Gierut (1986) assert:

> An accurate assessment and characterization of the speech sound problem is the first and perhaps most essential component in the clinical treatment of children with speech disorders. (op. cit.: 9)

Thus we have here two unequivocal statements emphasising the importance and primacy of phonological analysis and assessment as a basis for clinical decision-making, specifically treatment planning. Having established the clinical requirement for phonological investigations we must now consider what aims and objectives those investigations must attempt to fulfil. As we saw in Chapter One, one of the major insights that the clinical applications of phonology has contributed to clinical speech pathology is that speech is organised to function as the spoken medium of language. It is therefore essential that the phonological assessment procedures focus on the functional, i.e. communicative, aspects of disordered speech. The clinical investigation needs to discover how the person, child or adult, is using speech for spoken language, and how this usage is inadequate for the person's communicative intentions.

A second major contribution of clinical phonology has been to reveal through phonological analysis that there are patterns in the speech of disordered speakers, and that these patterns are related to the phonological patterns of the pronunciation system used by normal speakers of the person's language. Thus the communicative inadequacies of a disordered speaker's pronunciation patterns can be directly related, on the basis of a phonological analysis and assessment, to the organisation of the normal pronunciation system.

Given these fundamental insights into the phonological nature of disordered speech we can identify two critical aspects of any phonological investigation: the *data* and the *analysis.* The data are the samples of speech which are to be analysed in order to arrive at an assessment. If the assessment is to be regarded as valid, i.e. reliable and predictive, the data base must fulfil certain criteria. These criteria are determined from the characteristics of the phonological organisation of spoken language, observations of natural behaviour of speakers, especially disordered speakers, and the prerequisites for any empirical phonetic and phonological investigation. Thus the data sample should:

(1) contain a representative sampling of the different types of phonemes and phonotactic structures that constitute the target phonological system;
(2) be large enough to contain more than one token of several (preferably all) target-types to ensure that any variability in pronunciation can be detected;
(3) be representative of the speaker, and therefore obtained through a variety of relatively natural 'talking situations'; any non-spontaneous (i.e. repeated or imitated) utterances must be identified;
(4) be glossable; any utterances whose intended meaning and therefore normal pronunciation are not known are usually not amenable to assessment; this criterion can often restrict the range of situations in which data can be obtained from disordered speakers and thus impose constraints on the fulfilment of requirement (3);
(5) be recorded in such a way as to facilitate a detailed and comprehensive phonological analysis, whose validity can be checked by another analyst; as much as possible of the sample should be tape-recorded; the whole sample should be recorded in phonetic transcription, which should contain as much detail as possible about the pronunciations used, that is as detailed impressionistic transcription as is within the abilities of the transcriber.

These criteria are in themselves uncontroversial, but there are issues which are subject to some debate in achieving these criteria. In particular, there is controversy as to sample type and sample size. While the most desirable type of sample is spontaneous natural conversational speech, many speakers with communication disorders are less than forthcoming. Also their speech is frequently difficult to understand when the listener cannot guess the topic of conversation, and therefore the utterances are unglossable. In addition, it is difficult to ensure a representative sampling of the target system from spontaneous conversational types of samples. Given these potential shortcomings it is often advisable, and indeed necessary, to use a set of preselected elicitation materials which will obtain a representative sample and ensure that a majority of the speaker's utterances are glossable. However this need not, and indeed preferably should not, be the only type of sample analysed.

With regard to the size of the sample many authorities recommend between 80 and 100 words (Crystal 1982; Ingram 1981; Shriberg & Kwiatkowski 1980; Stoel-Gammon & Dunn 1985). Crary (1983) conducted a study of 100-word samples and on the basis of his findings claims that a 50-word sample provides descriptive information similar to samples of 100 words. In contrast Grunwell (1985c) regards 100 words as a minimum sample size and advocates 200–250 words as the preferred sample size. Crary's study points to the probable reason for the discrepancy between these recommendations. He investigated the total occurrence of phonological processes in the first 50 words compared with the second 50 words in a 100-word sample. He did not investigate the frequency of occurrence of the processes (i.e. total occurrence *v.* total possible occurrence), nor did he take into account whether a target phoneme was variably subject to different processes at one or several different positions in syllable and word structure. He is not therefore concerned to analyse the detailed patterns of pronunciation of a speaker, nor to establish whether there is variability in these pronunciation patterns. Grunwell's analytical and assessment procedures (PACS; op. cit.), on the other hand, are specifically designed to investigate in detail a speaker's pronunciation patterns. Furthermore particular attention is paid to the occurrence of variability, since this is regarded as being particularly significant for identifying aspects of a pronunciation pattern where there is potential for change. In the light of these points, for a reliable assessment which will provide an adequate basis for informed treatment planning the collection of as large a data sample as possible (at least 200 and preferably 200–250 words) is therefore recommended.

The issue of phonetic transcription is also not without controversy. Here once again the concerns are focused on the reliability of the transcription. Some authorities consider the problem of ensuring a reliable transcription of certain aspects of speech to be so great that they exclude analysis of these features from their assessments; for example Shriberg & Kwiatkowski (1980) exclude voicing completely from their Natural Process Analysis. This must be regarded as an extreme and undesirable solution to what is undeniably a problem area. There have been suggestions that acoustic analysis could be used to supplement and indeed verify auditory–articulatory phonetic transcription. This, however, is also not a simple task, and the phonetic transcription and instrumental analyses may not be compatible (Weismer 1984). Furthermore phonetic transcription is not simply a question of the analyst recording what he thinks he hears. Oller & Eilers (1975) demonstrated that knowledge of the lexical target attempted significantly influences the transcription; a phenomenon which they call *expectancy.* This study did, however, demonstrate that trained listeners do tend to converge if not exactly agree in their transcriptions. Shriberg *et al.* (1984) take up this point, and propose a procedure for establishing concensus transcriptions. The use of phonetic transcription is thus fraught with methodological problems. There is, however, no other basis available to us at present upon which to carry out a comprehensive phonetic and phonological assessment. It is after all most appropriate that an auditory–articulatory phonetic analysis is the entry point for our clinical evaluation, since it is the effect of a speaker's pronunciation upon listeners that has led to our initial identification that this particular speaker has a speech disorder. While being aware of their acknowledged limitations we must therefore continue to use detailed phonetic transcriptions as the data base for phonological analyses and assessments.

It is the analysis which is the core of the phonological assessment. As the preceding chapters have shown, there are a variety of procedures to choose from. For a procedure to be clinically applicable it must satisfy the following requirements:

(1) Provide a description of the pronunciation *patterns* of the disordered speaker.
(2) Identify the differences between the *patterns* used by normal speakers and those used by the disordered speaker; this is the first assessment function of a procedure in that it pinpoints which specific aspects of a disordered speaker's pronunciation patterns are not in conformity with, and therefore presumably not acceptable to, the normal-speaking linguistic community. While this is essentially an analysis of the 'errors' in a person's speech, the term 'patterns' indicates the crucial difference from traditional procedures, where there was apparently little appreciation of the need to consider recurrent regularities in the data.
(3) Indicate the communicative implications of the disordered speech patterns; this is the second assessment function of a procedure and is the essentially *phonological* dimension in that it examines the consequences of the disordered pronunciation patterns; that is the actual and implied failures to signal intended meanings unambiguously through the lack of adequate phonological contrasts. This provides an indication of how difficult the speaker would be to understand; this is therefore an assessment of functional adequacy of the pronunciation system and an indication of the probable level of communicative efficiency/inefficiency of the speaker.
(4) Enable the clinician to derive treatment aims and guidelines from the assessment; i.e. the assessment should pinpoint precisely which pronunciation patterns need to be modified for the speaker to achieve more adequate and efficient pronunciation.
(5) Provide a straightforward and informative method of assessing and evaluating changes on reanalysis, after a programme of treatment has been carried out and/or after a period of time has elapsed.

These are the *principles* of clinical phonological analysis and assessment. In seeking to achieve these aims a phonological assessment must also satisfy the general linguistic criteria for an adequate and reliable framework of analysis. These criteria are that an analysis should be: (1) exhaustive; (2) replicable;

(3) predictive (cf. Grunwell 1985c: 23).

(1) For an analysis to be adequate it should be capable of handling all the data it is required to describe: i.e. it must be *exhaustive.* As we have seen in preceding chapters (especially Chapter Five, but also in relation to some phonological process analyses in Chapter Seven), there are some clinical procedures which clearly fail to satisfy this criterion and which are therefore inadequate and potentially misleading.

(2) If an analysis is to be reliable it must be carried out according to an explicitly stated set of procedures and not be based upon implicitly unstated assumptions. This will ensure that the analysis will be *replicable*; i.e. it can be replicated by the same analyst or another analyst using the same procedures.

(3) When an analyst identifies patterns in a speaker's pronunciation we assume that, provided the analysis is based on a representative data sample, these patterns will recur in further data samples from the same speaker obtained under similar conditions; i.e. the analysis is *predictive.* Unless we can confidently make this assumption our analysis is of no clinical value; i.e. we cannot assess the pronunciation patterns nor plan treatment which is designed to facilitate a change in these pronunciation patterns without this confidence. It is therefore essential that we collect a representative speech sample and subject this to exhaustive comprehensive, replicable and clinically applicable analyses.

The main focus of the debate on the type of analysis is whether an applicable analysis for clinical purposes should provide an independent or relational description of a speaker's pronunciation patterns (Elbert & Gierut 1986; Stoel-Gammon & Dunn 1985). The criteria as listed above in fact require both types of analysis. However, as we have seen many phonological procedures in effect conflate criteria (1) and (2) of the list of clinical prerequisites, by identifying the pronunciation patterns through statements of the patterns in the relationships between target and disordered pronunciations (e.g. phonological processes). It is, however, possible to separate these two descriptive statements, as we have seen in Chapter Four. This approach has recently become increasingly popular (Grunwell 1985c; Elbert & Gierut op. cit.; Stoel-Gammon & Dunn op. cit.).

There is one significant omission from the criteria listed above: that is the need to carry out a developmental assessment. This is of course essential in the evaluation of the status of children's pronunciation patterns. Because these criteria were drawn up to have general clinical applicability this principle is omitted from the list, but should be included in any list defining the prerequisites for a clinical assessment of child speech (see Grunwell op. cit.).

A further requirement for phonological assessments that is of general applicability, and it is highly desirable that the assessment should provide a framework for the identification of different types of disordered speech. This would entail descriptions of the phonological characteristics of different types of speech disorders; on the basis of such comprehensive and explicit descriptions clinicians could make a diagnosis of the type of speech disorder exhibited by an individual speaker. This requirement is an aspiration for phonological analysis and assessment, not as yet a reality. It is issues related to this aim that are addressed in the next section. Before we address these issues, however, we must note an important implication of aspiring to use phonological assessments to inform diagnostic classifications. In so doing the phonological analysis and assessments cease to be just a description of the data sample; they become part of the explanation of the speaker's communication disorder. This point will be explored further in the last section of this chapter.

DIAGNOSIS

In Chapter One it was indicated that the distinction between phonetics and phonology is of crucial diagnostic significance. This linguistically based classification can be usefully applied in the descriptions of the characteristics (i.e. speech patterns) of speech and language disorders. On the basis of the phonetic and phonological characteristics of different types of speech disorders, descriptive typologies can be formulated. These can be related to and cross-referenced with the diagnostic categories used in clinical speech and language pathology in order to gain a clearer and deeper insight into the nature of speech and/or language disorders *per se*. This synthesis of the information from clinical phonological descriptions and the speech pathological investigations is essential; neither approach is adequate on its own. We shall explore this point further in the final section of this chapter. In this section we shall examine how clinical descriptions can be used for classifying speech disorders on the basis of their phonetic and phonological characteristics.

A speech disability at the phonetic level involves an apparent difficulty in the production of normal speech. This is usually associated with some organic deficiency in the speech-producing mechanism. Clearly a person who has a structural abnormality in the cranio-facial region, or a person who has a neurological lesion that in some way disrupts or impairs the neurophysiological functioning of the oral musculature will experience difficulty in producing normally articulated, auditorily acceptable speech.

In contrast, a speech disability at the phonological level involves an abnormal, or inadequate or disorganised system of sound patterns evidenced by deviations in the spoken language. Often an individual with an apparent phonological disability will give evidence of an ability to produce a full range of adequate articulatory movements, and indeed often uses sounds inappropriately in certain contexts and positions in speech, while failing to use them appropriately in other contexts and positions. This being so, it might be hypothesised that the disability is a neurolinguistic dysfunction at the phonological level of cortical representation and organisation of the language system.

The distinction between phonetic and phonological speech disorders is particularly important in the differential diagnosis of acquired speech disorders. The following quotation confirms that this fact has been appreciated:

> Patients with a *phonetic disorder* produce distorted sounds, allophonic variants, or sounds which are not part of the inventory of their native language. To transcribe their speech we need not only the phonemic symbols but diacritics to indicate explosive initiation, ingressive airstream, nasalisation, lengthening and so on, together with a description of paralinguistic features such as breathiness. For other speakers with deviancy at the phonological level however, a phonemic transcription without diacritics suffices. The sounds are well-

articulated, and are acceptable sounds in the phonemic inventory, but they may be inappropriate for their context, and differ from what is presumed to be their intended realisation. (Lesser 1978: 152)

Here, there is a clear differentiation between two types of disorder based on their phonetic/phonological characteristics. An error analysis format in the assessment procedure is adequate for such a diagnosis. Let us look more closely at the data, the characteristics of the two types of disorders referred to in the quotation (see also Mackenzie 1982).

Acquired dysphasia is traditionally defined as a language disorder. Phonetic and phonological analysis and classification of the speech errors produced by dysphasic patients demonstrate this to be so; they indicate a phonological disability, as defined above. Dysphasic mispronunciations — often called literal or phonemic paraphasias in the traditional speech pathology terminology — tend to be phonologically similar to the target pronunciations. Segments in error generally have features in common with the intended segment; and/or there may be evidence of the influence of a preceding or succeeding segment, perseverative or anticipatory assimilation, respectively. These assimilative influences are usually 'at a distance' or non-contiguous; that is another segment occurs between the affected segments, usually a vowel between two assimilated consonants. For example:

errors in the selection of phonemes
/p/ *lips* [lɪts] /g/ *gum* [dʌm]
/ʃ/ *shop* [ʧɒp] /ʧ/ *which* [wɪt]
involving perseveration
sugar ['ʃʊʒə]
involving anticipation
wireless ['waɪsɪs]

Errors also occur which can be classified as involving structural or sequencing errors. For example:

omission:
scratch [sæʧ] *crane* [keɪn]
insertion:
clock [kə'lɒk]

metathesis:
car rally [ˈkɑˌlæɹi]

The diagnostic characteristic of all pronunciation errors in dysphasic speech is that they result in phonemically and phonotactically permissible phonological units (cf. quotation from Lesser). They are therefore evidence of a *phonological* disability in which the *system is disorganised*, but not necessarily inadequate. This explanation is based on the observation that on occasions many dysphasic patients will produce correct pronunciations of words which previously and subsequently they might mispronounce. This suggests that in some patients the phonological system is not destroyed by the cerebral lesion, but that its functioning is impaired. The speech difficulties of the dysphasic patient usually appear to involve intermittent access and inconsistent organisation of the phonological constituents and sequential structure of linguistic units.

In contrast to the purely phonological errors in dysphasic speech, both phonological and phonetic difficulties are evidenced in *acquired articulatory dyspraxia* (often also referred to as *apraxia of speech*). Patients with this disability tend to exhibit great difficulties in achieving *their* intended pronunciations; they 'struggle' to control and direct their articulatory gestures. On many occasions they appear unable to locate and execute the target articulatory movement and placement; articulation is almost always effortful and frequently visibly so. The control and co-ordination of sequences of articulatory gestures present major difficulties. There is, however, no evidence of paralysis of the organs of articulation and the movements that may be presenting difficulties on one occasion may be adequately performed at another time, in speech and/or in non-speech oral activities. Nevertheless, in most attempts at speaking there is evidence of a disordered speech production mechanism, that is a *phonetic* disability.

The following phonetic phenomena appear to be characteristic of articulatory dyspraxia:

Phonetic experimentation. In attempting to locate and execute the intended target gesture, patients often 'experiment' with silent articulatory movements; sometimes these are audible as very weak articulations, or 'tentative realisations' (the traditional speech pathology terms for these phenomena include 'groping', 'struggle').

e.g. (1) *silent articulations:*
townhall [(t) — (t) tə̥, ˌtʰaʊn'ɔʊ̆]
(2) *tentative realisations:*
the railway line [ði — ə'ɹeɪɹ̥weɪ ɹ̥ə̥laɪ'ɹaɪn]
company [kʰʌmp̨ — kʰʌmpə̥ — 'kʰɒmpani]

Idiosyncratic substitutions. Often these patients will use phones outside the normal adult phonemic inventory; some patients have a 'favourite' or 'idiosyncratic' substitution, which they use fairly consistently for one, or a set of, segment type(s).

e.g. *fishing* ['fɪʂɪŋ] *just* [ʤ̡əst]
church [tʂɜʂ] *passengers* ['pʰæsəndʐəz]

Phonetic sequencing errors. The *dyspraxic* sequencing difficulties can result in the production of consonant combinations that contravene the phonotactic possibilities of the language.

e.g. *trains* [sɹeɪn — t̼ɹeɪnz]
driver ['vɹaɪvə — 'vɹaɪvə — — 'vɹaɪb̢ — d̥̠ɹ̥ — 'd̠ɹ̣aɪvə]

Self-correction. On becoming aware of an error, the dyspraxic patient often attempts to correct it; there is no guarantee, however, that the attempted self-corrections, usually involving several repeats, will result in the production of the intended target or, indeed, improved performance, or that any achieved improvement will be maintained. It is the occurrence of this type of disordered speech production together with phonetic experimentation that indicates that, more often than not, the person 'knows what he wants to say' but is patently 'unable to speak it'; that is this is definitely a *phonetic disability.*

e.g. *tunnel* ['dʊnʊ̃n — 'tʰʊnə — 'dʊnə — ə't͇ʊnəl — tʰʊnəɫ
signal [sɪŋ — 'sɪŋə̆lən — 'sɪŋələn — 'sɪŋlən]
everybody P. ['ɛw͡ɹ̥i'bəri — 'ɛvɹiɹʷə — 'ɛvɹi'beɪ — 'ɛvɹ
— 'beɪbdi]
T. /'ɛvɹi, bɒdi/
P. ['bɒdi — 'ɛvɹi'bɒbli — 'bɒbdi]

T. : *do you want another go*
P. ['ɛvɹi'bɒdi]

(All the above examples of dyspraxic speech are taken from the same sample of one patient.)

It must be appreciated that many of the errors in acquired dyspraxia are in fact similar to the phonological errors in dysphasia. Indeed the majority of patients with dyspraxia also have some degree of dysphasic impairment. This leads MacKenzie (1982) to use the terms aphasic articulatory defect and aphasic phonological defect. Along the lines indicated above she also identifies two distinct impairment patterns — one articulatory and one linguistic. However, she highlights the necessity to include the term *aphasic* with reference to both patterns: 'a sparing of the phonological level in the patient with aphasic articulatory impairments is unlikely. Those with language defects [aphasic phonological defects, P.G.] do not necessarily have articulatory impairments, but if aphasia exists, phonological level disruption is likely to be present' (Mackenzie op. cit.: 44). It is essential therefore that the characteristically different phonetic errors are recognised, since they are the basis of this differential diagnosis and are crucial for devising appropriate treatment strategies (see further Mackenzie op. cit.). A detailed impressionistic phonetic transcription and analysis are obviously required; a phonetic representation that records the data in terms of the phonemic categories of normal speech will be completely inadequate and will fail to identify the characteristics of the phonetic/aphasic articulatory disorder. Unfortunately many researchers restrict their transcriptions and analyses to this level (Klich *et al.* 1979; Marquardt *et al.* 1979). We shall return to consideration of the nature of this phonetic disorder later in the chapter, as it presents an interesting problem in formulating a psycholinguistic explanation of the nature of the speech production disturbances.

For the sake of completeness, mention must be made here of the acquired speech disorders which are classified neurologically as *dysarthrias.* These disorders result from clearly observable neuromuscular impairments, involving breakdowns in the accuracy, mobility, general control, timing and co-ordination of movements of the speech musculature (for details see Darley *et al.* 1975; see also Grunwell & Huskins 1979). The impairments are consistently present in both speech and non-speech contexts, though fatigue and other factors may exacerbate the condition in certain circumstances for individual patients. It will therefore be evident that dysarthric impairments entail a phonetic disability in speech production.

The distinction between phonetic and phonological levels of speech production has also facilitated the recognition of *developmental phonological disorders* in children. For many years clinical speech pathology employed the term 'functional articulation disorder' to describe the speech disability of children with no identifiable condition which would account for their inadequate speech development and production. These children are capable of making all the necessary articulatory movements, are not hearing-impaired and exhibit no major social or intellectual handicaps. Theirs was obviously *not* a phonetic disability and therefore the term 'articulation disorder' was inappropriate.

It is here that clinical phonology has made a highly significant contribution to clinical speech pathology. Once speech pathologists became aware of the possibility of a phonological as well as a phonetic disability of speech production then the phonological nature of this developmental speech disorder was appreciated. Developmental phonological disorder is now a widely understood, accepted and applied diagnostic category. For the assessment of phonological disorders in children, phonological analysis procedures truly come into their own, as has been demonstrated throughout this book. The majority of the examples and exercises use data samples from children with developmental phonological disorders (see especially Grunwell 1981b, 1985; Stoel-Gammon & Dunn 1985).

It cannot necessarily be assumed that children with this disability form a homogeneous group. The growing number of studies of the pronunciation patterns of the children suggest that there is the possibility of identifying different types of developmental phonological disorders; see for example Ingram 1983; Camarata & Gandour 1984; Grunwell 1981b; Lahey *et al.* 1985; Leonard 1985; Leonard & Brown 1984. The majority of these studies employ the descriptive framework of natural phonological process analysis (see Chapter Seven) in attempting to characterise the disorder. In contrast Grunwell (1985c) suggests a phonologically based set of potential diagnostic indicators together with a classification of the developmental characteristics. The suggested phonological indicators are:

Systemic Indices
— i.e. the function and organisation of the contrastive system of phones in the pronunciation system.
Phonotactic Indices
— i.e. the organisation of the system of phones to form combinations and sequences of units in the pronunciation system.
Phonetic Dimensions
— i.e. restrictions on the contrastive potential of the pronunciation system due to a reduced phonetic range and/or signs of specific phonetic problems.

With regard to the developmental characteristics, the five categories of developmentally disordered phonological patterns are identified within a general classification of developmental disorders:

Delayed Development: Persisting Normal Processes.
Uneven Development: Chronological Mismatch — which implies persisting normal processes; Variable Use of Processes — in those instances where variability is between processes from two or more stages of development.
Deviant Development: Unusual/Idiosyncratic Processes; Systematic Sound Preference; Variable Use of Processes — where variability is between normal and unusual/idiosyncratic processes of approximately the same stage of development.

At present this represents a logical framework on which we can expect to build in the next stage of the development of the discipline of clinical phonology. In this next stage descriptions of the phonological characteristics of disordered pronunciation systems need to be related to the individual speaker's response to explicitly principled remediation strategies. With this information clinical phonology will begin to move from just describing speech and language disorders to providing explanations of their underlying nature.

Drawing the distinction between phonetic and phonological problems also allows clinicians to conceptualise and identify their co-occurrence. After all a child with a repaired cleft to the palate is developing a phonological system as well as coping with and compensating for the effects of the organic malformation. Further valuable diagnostic insights are therefore potentially available: by carrying out phonetic and phonological investigations the clinician can 'determine the extent to which an adequate phonological system is being obscured by purely phonetic deviance, or whether there is in addition an underlying disturbance of a phonological type; if the latter, is it something unique to the cleft palate condition or a manifestation of some general pattern of delay' (Crystal 1981: 193; see also Grunwell & Russell 1987). These diagnostic investigations clearly have major implications for identifying the need for and implementing appropriately differentiated treatment strategies.

TREATMENT

Phonological therapy has only just become a current term in speech and language pathology during the 1980s; indeed after the publication of the first edition of this book. Phonological therapy is essentially a principled approach to the treatment of phonological disorders within a clearly stated conceptual framework. We shall examine the conceptual framework – the premises – and the principles in this section. The discussion will be at a general level; specific procedures and the devising of treatment programmes will not be discussed as these aspects of remediation have to take account of the nature of an individual patient's communication disorder and his/her personal characteristics and abilities.

The premises of phonological therapy are the theoretical bases which provide the conceptual framework for a principled approach to remediation. They reflect assumptions about the nature of phonological organisation, a speaker's knowledge of that organisation and how this knowledge is acquired in childhood and might be changed; and finally assumptions about how that knowledge is implemented in the production of spoken language. The first assumption we must make is that the person's communication difficulties stem at least in part from a phonological disorder. It is often found that a person with speech problems has two types of disorders, i.e. both a phonological disorder and some phonetic difficulties. It is very important to distinguish between these two types of disorders, as they each require different approaches in therapy (see for example Stackhouse 1984). The difference in the approaches is captured in the following statements:

> the fundamental premise of phonological therapy must surely be that the changes in speech production need to take place not so much in the mouth but in the mind of the child. The aim of treatment is to effect cognitive reorganisation rather than articulatory retraining. (Grunwell 1983)

> The techniques focus on teaching meaningful concepts (e.g. that sound contrast meaning) rather that on production practice. (Stoel-Gammon & Dunn 1985: 165)

As can be seen from these statements, we assume that we are dealing with a person with a phonological disorder and thus we immediately move on to consider the nature of that disorder with reference to the implications for the nature of the intervention process. As the quotation from Stoel-Gammon & Dunn indicates, the second assumption that is made is that phonological knowledge is fundamentally knowledge of the organisation and function of the system of sound contrasts which signal meaning contrasts. The implications of this for treatment are that procedures must concentrate on speech as the medium of communication. Thus the structure of the treatment programme must facilitate the induction of both the contrastive value of the elements in the phonological system and their relationships with each other, both paradigmatic and syntagmatic. Treatment will not therefore be aimed just towards promoting the learning of the correct pronunciation of words, but will be aiming to assist the person to discern the similarities between contrastive sounds and sequences which provide the bases for grouping sounds into classes and sequences into structures (Dean & Howell 1986). From these two fundamental premises we can derive the principles of phonological therapy. The issue of the way in which this phonological knowledge is implemented is addressed in the final section of this chapter.

A principled approach to treatment based on the conceptual framework of phonological therapy should:

(1) Distinguish between phonetic and phonological treatment aims; symptoms which result from a phonetic disability require different remediation procedures from

phonologically-based disorders. For example, the treatment of acquired dysphasia is purely language-based; the disability is phonological. For acquired dyspraxia, the treatment is directed towards improving articulatory gestures, movements and sequences; that is the disability and the treatment are phonetic (see Huskins 1986).

(2) Be based on the assessment; this criterion requires that the treatment should be explicitly principled in that each programme should be devised to suit the requirements of each individual patient as indicated by the phonological analysis and assessment.

(3) Be planned to follow an ordered progression of treatment aims based on the assessment of the relative severity of the speech deviations and relative difficulty for the individual of learning the new patterns; this is another criterion which requires explicit statements of the structure of the treatment programme based on the phonological assessment.

(4) Be aimed as far as possible at changing the *patterns* of deviant speech production; in most circumstances treatment should *not* be concerned only with achieving the correct pronunciation of individual sounds.

(5) Be organised on phonological principles (where, of course, the disability is phonological); that is the procedures should concentrate on the communicative value of the phonological units being learnt, placing them in a meaningful context, thus facilitating the induction of the organisation and contrastive function of the elements in the phonological system; therapy therefore aims to change the person's disordered and inadequate phonological patterns in order to build up a more adequate system of sound contrasts to signal meaning contrasts.

Given these principles we now need to consider in general terms what kinds of treatment procedures comply with these criteria. A number of approaches have been proposed as exemplifying phonological therapy (Weiner 1981; Blache 1985; Cooper 1985; Low, Newman & Ravsten 1985; Neville 1984; Stackhouse 1984; Howell & Dean 1983; Dean & Howell 1986; Hodson & Paden 1983; Ingram 1986; Elbert & Gierut 1986). It is evident from the variety of approaches proposed that we need to distinguish two dimensions of strategic planning for phonological therapy. Firstly, the control that is imposed upon the linguistic environment, at least in the clinical situation, but often also outside the clinic to a certain extent too. The clinician selects specific phonological targets which are pinpointed through relatively controlled exposure to selected stimuli. The targets are selected on the basis of the phonological assessment and on the assumption that appropriate learning will take place through focused exposure to these targets in words, phrases, conversation and other communicative contexts.

Secondly the phonological information that the person is assumed to lack and needs to learn is presented in a more or less explicit way to facilitate learning. This second dimension thus concerns the structure of the treatment procedures and activities. Many of the approaches mentioned above emphasise the use of minimal pairs, which focuses attention on the function of sound differences to signal meaning differences (e.g. Weiner; Blache; Cooper; Low, Newman & Ravsten). Other approaches, while using minimal pairs, introduce other principled strategies. Hodson & Paden (1983) advocate auditory bombardment with words containing the target sound and a cyclical organisation for treatment programmes. Ingram (1986) demonstrates how these two strategies are consistent with our current understanding of phonological learning in children. He shows that there is a relationship between lexical frequency and order of phonological acquisition, and that phonological development is gradual. These two characteristics of learning respectively support the auditory bombardment technique and the cyclical structure of programmes. Dean & Howell's approach (1986) is based on a very different conceptualisation of the learning process. Their aim is to promote the development of metalinguistic awareness so that the person, in this instance a child, gains an understanding of the properties of the phonological system and of his/her effectiveness (and ineffectiveness) in communicating. Elbert & Gierut (1986) identify three types of learning and structure their treatment programmes accordingly: (1) acquisition, i.e. motor learning for accurate and automatic sound production; (2) conceptualisation, i.e. learning that specific sound differences signal specific meaning differences; (3) integration, i.e. incorporation of the new contrasts into spontaneous speech.

In fact, none of these approaches are logically incompatible. It would be possible to combine them all. We do not know, however, whether it is necessary or desirable so to do. In order to discover which strategies are most effective studies are needed which match the outcomes of explicitly principled remediation procedures to the characteristics of individual speakers' phonological disorders and other clinically relevant information. In such studies the clinical applications of phonology would be brought to fruition as they would require a phonological assessment and descriptive diagnosis on the basis of which a phonological therapy programme would be planned and implemented, and then subsequently assessed again using phonological procedures.

> Phonological descriptions would be of value clinically if it could be shown for example that they result in predictions that account at least in part for individual differences in learning as a result of training. (Dinnsen & Elbert 1984: 59)

The questions addressed by such studies are fundamental to phonological therapy. They are: what is a person learning and how is that learning process taking place? When we ask such questions we are seeking an explanation of the nature of phonological knowledge and phonological learning, and thus indirectly an explanation of the nature of disordered phonological learning.

EXPLANATION IN CLINICAL PHONOLOGY

Throughout this book, but most especially in the first chapter and in this last chapter, the impact of phonology upon the clinical investigation of speech disorders has been emphasised. As we have seen, this impact has been felt in particular in the assessment procedures employed for clinical investigations and the resultant descriptions of the characteristics of the speech disorders. Unfortunately in many instances these descriptions have also been offered as explanations. For example Oller wrote in 1973:

> Perhaps the major conclusion that can be drawn from this

> application of generative notational conventions to abnormal child speech is that there seems to be a terrific amount of delicacy in the substitution processes these children possess. The complexity and intricacy of these processes is only approximated by our description. I stand in awe of the abilities these 'abnormal' children have demonstrated. (op. cit.: 42–3)

As Locke (1983b) points out, there has been a strong tendency to extrapolate directly from labels to explanations without addressing the question as to the nature of behaviours that are to be explained. However, this issue is now being addressed in more appropriate and insightful ways. In fact there are two issues to be addressed: the nature of disordered phonology and the nature of disordered phonological development. We shall examine the latter first as there are more studies which have addressed this issue.

Studies seeking an explanation of disordered phonological development have taken the lead from current trends in the description of normal phonological development. This is currently being accounted for by the cognitive model of phonological acquisition, which views the child as playing an active role in the learning process by formulating and testing hypotheses, creating sound patterns and words, and selecting and avoiding words and sounds with certain phonological characteristics. This approach to normal phonological development also provides an explanation in which both universal tendencies and individual differences, strategies and styles can be accounted for.

As Grunwell (1985a) indicates, this account of normal phonological development also informs our understanding of the phonological problems of children with language learning disabilities. We have seen in Chapter Seven that in many respects the pronunciation patterns of such children are systematic and organised in conformity with strategies that children normally exhibit when they are developing the pronunciation patterns of their language. In addition to these normal patterns these children exhibit unusual and idiosyncratic patterns which are suggestive of creativity and inventive hypothesis formation. Leonard (1985) offers a similar explanation for the occurrence of unusual and subtle behaviours in the speech of children with disordered phonological development (see Chapter Seven). He discusses in some detail the interaction between perceptual constraints, organisational devices and output constraints and preferences in individual children's solutions in phonological learning. Specifically he points out that:

> the child stores for recognition some of the information available from the adult words spoken in the environment. This stored information does not necessarily preserve all of the characteristics of the adult form. Differences between the child's stored form and the adult form may be the result of perceptual encoding rules or a failure to adequately store in memory less familiar though correctly perceived phonetic details. Output rules then relate the child's stored form for a word to his or her produced form. Importantly these rules are both motivated and restricted by severe output constraints. These constraints may be the result of the child's limited ability to hit particular articulatory targets or to plan sequences of articulatory gestures.

He also points out, however, that there are instances where the output rules apparently derive from constraints upon the organisational strategies in the absence of any apparent articulatory limitations.

This approach to children's phonological learning has also influenced the conceptualisation of facilitated learning in the clinic. For example Elbert & Gierut (1986) state:

> If we accept the idea that the phonologically disordered child like the normal child is an active creative participant in the learning process, then it is important that we as clinicians facilitate this mode of learning by modifying the clinic environment and clinic programs. We need to utilize the cognitive abilities and knowledge that the child brings to the clinical situation and to assist the child in continuing the acquisition process. (op. cit.: 6)

Similarly Dean & Howell (1986) propose a therapeutic model which is directed towards increasing a child's metalinguistic awareness of the phonological aspects of language and by focusing on his communicative adequacies and inadequacies to promote phonological learning. This model approaches phonological learning as essentially a cognitive process (see also

Schwartz & Prelock 1982; Grunwell 1983; Stackhouse 1984).

So far the discussion has concentrated upon the nature of phonological learning. We now need to address the issue of what is being learned, and in consequence what is disordered phonology. Once again, however, we can take the lead from studies of normal phonological development. In 1980 Menn suggested that:

> a theory devised to account economically for an adult behaviour cannot generally account for the acquisition of that behaviour. The relation between child and adult is among other things the relation between a skilled and an unskilled performer. If the adult produces no unskilled acts the central theory is unlikely to have a way of modelling the production of unskilled acts. Therefore the child cannot be modelled merely as one who possesses a subset of the capacities of the adult. (op. cit.: 27)

Menn here is talking about normal child phonologies but her comments are equally applicable to clinical phonology. Clinical phonology should aspire to produce applicable descriptions and explanations of disordered speech which provide insights into the nature of the speech disorders described. In order to realise this aspiration the approach to description and explanation needs to be speaker-oriented rather than data-oriented (see Grunwell 1985b). Harris & Cottam (1985: 73–4) clearly point to one of the implications of this approach:

> the term *natural* when used in the context of clinical phonology is, in principle at least, independent of the term *normal.* Measures of normality versus deviance in speech assessment are made with reference to adult or developmental norms. The naturalness of particular phonological phenomena, on the other hand, has to do with the extent to which their occurrence can be accounted for by reference to external factors ... [derived] ... from such areas as articulatory physiology, acoustic phonetics or perceptual psychology. It is thus perfectly possible for a child's speech to exhibit phonological patterns which are deviant but which are nonetheless natural to the extent that they are attributable to external phenomena of this type.

Here we have a proposed framework for the explanation of disordered child phonologies which precisely answers the point made by Menn.

In addressing the challenges presented by a speaker-oriented approach to explanation in clinical phonology we must also be prepared to abandon other traditional concepts in phonological description. Hewlett (1985) argues that the two-way distinction between phonetics and phonology, as presented in the opening chapter of this book and in the earlier section of this chapter, is inadequate when attempting to explain the psycholinguistic mechanisms underlying different types of speech disorders. This view is also taken by Ball & Code (1986), who follow a proposal of Tatham (1984). Both Hewlett, and Ball & Code, suggest that a three-way distinction provides a more insightful characterisation of the different natures of speech disorders. This three-way distinction is presented by Hewlett employing the familiar terms: articulatory, phonetic and phonological. Ball & Code discuss Tatham's term 'cognitive phonetics', but opt for the new term (coined by Bailey 1985) 'phonetology' for Hewlett's phonetic level. The three-way distinction that is being drawn is between:

phonology:	abstract conceptual linguistic level of representation;
phonetics:	motor speech planning, programming and control;
articulation:	peripheral output sequences of movements resulting in sounds.

With these three levels it is possible to distinguish between output constraints that are articulatory and peripheral, for example in speakers with identifiable organic disabilities such as cleft palate and dysarthria, and output constraints that are phonetic, i.e. not attributable to any peripheral production handicap. These latter disorders have always presented clinical phonologists with problems, especially the condition of articulatory dyspraxia, but also many aspects of children's speech development. In the instance of dyspraxia the three-way distinction provides an explanation which clearly separates the potentially confusable conditions of dysarthria — an articulation disorder; dyspraxia — a phonetic disorder; and dysphasia — a phonological disorder. It should be appreciated that this newly proposed explanation of dyspraxia is not incompatible with the account presented earlier in this chapter, where the condition was identified as a phonetic programming disorder and thus different in nature from a phonetic realisation disorder such as dysarthria. It does, however, considerably clarify these differences, and furthermore locates the programming difficulties at the level of cortical organisation and therefore with a close interface to the phonological level.

In the instance of explaining children's speech development this model enables us to explain apparent discrepancies between children's abilities in articulatory production and their pronunciation patterns in spoken language. Very often it is observed that children understand, and appear to perceive adequately, words that they pronounce inaccurately. Furthermore they demonstrate an ability to produce the articulatory gestures that are required to pronounce the words accurately. In some instances the explanation may lie in the constraints currently operating on the child's phonetic planning mechanism at the cortical level which is responsible for motor programming and control. There is increasing evidence that this is a significant dimension of children's speech development.

It should not, however, be assumed that this explanation is appropriate in all instances. As indicated in the quotation from Leonard (1985), we need to consider the possibility that several different levels of processing and planning may be involved. Indeed there is more than likely to be an interaction between the outputs of the various processing mechanisms involved:

> The mismatches between adult model and child word are the results of the child's trial and error attempts; they are shaped by the child's articulatory and auditory endowments (and thus to that extent 'natural') and by the child's previous successes at sound production. All rules of child phonology are learned in the sense that the child must discover for herself each correspondence between the sounds she hears and what she does with her vocal tract in an attempt to produce these sounds. (Menn 1983: 44)

A similar explanatory model is proposed by Grunwell (1981b: 177–81) in accounting for disordered phonological development.

From this final section it is evident that clinical phonology as an area of study is moving into a new phase of development. The orientation of the subject is shifting from descriptions of the data of disordered speech to explanations of the nature of speakers' speech disorders. These explanations provide clinical insights which facilitate the planning of more appropriate and thus potentially more effective intervention strategies. This shift in emphasis entails a broadening of the scope of the subject in order to create psycholinguistic models which take into account all the relevant aspects of speech behaviour. Nevertheless the concerns of clinical phonology still derive clearly from its origins: phonetic descriptions of speech production and phonological analyses of the functions of speech for communicating through the medium of spoken language.

Appendix: Phonetic Representation

The International Phonetic Alphabet (revised to 1979)

		Bilabial	Labiodental	Dental, Alveolar, or Post-alveolar	Retroflex	Palato-alveolar	Palatal	Velar	Uvular	Labial-Palatal	Labial-Velar	Pharyngeal	Glottal
CONSONANTS (pulmonic air-stream mechanism)	*Nasal*	m	ɱ	n	ɳ		ɲ	ŋ	ɴ				
	Plosive	p b		t d	ʈ ɖ		c ɟ	k g	q ɢ		k͡p g͡b		ʔ
	(Median) Fricative	ɸ β	f v	θ ð s z	ʂ ʐ	ʃ ʒ	ç ʝ	x ɣ	χ ʁ		ʍ	ħ ʕ	h ɦ
	(Median) Approximant		ʋ	ɹ	ɻ		j	ɰ		ɥ	w		
	Lateral Fricative			ɬ ɮ									
	Lateral (Approximant)			l	ɭ		ʎ						
	Trill			r					ʀ				
	Tap or Flap			ɾ	ɽ				ʀ				
(non-pulmonic air-stream)	*Ejective*	p'		t'				k'					
	Implosive	ɓ		ɗ				ɠ					
	(Median) Click	ʘ		ʇ ʗ									
	Lateral Click			ʖ									

Source: Reproduced with the permission of the International Phonetic Association, London.

DIACRITICS

̥ Voiceless n̥ d̥
̬ Voiced s̬ t̬
ʰ Aspirated tʰ
̤ Breathy-voiced b̤ a̤
̪ Dental t̪
̫ Labialized t̫
̡ Palatalized t̡
~ Velarized or Pharyngealized ɫ, ɫ
̩ Syllabic n̩ l̩
͡ or ͜ Simultaneous s͡f (but see also under the heading Affricates)

˔ or ˕ Raised e˔, e̝, e̝ ʍ
˕ or ̞ Lowered e˕, e̞, e̞ ʁ̞
̟ Advanced u̟, u̟
- or ̠ Retracted i̠, i-, t̠
̈ Centralized ë
̃ Nasalized ɑ̃
˞ r-coloured ɑ˞
ː Long ɑː
ˑ Half-long ɑˑ
̆ Non-syllabic ŭ
̹ More rounded ɔ̹
̜ Less rounded y̜

OTHER SYMBOLS

ɕ, ʑ Alveolo-palatal fricatives
ʆ, ʓ Palatalized ʃ, ʒ
ɼ Alveolar fricative trill
ɺ Alveolar lateral flap
ɧ Simultaneous ʃ and x
ʃˢ Variety of ʃ resembling s, etc.
ɪ = ɩ
ʊ = ɷ
ɜ = Variety of ə
ɚ = r-coloured ə

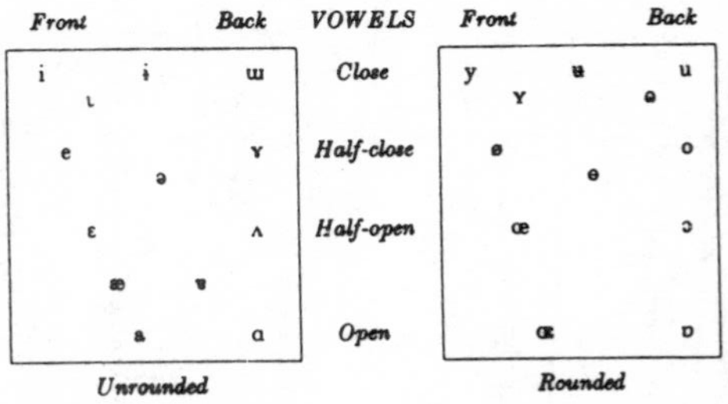

Front		Back	VOWELS
i	ɨ	ɯ	Close
ɩ			
e	ə	ɤ	Half-close
ɛ		ʌ	Half-open
æ	ɐ		
a		ɑ	Open

Unrounded

Front		Back
y	ʉ	u
ʏ		ɷ
ø	ɵ	o
œ		ɔ
ɶ		ɒ

Rounded

STRESS, TONE (PITCH)

ˈ stress, placed at beginning of stressed syllable: ˌ secondary stress: ˉ high level pitch, high tone: ˍ low level: ˊ high rising: ˏ low rising: ˋ high falling: ˎ low falling: ˆ rise-fall: ˇ fall-rise.

AFFRICATES can be written as digraphs, as ligatures, or with slur marks; thus ts, tʃ, dʒ: ʦ ʧ ʤ: t͡s t͡ʃ d͡ʒ.
c, ɟ may occasionally be used for tʃ, dʒ.

PRDS – Recommended additional phonetic symbols

For the representation of segmental aspects of disordered speech.

A. Relating mainly to place of articulation

1. Bilabial trills		p͜pp b͡bb
2. Lingualabials (tongue tip/blade to upper lip)	plosives, nasal	P B M
	fricatives	p 8
	lateral	L
3. Labiodental plosives and nasal (m̺ is an alternative to the usual ɱ)		p̺ b̺ m̺
4. Reverse labiodentals (lower teeth to upper lip)	plosives, nasal	p̪ b̪ m̪
	fricatives	f̪ v̪
5. Interdentals (using existing IPA convention for advancement)	plosives, nasal	ẗ̺ d̺̈ n̺̈ (or t̺̟ etc.)
6. Bidentals (lower teeth to upper teeth)	fricatives	h̪̺ ɦ̺ (or ʔ̺ etc.)
	percussive	ʭ
7. Voiced palatal fricative (reserving j for palatal approximant)		ʝ
8. Voiced velar lateral (using existing IPA convention for retraction)		ʎ̠
9. Pharyngeal plosives (using existing IPA convention for retraction)		q̠ ɢ̠

B. Relating mainly to manner of articulation

10. Segments with nasal escape:

(i) nasal fricatives (audible turbulent nasal egressive air-flow; no oral escape)	m̥^{F} m^{F} n̥^{F} ŋ^{F} etc.
(ii) nasalized fricatives	s̃ z̃ x̃ etc.; also s̃^{F} etc.
(iii) sounds intermediate between oral stop and nasal	t̃ d̃ p̃ etc.

NOTE: The nasality diacritic, [˜], may be freely used to denote nasal resonance or escape; it does not in itself imply nasal *friction*, for which the raised [^{F}] is recommended.

11. Lateral fricatives with sibilance	ɬʃ ɮʒ etc.; or ɬ͜ʃ etc.
12. Strong/tense articulation }*	f͈ m͈
13. Weak/lax/tentative articulation }*	f͉ m͉
*as compared with the norm for the segment in question	
14. Reiterated articulation (as in dysfluencies and palilalia)	pˆpˆp etc.
15. Alveolar slit fricatives (using existing IPA convention for retraction)	θ̠ ð̠
16. Blade (as opposed to tip of tongue) articulation	s̻ t̻
17. Plosive with non-audible release	p˺ b˺

C. Relating to vocal fold activity

18. Unaspirated (where explicit symbolization is desired)	p$^{=}$ t$^{=}$ etc.

19. Pre-voiced; post-voiced (i.e. with voicing starting earlier/ continuing later than the norm for the segment in question) — ˬz zˬ etc.
20. Partially voiced (for segments normally voiceless; use where 's̬' etc. is not sufficiently explicit) — ˬs sˬ etc.
21. Partially voiceless (for segments normally voiced; use where 'z̥' etc. is not sufficiently explicit) — ̥z z̥
22. Preaspirated — ʰp ʰt etc.

D. Relating to air-stream mechanism

23. Pulmonic ingressive — s̰ m̰ etc.
24. Oral (velaric) egressive ('reverse click') — ɿ etc.
25. Zero air-stream (absence of air-stream mechanism, but articulation present; 'silent articulations', 'mouthing') — (f) (m) etc.

NOTE: This may occur simultaneously with an articulation using some other air-stream mechanism, e.g. — ʔ(f) ŋ(f)

E. Relating to duration, coarticulation, and pausing

26. Excessively short — m̆ θ̆ ɜ̆ etc.

NOTE: It is felt that confusion is unlikely to arise between this use and the customary IPA use to denote non-syllabicity; but this diacritic should *not* be used to denote mere absence of length.

27. Prolonged (using existing IPA conventions) — m: (or m::) etc. p: (i.e. with prolonged hold/closure stage)
28. Silence, with absence of coarticulatory effects between segments or words

short	–	thus ʌn–də
long	– –	ʌn – – də
extra long	– – –	ʌn – – – də

F. Relating to secondary articulation

29. Lip rounding (using existing IPA convention for labialization) — s̫
30. Lip spreading — s̈

G. Relating to inadequacy of data or transcriptional confidence

31. 'Not sure' — Ring doubtful symbols or cover symbols, thus:

◯	entirely unspecified articulatory segment
Ⓒ	unspecified consonant
Ⓥ	unspecified vowel
Ⓢ	unspecified stop
Ⓕ	unspecified fricative
Ⓐ	unspecified approximant
(NAS)	unspecified nasal

(AFF)	unspecified affricate
(LAT)	unspecified lateral
(PAL)	probably palatal, unspecified manner (etc)
(ɬ)	probably [ɬ], but not sure (etc.)
mɪ(ʉ)(k)	probably [ʉk], but not sure (etc.)

Note: A voiced, but otherwise unspecified, fricative may be shown as (F); similarly, a voiceless, but otherwise unspecified, stop as (S); and so on.

32. Speech sound(s) masked by extraneous noise — (( )) thus bɪg ((bæd wʊl))f or bɪg ((2 sylls))

33. *The asterisk*. It is recommended that free use be made of asterisks (indexed, if necessary) and footnotes where it is desired to record some segment or feature for which no symbol is provided.

REPRESENTATION OF VOWELS

As indicated in Chapter Two, systematic transcription of vowels is often adequate for clinical purposes, as the most frequently occurring phonetic and phonological disabilities involve the pronunciation of consonants. The representation of vowels throughout the text and in the exercises is phonemic. The transcriptions of adult pronunciations are based on a Southern British Standard accent (see especially Wells & Colson 1971: 17). The symbols used are as follows:

Key Word		Key Word	
bead	/i/	bird	/ɜ/
bid	/ɪ/	a̱bout	/ə/
bed	/ɛ/	bay	/eɪ/
bad	/æ/	buy	/aɪ/
bar	/ɑ/	boy	/ɒɪ/
bog	/ɒ/	boat	/əʊ/
board	/ɔ/	bout	/ɑʊ/
good	/ʊ/	beer	/ɪə/
food	/u/	bear	/ɛə/
bud	/ʌ/	poor (for some speakers)	/ʊə/

Many of the children whose speech data are used in the examples had regional accents, primarily from the Midlands and North of England. In order to indicate more accurately the vowel qualities of their pronunciations the following representations are used in some of the data samples:

bad [a] (also usually used in bath, grass, etc)
bud [ə] or [ʊ]
boat [oʊ]

The vocalic lateral is often a locally acceptable pronunciation in many of the communities in which these children lived; whether this was so or not, it was used very frequently by many of the children. It is represented here by [ʊ]:

e.g. milk [mɪʊk] ball [bɔʊ].

References

Abercrombie, D. (1967) *Elements of general phonetics*, Edinburgh University Press, Edinburgh

Anthony, A., Bogle, D., Ingram, T.T.S. & McIsaac, M.W. (1971) *Edinburgh Articulation Test*, Churchill Livingstone, Edinburgh

Bailey, C.-J.N. (1985) *English phonetic transcription*, University of Texas/SIL, Arlington

Ball, M. & Code, C. (1986) Apraxia of speech — does linguistics apply? Paper presented at BAAL Seminar, Leicester, April

Benjamin, B.J. & Greenwood, J. (1983) 'A comparison of three phonological assessment procedures', *J. Childhood Commun. Disord.*, *7*, 19-27

Berko, J. & Brown, R. (1960) 'Psycholinguistic research methods', in Mussen, P. (ed.) *Handbook of research methods in child development*, Wiley, New York, pp. 517-57

Bernthal, J.E. & Bankson, N.W. (1981) *Articulation disorders*, Prentice Hall, Englewood Cliffs, NJ

Bernthal, J.E. & Bankson, N.W. (1984) 'Phonologic disorders: an overview', in Costello, J.M. (ed.) *Speech disorders in children*, NFER-Nelson, Windsor, UK, pp. 3-24

Blache, S.E. (1985) 'A distinctive feature approach to articulation therapy', in Newman, P.W., Creaghead, N. & Secord, W. (eds) *Assessment and remediation of articulatory and phonological disorders*, Merrill, Columbus, OH, pp. 383-407

Bleile, K. (1982) 'Consonant ordering in Down's syndrome phonology', *J. Commun. Disord.*, *15*, 275-85

Bleile, K. & Schwartz, R. (1984) 'Three perspectives on the speech of children with Down's syndrome', *J. Commun. Disord.*, *17*, 87-94

Blumstein, S. (1973) *A phonological investigation of aphasic speech*, Mouton, The Hague

Braine, M.D.S. (1974) 'On what might constitute learnable phonology', *Language*, *50*, 270-99

Camarata, S. & Gandour, J. (1984) 'On describing idiosyncratic phonologic systems', *J. Speech Hear. Disord.*, *49*, 262-6

Carney, E. (1979) 'Inappropriate abstraction in speech assessment procedures', *Brit. J. Disord. Commun.*, *14*, 123-35

Chomsky, N. & Halle, M. (1968) *The sound pattern of English*, Harper & Row, New York

Compton, A.J. (1970) 'Generative studies of children's phonological systems', *J. Speech Hear. Disord.*, *35*, 315-39

Compton, A.J. (1975) 'Generative studies of children's phonological disorders: a strategy for therapy', in Singh, S. (ed.) *Measurement procedures in speech hearing and language*, University Park Press, Baltimore, MD, pp. 55-90

Compton, A.J. (1976) 'Generative studies of children's phonological disorders: clinical ramifications', in Morehead, D.M. & Morehead,

A.E. (eds) *Normal and deficient child language*, University Park Press, Baltimore, MD, pp. 61-96

Compton, A. J. & Hutton, J.S. (1978) *Compton–Hutton phonological assessment*, Carousel House, San Francisco, CA

Cooper, R. (1985) 'The method of meaningful minimal contrasts', in Newman, P.W., Creaghead, N. & Secord, W. (eds) *Assessment and remediation of articulatory and phonological disorders*, Merrill, Columbus, OH, pp. 369-82

Crary, M.A. (1983) 'Phonological process analysis from spontaneous speech: the influence of sample size', *J. Commun. Disord.*, *16*, 133-41

Crary, M.A. & Fokes, J. (1980) 'Phonological processes in apraxia of speech: a systemic simplification of articulatory performance', *Aphasia, Apraxia, Agnosia*, *4*, 1-13

Crocker, J.R. (1969) 'A phonological model of children's articulation competence', *J. Speech Hear. Disord.*, *34*, 203-13

Cruttenden, A. (1972) 'Phonological procedures for child language', *Brit. J. Disord. Commun.*, *7*, 30-7

Cruttenden, A. (1979) *Language in infancy and childhood*, Manchester University Press, Manchester

Crystal, D. (1980) *An introduction to language pathology*, Edward Arnold, London

Crystal, D. (1982) *Profiling linguistic disability*, Edward Arnold, London

Crystal, D., Fletcher, P. & Garman, M. (1976) *The grammatical analysis of language disability*, Edward Arnold, London

Dale, P.S. (1976) *Language development: structure and function*, 2nd edition, Holt, Rinehart & Winston, New York

Darley, F.L., Aronson, A.E. & Brown, J.R. (1975) *Motor speech disorders*, W.B. Saunders Co., Philadelphia, PA

Dean, E. & Howell, H. (1986) 'Developing linguistic awareness: a theoretically based approach to phonological disorders', *Brit. J. Disord. Commun.*, *21*, 223-38

De Villiers, J.G. & De Villiers, P.A. (1978) *Language acquisition*, Harvard University Press, Cambridge, MA

Dinnsen, D. & Elbert, M. (1984) 'On the relationship between phonology and learning', in Elbert, M., Dinnsen, D. & Weismer, G. (eds) *Phonological theory and the misarticulating child*, ASHA Monograph No. 22, ASHA, Rockville, MD

Donegan, P.J. & Stampe, D. (1979) 'The study of natural phonology', in Dinnsen, D.A. (ed.) *Current approaches to phonological theory*, Indiana University Press, Bloomington, IN, pp. 126-73

Edwards, M.L. (1978) 'Phonological aspects of adult aphasia: evidence from three aphasic patients'. Unpublished paper; see Edwards, M.L. & Shriberg, L.D. (1983), pp. 263-7

Edwards, M.L. & Bernhardt, B.H. (1973) 'Phonological analysis of the speech of four children with language disorders'. Unpublished paper; see Ingram, D. (1976)

Edwards, M.L. & Shriberg, L.D. (1983) *Phonology: applications in communicative disorders*, College Hill Press, San Diego, CA

Elbert, M. (1983) 'A case study of phonological acquisition', *Topics in Lang, Disord.*, *3*, 1-9

Elbert, M. & Gierut, J. (1986) *Handbook of clinical phonology*, Taylor & Francis, London

Emerick, L.L. & Hatten, J.T. (1979) *Diagnosis and evaluation in speech pathology*, Prentice Hall, Englewood Cliffs, NJ

Fee, J. & Ingram, D. (1982) 'Reduplication as a strategy of phonological development', *J. Child Lang.*, *9*, 41-54

Ferguson, C.A. (1968) 'Contrastive analysis and language development', reprinted in Dil, A.S. (ed.) (1971) *Language structure and language use*, Stanford University Press, Stanford, CA, pp. 233-48

Ferguson, C.A. (1976/8) 'Learning to pronounce: the earliest stages of phonological development in the child'; reprinted in Minifie, F.L. & Lloyd, L.L. (eds) *Communicative and cognitive abilities: early behavioral assessment*, University Park Press, Baltimore, MD, pp. 273-97

Fey, M.E. & Gandour, J. (1982) 'Rule discovery in phonological acquisition', *J. Child Lang.*, *9*, 71-81

Fisher, H.B. & Logemann, J.A. (1971) *The Fisher–Logemann test of articulation competence: therapist's manual*, Houghton Mifflin, Boston, MA

Foster, D., Riley, K. & Parker, F. (1985) 'Some problems in the clinical application of phonological theory', *J. Speech Hear. Disord.*, *50*, 294-7

Fudge, E. (1970) 'Phonology', in Lyons, J. (ed.) *New horizons in linguistics*, Penguin, Harmondsworth, pp. 76-95

Fudge, E. (1973) (ed.) *Phonology*, Penguin, Harmondsworth

Gandour, J. (1981) 'The non-deviant nature of deviant phonological systems', *J. Commun. Disord.*, *14*, 11-29

Garman, M. (1982) 'Is Broca's aphasia a phonological deficit?', in Crystal, D. (ed.) *Linguistic controversies*, Edward Arnold, London, pp. 152-71

Gimson, A.C. (1980) *An introduction to the pronunciation of English*, 3rd edition, Edward Arnold, London

Goldman, R. & Fristoe, M. (1972) *Goldman–Fristoe test of articulation*, AGS Inc., Minnesota, MN

Grady, P.A.E. (1966) 'Towards a new concept of dyslalia', in Mason, S. (ed.) *Signs, signals and symbols*, Methuen, London, pp. 159-65

Grunwell, P. (1975) 'The phonological analysis of articulation disorders', *Brit. J. Disord. Commun.*, *10*, 31-42

Grunwell, P. (1977) 'The analysis of phonological disability in children'. Unpublished PhD thesis, University of Reading

Grunwell, P. (1980a) 'Developmental language disorders at the phonological level', in Jones, F.M. (ed.) *Language disability in children*, MTP Press, Lancaster, pp. 129-58

Grunwell, P. (1980b) 'Procedures for child speech assessment: a review', *Brit. J. Disord. Commun.*, *15*, 189-204

Grunwell, P. (1981a) 'The development of phonology: a descriptive profile', *First Lang.*, *3*, 161-91

Grunwell, P. (1981b) *The nature of phonological disability in children*,

Academic Press, London and New York
Grunwell, P. (1983) 'Phonological therapy: premises, principles and procedures', Proceedings XIX IALP Congress, Edinburgh
Grunwell, P. (1985a) 'Developing phonological skills', *Child Lang. Teaching & Therapy*, *1*, 65-72
Grunwell, P. (1985b) 'Comment on the terms "phonetics" and "phonology" as applied in the investigation of speech disorders', *Brit. J. Disord. Commun.*, *20*, 165-70
Grunwell, P. (1985c) *Phonological assessment of child speech (PACS)* NFER–Nelson, Windsor, UK/College-Hill Press, San Diego, CA
Grunwell, P. & Huskins, S. (1979) 'Intelligibility in acquired dysarthria: a neurophonetic approach', *J. Commun. Disord.*, *12*, 9-22
Grunwell, P. & Pletts, M.M.K. (1974) 'Therapeutic guidelines from linguistics — a case study'. Unpublished paper
Grunwell, P. & Russell, J. (1987) 'Vocalisations before and after cleft palate surgery: a pilot study', *Brit. J. Disord. Commun.* (forthcoming)
Halle, M. & Stevens, K.N. (1979) 'Some reflections on the theoretical basis of phonetics', in Lindblom, B. & Ohman, S. (eds), *Frontiers of speech communication research*, Academic Press, London
Harris, J. & Cottam, P. (1985) 'Phonetic features and phonological features in speech assessment', *Brit. J. Disord. Commun.*, *20*, 61-74
Henderson, E.J.A. (1971) 'Structural organisation of language: phonology', in Minnis, N. (ed.), *Linguistics at large*, Paladin, London
Hewlett, N. (1985) 'Phonological versus phonetic disorders: some suggested modifications to the current use of the distinction', *Brit. J. Disord. Commun.*, *20*, 155-64
Higgs, J.A.W. (1970) 'The articulation test as linguistic technique', *Lang. Speech*, *13*, 262-70
Hodson, B.W. (1980) *The assessment of phonological processes*, Interstate Inc., Danville, IL
Hodson, B.W. & Paden, E.P. (1981) 'Phonological processes which characterize unintelligible and intelligible speech in early childhood', *J. Speech Hear. Disord.*, *46*, 369-73
Hodson, B.W. & Paden, E.P. (1983) *Targetting intelligible speech*, College Hill Press, San Diego, CA
Howell, J. & Dean, E. (1983) 'Phonological disorders revisited', *CST Bulletin*, *377*, 11-13
Hughes, G. & Trudgill, P. (1979) *English accents and dialects*, Edward Arnold, London
Huskins, S. (1986) *Working with dyspraxics*, Winslow Press, London
Hyman, L.M. (1975) *Phonology: theory and analysis*, Holt, Rinehart & Winston, New York
Ingram, D. (1976) *Phonological disability in children*, Edward Arnold, London
Ingram, D. (1981) *Procedures for the phonological analysis of children's language*, University Park Press, Baltimore, MD
Ingram, D. (ed.) (1983) 'Case studies of phonological disorders', *Topics in Lang. Disord.*, *3* (2)

Ingram, D. (1986) 'Explanation and phonological remediation', *Child Lang. Teaching & Therapy, 2,* 1-16

Jakobson, R. (1942) *Kindersprache, Aphasie und allgemeine Lautgesetze*; in translation (1968) *Child Language, Aphasia and Phonological Universals,* Mouton, The Hague

Jakobson, R., Fant, G. & Halle, M. (1952) *Preliminaries to speech analysis,* MIT Press, Cambridge, MA

Kean, M.L. (1977) 'The linguistic interpretation of aphasic syndromes agrammatism in Broca's aphasia, an example', *Cognition, 5,* 9-46

Kean, M.L. (1979) 'Agrammatism: a phonological deficit?', *Cognition, 7,* 61-8

Kiparsky, P. & Menn, L. (1977) 'On the acquisition of phonology', in Macnamara, J. (ed.) *Language learning and thought,* Academic Press, New York, pp. 47-78

Klich, R.J., Ireland, J.V. & Weidner, W.E. (1979) 'Articulatory and phonological aspects of consonant substitutions in apraxia of speech', *Cortex, 15,* 451-70

Ladefoged, P. (1971) *Preliminaries to linguistic phonetics,* Chicago University Press, Chicago, IL

Ladefoged, P. (1982) *A course in phonetics,* 2nd edition, Harcourt, Brace, Jovanich, New York

Lahey, M., Flax, J. & Schlisselberg, G. (1985) 'A preliminary investigation of reduplication in children with specific language impairment', *J. Speech Hear. Disord., 50,* 186-94

Leinonen-Davies, E.K. (1987) 'Assessing the functional adequacy of children's phonological systems', CNAA PhD thesis, Leicester Polytechnic

Leonard, L.D. (1985) 'Unusual and subtle phonological behavior in the speech of phonologically disordered children', *J. Speech Hear. Disord., 50,* 4-13

Leonard, L.D. & Brown, B.L. (1984) 'Nature and boundaries of phonologic categories: a case study of an unusual phonologic pattern in a language impaired child', *J. Speech Hear. Disord., 49,* 419-28

Lesser, R. (1978) *Lingustic investigation of aphasia,* Edward Arnold, London

Locke, J.L. (1983a) *Phonological acquisition and change,* Academic Press, New York

Locke, J.L. (1983b) 'Clinical phonology: the explanation and treatment of speech sound disorders', *J. Speech Hear. Disord., 48,* 339-41

Lorentz, J.P. (1976) 'An analysis of some deviant phonological rules of English', in Morehead, D.M. & Morehead, A.E. (eds) *Normal and deficient child language,* University Park Press, Baltimore, MD

Low, G.M., Newman, P.W. & Ravsten, M.T. (1985) 'Communication centred articulation treatment', in Newman, P.W., Creaghead, N. & Secord, W. (eds), *Assessment and remediation of articulatory and phonological disorders,* Merrill, Columbus, OH, pp. 217-48

Lund, N.L. & Duchan, J.F. (1978) 'Phonological analysis: a multifaceted approach', *Brit. J. Disord. Commun., 13,* 119-26

Lyons, J. (1969) *Introduction to theoretical linguistics,* Cambridge University Press, Cambridge

Lyons, J. (1970) *Chomsky*, Fontana/Collins, London

McDonald, E.T. (1964a) *A Deep Test of Articulation*, Stanwix House Inc., Pittsburgh, PA

McDonald, E.t. (1964b) *Articulation testing and treatment: a sensory-motor approach*, Stanwix House Inc., Pittsburgh PA

McReynolds, L.V. & Bennett, S. (1972) 'Distinctive feature generalisation in articulation training', *J. Speech Hear. Disord.*, *37*, 462-70

McReynolds, L.V. & Engmann, D. (1975) *Distinctive feature analysis of misarticulations*, University Park Press, Baltimore, MD

McReynolds, L.V. & Huston, K. (1971) 'A distinctive feature analysis of children's misarticulations', *J. Speech Hear. Disord.*, *36*, 155-66

McReynolds, L.V., Engmann, D. & Dimmitt, K. (1974) 'Markedness theory and articulation errors', *J. Speech Hear. Disord.*, *39*, 93-103

Mackay, L. & Hodson, B.W. (1982) 'Phonological process identification of misarticulations of mentally retarded children', *J. Commun. Disord.*, *15*, 243-50

Macken, M.A. (1986) 'Phonological development; a crosslinguistic perspective', in Fletcher, P. & Garman, M. (eds) *Language acquisition*, 2nd edition, Cambridge University Press, Cambridge, pp. 251-68

Macken, M.A. & Barton, D. (1979) 'The acquisition of the voicing contrast in English: a study of voice onset time in word-initial stop consonants', *J. Child Lang.*, *7*, 41-74

Macken, M.A. & Ferguson, C.A. (1983) 'Cognitive aspects of phonological development: model, evidence and issues', in Nelson, K.E. (ed.) *Children's language*, vol. 4, Erlbaum, Hillsdale, NJ, pp. 256-82

Mackenzie, C. (1982) 'Aphasic articulatory defect and aphasic phonological defect', *Brit. J. Disord. Commun.*, *17*, 27-46

Marquardt, T.P., Reinhart, J.B. & Peterson, H.A. (1979) 'Markedness analysis of phonemic substitution errors in apraxia of speech', *J. Commun. Disord.*, *12*, 481-94

Maxwell, E.M. (1979) 'Competing analyses of a deviant phonology', *Glossa*, *13*, 181-205

Menn, L. (1980) Phonological theory and child phonology', in Yeni-Komshian, G.H., Kavanagh, J.F. & Ferguson, C.A. (eds) *Child phonology*, vol. 1, Academic Press, New York, pp. 23-41

Menn, L. (1983) 'Development of articulatory, phonetic and phonological capabilities', in Butterworth, B. (ed.) *Language production*, vol. 2, Academic Press, London, pp. 3-50

Menyuk, P., Menn, L. & Silber, R. (1986) 'Early strategies for the perception and production of words and sounds', in Fletcher, P. & Garman, M. (eds) *Language acquisition*, 2nd edition, Cambridge University Press, Cambridge, pp. 198-222

Michel, L.I. (1978) 'Evaluation of articulation disorders: a traditional approach', in Singh, S. & Lynch, J. (eds) *Diagnostic procedures in hearing speech and language*, University Park Press, Baltimore, MD, pp. 417-57

Milloy, N.R. (1985) 'The assessment and identification of developmental articulatory dyspraxia and its effect on phonological development', CNAA PhD thesis, Leicester Polytechnic

Neville, A. (1984) 'Phonological therapy — from ear to mouth', *CST*

Bulletin, 390, 10-11

Newman, P.W., Creaghead, N.A. & Secord, W. (eds) (1985) *Assessment and remediation of articulatory and phonological disorders*, Merrill, Columbus, OH

Norris, M. & Harden, J. (1981) 'Natural processes in the phonologies of four error-rate groups', *J. Commun. Disord., 14*, 194-213

O'Connor, J.D. & Trim, J.L.M. (1953) 'Vowel, consonant and syllable: a phonological definition', *Word, 9*, 103-22

Oller, D.K. (1973) 'Regularities in abnormal child phonology', *J. Speech Hear. Disord., 38*, 35-46

Oller, D.K. & Eilers, R. (1975) 'Phonetic expectation and transcription validity', *Phonetica, 31*, 288-304

Oller, D.K. *et al.* (1972) 'Five studies in abnormal phonology'. Unpublished paper

Oller, D.K., Wieman, L.A., Doyle, W.J. & Ross, C. (1976) 'Infant babbling and speech', *J. Child Lang., 3*, 1-11

Olmsted, D.L. (1971) *Out of the mouth of babes*, Mouton, The Hague

Paden, E.P. & Moss, S.A. (1985) 'Comparison of three phonological analysis procedures', *Lang. Speech Hear. Services Schools, 16*, 103-9

Parker, F. (1976) 'Distinctive features in speech pathology: phonology or phonemics', *J. Speech Hear. Disord., 41*, 23-39

Perkins, W.H. (1977) *Speech pathology: an applied behavioral science*, 2nd edition, C.V. Mosby, St Louis, MI

Pollack, E. & Rees, N.S. (1972) 'Disorders of articulation; clinical applications of distinctive feature theory', *J. Speech Hear Disord., 37*, 451-61

PRDS (1980) 'The phonetic representation of disordered speech', *Brit., J. Disord. Commun., 15*, 217-23

PRDS (1983) *The phonetic representation of disordered speech: final report*, King's Fund, London

Prater, R.J. (1982) 'Functions of consonant assimilation and reduplication in the early words of mentally retarded children', *Amer. J. Ment. Deficiency, 86*, 399-404

Priestly, T.M.S. (1977) 'One idiosyncratic strategy in the acquisition of phonology', *J. Child Lang., 4*, 45-66

Priestly, T.M.S. (1980) 'Homonymy in child phonology', *J. Child Lang., 7*, 413-27

Renfrew, C. (1966) 'Persistence of the open syllable in defective articulation', *J. Speech Hear. Disord., 31*, 370-3

Schane, S.A. (1973) *Generative phonology*, Prentice Hall, Englewood Cliffs, NJ

Schwartz, R.G. & Leonard, L.B. (1983) 'Some further comments on reduplication in child phonology', *J. Child Lang., 10*, 441-8

Schwartz, R.G. & Prelock, P.A. (1982) 'Cognition and phonology', *Seminars in Speech, Language and Hearing, 3*, 149-61

Schwartz, R.G., Leonard, L.B., Wilcox, M.J. & Folger, M.K. (1980) 'Again and again: reduplication in child phonology', *J. Child. Lang., 7*, 75-88

Shriberg, L.D. & Kwiatkowski, J. (1980) *Natural process analysis*

(NPA), John Wiley, New York

Shriberg, L.D., Kwiatkowski, J. & Hoffmann, K. (1984) 'A procedure for phonetic transcription by consensus', *J. Speech Hear. Res.*, *27*, 456-65

Smit, A.B. & Bernthal, J.E. (1983) 'Voicing contrasts and their phonological implications in the speech of articulation disordered children', *J. Speech Hear. Res.*, *26*, 486-500

Smith, B.L. & Stoel-Gammon, C. (1983) 'A longitudinal study of the development of stop consonant production in normal and Down's syndrome children', *J. Speech Hear. Disord.*, *48*, 114-18

Smith, N.V. (1973) *The acquisition of phonology: a case study*, Cambridge University Press, Cambridge

Smith, N.V. (1978) 'Lexical representation and the acquisition of phonology'. Paper given as Forum Lecture, Linguistic Institute, Linguistic Society of America

Smith, N.V. & Wilson, D. (1979) *Modern linguistics*, Penguin, Harmondsworth

Snow, K. (1963) 'A detailed analysis of articulation responses of normal first-grade children', *J. Speech Hear. Res.*, *6*, 277-90

Sommerstein, A.H. (1977) *Modern phonology*, Edward Arnold, London

Spencer, A. (1984) 'A non-linear analysis of phonological disability', *J. Commun. Disord.*, *17*, 325-48

Stackhouse, J. (1984) 'Phonological therapy; a case and some thoughts', *CST Bulletin*, *381*, 10-11

Stampe, D. (1969) 'The acquisition of phonetic representation'. Paper from Vth Regional Meeting, Chicago Linguistic Society, pp. 443-54; reprinted in Stampe (1979): vii–xxv

Stampe, D. (1979) *A dissertation on natural phonology*, Hankamer, I. (ed.), Garland, New York

Stoel-Gammon, C. (1980) 'Phonological analysis of four Down's syndrome children', *J. Appl. Psycholing.*, *1*, 31-45

Stoel-Gammon, C. & Cooper, J. (1984) 'Patterns of early lexical and phonological development', *J. Child Lang.*, *11*, 247-71

Stoel-Gammon, C. & Dunn, C. (1985) *Normal and disordered phonology in children*, University Park Press, Baltimore, MD

Straight, H.S. (1980) 'Auditory versus articulatory phonological processes and their development in children', in Yeni-Komshian, G.H., Kavanagh, J.F. & Ferguson, C.A. (eds) *Child phonology*, vol. 1, Academic Press, New York, pp. 43-71

Tallal, P., Stark, R.E., Kallman, C. & Mellitts, D. (1980) 'Perceptual constancy for phonemic categories: a developmental study with normal and language impaired children', *J. Applied Psycholing.*, *1*, 49-64

Tatham, M.A.A. (1984) 'Towards a *cognitive* phonetics', *J. Phonetics*, *12*, 37-47

Templin, M.C. (1957) *Certain language skills in children*, University of Minnesota Press, Minnesota, MN

Templin, M.C. & Darley, F.L. (1960) *Templin–Darley tests of articulation*, University of Iowa Press, Iowa, IA

Toombs, M.S., Singh, S. & Hayden, M.E. (1981) Markedness of features in the articulatory substitutions of children. *J. Speech Hear. Disord.*, *46*, 184-90

Trubetzkoy, N. (1939) *Grundzuge der Phonologie*, translated by Baltaxe, C.A.M. (1969) *Principles of phonology*, University of California Press, Berkeley, CA

Van Riper, C. & Irwin, J. (1958) *Voice and articulation*, Prentice Hall, Englewood Cliffs, NJ

Vihman, M.M. (1984) 'Individual differences in phonological development: age one and age three'. Unpublished paper

Walsh, H. (1974) 'On certain practical inadequacies of distinctive feature systems', *J. Speech Hear. Disord.*, *39*, 32-43

Waterson, N. (1970) 'Some speech forms of an English child: a phonological study', *Trans. Philol. Soc.*, pp. 1-24

Weiner, F.F. (1979) *Phonological process analysis (PPA)*, University Park Press, Baltimore, Md

Weiner, F.F. (1981) 'Systematic sound preference as a characteristic of phonological disability', *J. Speech Hear. Disord.*, *46*, 281-6

Weiner, F.F. (1984) 'A phonologic approach to assessment and treatment', in Costello, J.M. (ed.) *Speech disorders in children*, NFER–Nelson, Windsor, UK, pp. 75-91

Weinreich, U. (1964) *Languages in contact*, Mouton, The Hague

Weismer, G. (1984) 'Acoustic analysis strategies for the refinement of phonological analysis', in Elbert, M., Dinnsen, D. & Weismer, G. (eds) *Phonological theory and the misarticulating child*, ASHA Monograph No. 22, ASHA, Rockville, MD

Wells, J.C. (1982) *Accents of English*, vols 1-3, Cambridge University Press, Cambridge

Wells, J.C. & Colson, G. (1971) *Practical phonetics*, Pitman, London

Williams, F., Cairns, H.S., Cairns, C.E. & Blosser, D.F. (1971) 'Analysis of production errors in the phonetic performance of school-age standard English-speaking children', University of Texas, Austin, TX

Winitz, H. (1969) *Articulatory acquisition and behavior*, Appleton Century Crofts, New York, NY

Wolk, L. (1986) 'Markedness analysis of consonant error productions in apraxia of speech', *J. Commun. Disord.*, *19*, 133-60

Index

Page references including 'n' refer to notes e.g.: 83n5 refers to page 83, note 5.